School PROMOTION, PUBLICITY, & PUBLIC RELATIONS
...NOTHING BUT BENEFITS

by

Tracey H. MacPhee
Author of *Management Vision*

Robert L. DeBruyn
Author of *The MASTER Teacher*

The Master Teacher, Inc.   •   Publisher   •   Manhattan, Kansas   •   U.S.A.

THE MASTER TEACHER, INC.
Publisher
Leadership Lane
P.O. Box 1207
Manhattan, Kansas 66502

Library of Congress Catalog Card Number: 87-060751
ISBN 0-914607-25-1
Printed in the United States of America

As with any effort in any organization, it is the cooperative spirit which makes all things possible. So it is with this book; and we dedicate it to three valued colleagues, Kym Nies, Norreen Furness, and Barry Anderson, who helped make the journey as well as the destination a productive and satisfying experience. Thank you.

— Tracey H. MacPhee
Robert L. DeBruyn

TABLE OF
CONTENTS

PAGE

INTRODUCTION 6

CHAPTER I.   PROMOTION, PUBLICITY, AND PUBLIC
              RELATIONS . . . WHAT'S THE
              DIFFERENCE? 9
              ● SOME DEFINITIONS WE SHOULD KNOW 11
              ● WHAT SCHOOL PUBLIC RELATIONS IS
                AND IS NOT 13
              ● THE BENEFITS OF A STRONG, WELL-PLANNED
                PUBLIC RELATIONS PROGRAM 17
              ● A STANCE FOR SUCCESS 19

CHAPTER II.   STEP ONE: DECIDE HOW YOU WANT
              TO APPEAR 21
              ● THE THREE MOST IMPORTANT DECISIONS WE
                WILL MAKE AS EDUCATORS...................22
              ● DECISION NUMBER ONE: HOW WILL YOU
                POSITION YOURSELF? 23
              ● DECISION NUMBER TWO: MAKE YOUR
                STUDENTS/COMMUNITY A PROMISE 25
              ● DECISION NUMBER THREE: BUILD YOUR
                IMAGE ON POSITIVE IDEAS 29

CHAPTER III. PEOPLE BUY WHAT YOU BUY—BENEFITS...31
              ● THE INDIVIDUAL PEOPLE MOTIVATORS
                AND HOW THEY AFFECT PUBLIC
                RELATIONS EFFORTS.........................31
                1. PERSONAL GAIN 32
                2. PRESTIGE 33
                3. PLEASURE..............................35
                4. IMITATION.............................37
                5. SECURITY 38
                6. CONVENIENCE 39
                7. DESIRE TO AVOID FEAR 40
                8. NEW EXPERIENCES 40

9. LOVE/CARING 41
  ● WE MUST FOCUS ON DELIVERING BENEFITS 42

CHAPTER IV.   THE LAWS AND PRINCIPLES OF
               MANAGEMENT AS THEY APPLY TO
               SCHOOL PUBLIC RELATIONS 45
  ● THE LAW OF ORIGIN 46
  ● THE LAW OF POSITIVE REINFORCEMENT 49
  ● THE LAW OF TRUST 51
  ● THE THEORY OF GROUP COMMUNICATION 53
  ● THE LAW OF PLANNING 54
  ● THE LAW OF REAL TRUTH AND TIME 56
  ● THE PRINCIPLE OF OWNERSHIP 57
  ● THE LAW OF BLAME AND CREDIT 59
  ● THE LAW OF TOP-DOWN MANAGEMENT 61
  ● ADMINISTRATIVE UNDERSTANDINGS THAT
    PROMOTE SOUND PROFESSIONAL
    RELATIONSHIPS 63
    —UNDERSTANDING #1: FEAR IS A POWERFUL
        EMOTION WHICH HAS A DIRECT IMPACT
        ON INTELLECT AND ACHIEVEMENT 63
    —UNDERSTANDING #2: THE POWER OF FEAR
        IS ULTIMATELY DESTRUCTIVE, WHEREAS
        THE POWER OF JOY IS A POSITIVE
        AND CONSTRUCTIVE FORCE 63
    —UNDERSTANDING #3: WHEN YOU LOOK
        DOWN ON JOBS, YOU LOOK DOWN ON
        THE PEOPLE WHO HAVE THEM 67
    —UNDERSTANDING #4: PEOPLE ARE MORE
        IMPORTANT THAN THINGS 69
    —UNDERSTANDING #5: DON'T TAKE YOUR
        PERSONAL LIFE OR YOUR PERSONAL
        TROUBLES TO SCHOOL—AND DON'T
        PROCLAIM ALL YOUR PROFESSIONAL
        PROBLEMS IN SCHOOL 71
    —UNDERSTANDING #6: STRIVE FOR ESTEEM,
        NOT ENVY 73
    —UNDERSTANDING #7: AVOID THE "I, ME,
        AND MY" SYNDROME 74
    —UNDERSTANDING #8: THERE MUST BE
        ROOM FOR DISAGREEMENT 77
    —UNDERSTANDING #9: WE MUST OBSERVE

AND TEACH SIX ABSOLUTES OF
PROFESSIONAL COURTESY 79

CHAPTER V.   DEFINING YOUR MARKET AND GIVING
THE PUBLIC WHAT IT WANTS 81
- WHAT IS YOUR MARKET? 81
- WHAT THE PUBLIC WANTS AND NEEDS IN
  ORDER TO BE AN ADVOCATE FOR SCHOOLS 82
- THE QUESTION OF PARAMOUNT SIGNIFICANCE:
  DO YOU REALLY WANT PUBLIC
  INVOLVEMENT? 85
- EMOTIONAL INVOLVEMENT 87
- SEVEN TYPES OF EMOTIONAL INVOLVEMENT
  TO USE IN PUBLIC RELATIONS EFFORTS 89
  —VICARIOUS EXPERIENCE 89
  —CURIOSITY 89
  —HUMOR 89
  —AESTHETIC PLEASURE 90
  —SELF-RATING APPEAL 90
  —HUMAN CONTACT 90
  —FRIENDSHIP 91

CHAPTER VI.   DEALING WITH MASS COMMUNICATION
VEHICLES 93
- MEDIUM NUMBER ONE: DIRECT MAIL 96
  —LETTERHEADS 97
  —THE NEWSLETTER 107
  —MEMOS 135
  —STAFF BULLETINS 136
  —PURCHASE ORDERS .138
  —PROGRESS REPORTS .138
  —THE GRADE CARD 140
- NEWSPAPERS 141
- RADIO AND TELEVISION 150
- VIDEOTAPE 152
- SCHOOL SIGNS 154
- DEVELOPING A REPORT CARD FOR
  YOUR SCHOOL 155
- DEVELOPING A BROCHURE ABOUT
  YOUR SCHOOL OR DISTRICT 162

CHAPTER VII. FACE-TO-FACE COMMUNICATION 163
  ● ADMINISTRATOR-ADMINISTRATOR 164
  ● ADMINISTRATOR-TEACHER 165
    —THE THREE MAJOR STYLES OF
       COMMUNICATION 167
    —FACULTY MEETINGS 170
    —SOCIAL ACTIVITIES: A PART OF
       ADMINISTRATOR-STAFF
       COMMUNICATION AND INTERACTION ...191
  ● ADMINISTRATOR-STUDENT 193
    —ASSEMBLIES 193
    —MEETINGS WITH STUDENTS 195
  ● ADMINISTRATOR-SUPPORT STAFF 198
    —WHEN THE PUBLIC CALLS—A TELEPHONE
       POLICY FOR SCHOOLS 209
  ● TEACHER-STUDENT 214
    —A PUBLIC RELATIONS PROBLEM: SAYING
       YES OR NO TO STUDENT REQUESTS 221
    —GRADE CARDS: THE PROCESS REQUIRES
       A PLAN 223
  ● COMMUNICATION TO THE PUBLIC
       AT LARGE............................228
    —OPINION POLLS 230

CHAPTER VIII. WHEN THE SCHOOLS ARE CRITICIZED 241
  ● IN PUBLIC RELATIONS, PUBLIC CONFIDENCE
     REJOINS WITH TRUTH.....................241
  ● RUMOR: IGNORE OR CONFRONT IT 244
  ● TAKING THE FIGHT OUT OF OPPONENTS 247
  ● WHEN THE PUBLIC ADDRESSES THE BOARD
     OR AN ADMINISTRATOR 250
  ● HIDING BEHIND FIGURES ALWAYS
     HURTS PUBLIC RELATIONS 255

CHAPTER IX. PROMOTING SCHOOL EVENTS—SOME
             DEFINITE HOW-TO'S 257
  ● PROMOTING TO PARENTS 258
    —FLYERS 259
    —NOTES HOME 261
    —PHONE CALLS 262

● PROMOTING TO STUDENTS................264
  —THE ACTIVITIES HANDBOOK 266
  —PARENT AND STUDENT INFORMATION
      HANDBOOKS.........................268
  —POSTERS 270

CHAPTER X.   THE PHYSICAL PLANT.................273
      ● THE PRINCIPAL'S OFFICE: THE IMAGE OF
        JUDGE, JURY, AND EXECUTIONER—OR
        CHIEF EXECUTIVE AND FACILITATOR? 274
      ● THE FACULTY LOUNGE—A PLACE FOR
        EVERYONE..............................276
      ● THE CAFETERIA 281
      ● HALLWAYS 282

CHAPTER XI.   DRESS—AN IMPORTANT PUBLIC
      RELATIONS INGREDIENT.................285
      ● HOW DO YOU LOOK?...IT DOES
        MAKE A DIFFERENCE 285
      ● PERSONAL CHOICE VS.
        PROFESSIONAL CHOICE 288

CHAPTER XII.   MORE POSITIVE PUBLIC RELATIONS
      IDEAS.................................293
      ● IDEAS FOR ADMINISTRATORS TO USE WITH
        STAFF MEMBERS........................293
      ● IDEAS FOR ADMINISTRATORS TO USE WITH
        STUDENTS 298
      ● IDEAS FOR ADMINISTRATORS TO USE WITH
        PARENTS 302
      ● IDEAS FOR ADMINISTRATORS TO USE WITH
        THE COMMUNITY 305
      ● IDEAS FOR BOARD MEMBERS TO USE WITH
        STAFF, STUDENTS, AND THE COMMUNITY 309

INDEX OF PUBLIC RELATIONS IDEAS 325

INTRODUCTION

"Such is the irresistible nature of truth that all it asks, and all it wants, is the liberty of appearing."
—Thomas Paine

There are numerous practices in the world of business which many educators and boards of education feel are forever out of their reach. The techniques of promotion, publicity, advertising, marketing, and public relations are among those social sciences about which educators and school boards most frequently say they would like to have more knowledge. Yet, in the same breath, many educators admit that they feel that developing expertise in such areas would be like learning a foreign language. Perhaps they could learn to speak it technically—but they openly and truthfully wonder if they could ever learn to master and work in this "foreign tongue."

That's one of the major reasons we wrote this book. For too long, educators have believed they can't be good public relations people, good advertisers, and good marketers. And to that notion we say, "Phooey!" When you finish reading and studying this book, you will probably know more about how to sell the services provided by your school or district than average business people know about how to sell theirs.

Why?

First, most business people know their products, but they don't know the laws, principles, and techniques that cause people to want to buy them. Second, it is the rare business that naturally lends itself to so many different methods of promotion as does the work and mission of education. And there are few products or services as profoundly necessary to enjoying a quality life. Most important, few businesses have had the successes that are known to most schools.

As you read and study, you will begin to understand what compels people to "buy into" and support the work and workers of organizations—whether they are businesses, clubs, industries, churches, or schools. And you will also have, at your disposal, over 200 methods and techniques to use in your school or district to cause interest and support for your work and the work of your colleagues.

As you read, we hope you will agree that there is much for you to shout about to the world. You are doing wonderful things for children. This country could not enjoy either a high standard of living or a high quality of life without schools. And yet, there is much more that you could do—if the public had the knowledge that you have of your successes. We will feel privileged and rewarded if, after reading this book, you feel a renewed commitment to inform the public of these successes. You owe it to yourself and to the glorious profession that you serve to do just that.

6

The Educator's Oath

I solemnly pledge to dedicate my life to the science of teaching.

I will give to those who are or have been my teachers the respect and gratitude which is their due.

I will practice my profession with conscience and dignity; the well-being of my students will be my primary concern always.

I will honor the position of parents and uphold public trust.

I will maintain by all the means in my power the honor of my profession.

I will respect the privacy of students.

I will teach toward meeting the individual needs and abilities of students.

I will accept all engaged in education and regard all as my colleagues.

I will not permit considerations of religion, nationality, race, party politics, social standing, or the monetary rewards received from my labors to intervene between my duty and my students.

I will maintain utmost respect for human dignity and human values, and I will hold human caring and consideration as the fundamental value in the student-teacher relationship.

I make this promise solemnly, freely, and upon my oath for as long as I am engaged in education.

—Robert L. DeBruyn

This oath is, indeed, the foundation of any public relations effort for any teacher, administrator, school, or district. It is all-inclusive of the work, mission, and ideals of our profession. Remember, foundations are vitally important to getting our work accomplished. That's why this book has been written in a specific format. First, we give you the management foundations—as they relate to public relations. Second, we give you the application of these foundations in carrying out a public relations program. This is done for good reason: Not only must we have public relations programs and be given the methods and techniques for carrying them out, but we need to know why it is important to have such programs and how we can carry them out in agreement with the highest standards of character and dignity. And these standards must be in agreement with the reason we have schools in the first place. Providing you with applications and no foundations would be meaningless and could, in fact, lead you astray. Make no mistake: Public relations is not a bag of tricks. It does not contain deception devices. It is founded on truth. Therefore, we invite you to return continually to this page. Read the Educator's Oath. Hang it in every office and in every classroom. Let it be your constant guide in the years ahead as you initiate a public relations effort and carry out the work and mission of the schools. It will tell you when you're right, and it will tell you immediately if you have gone astray.

ONE

PROMOTION, PUBLICITY, AND PUBLIC RELATIONS... WHAT'S THE DIFFERENCE?

"The purpose of public relations in its best sense is to inform and to keep minds open...."
—John W. Hill

We have worked with many school systems over the years to help them develop solid public relations programs. Not too many years ago, we were asked to do one such consultation with a school that we will refer to as the XYZ Hearing School. It was not a public school. It was a private school. But it is representative of the various kinds of problems that many schools encounter, and, therefore, is a good example for illustrative purposes. Administrators of the school said they had an image problem. We have heard many statements like that before—and so have you. As a result of their image problem, they were experiencing a decline in enrollment—thus, the need for our help.

Immediately upon our arrival at the school, members of the administrative staff took us on a long and detailed tour where we watched classes in session. When we returned to the office, we asked them one solitary question:

"What do you do here?"

"What do you mean what do we do here?" they asked, a little hurt by our apparent inability to see for ourselves.

"Do you teach deaf children to hear?" we asked.

"Well, of course not. You can't teach a deaf child to hear. We teach deaf children to speak."

"Why, then, do you call yourselves the XYZ Hearing School?" we questioned.

Stunned, they replied, "That's what the name has been for the last 25 years. We've never even given it a thought."

One of the first principles of public relations is that the image problems we incur are usually rooted in something very simple and very basic. In fact, this is the reason we can't always easily identify either the problems or their solutions. As a result, we often spend our time and energy looking for something far more complex. And that's precisely why, when we are searching for public relations answers, we need to look back to the basics of "What do we do?" and "What do we stand for?" Then we need to examine all our public relations messages to see if they do, indeed, communicate our fundamental purpose.

It was immediately clear to the people at the XYZ Hearing School that for 25 years they had not looked at their public relations message in light of the school's main objective. Without question, this was the primary reason that the general public did not know what was going on there. Such failure to examine a school's public relations messages in relation to its chief objective is also the main reason the public at large doesn't really know what's going on in most of our public, private, and parochial learning institutions. This lack of knowledge hinders the public's ability to form strong, positive opinions and to be supportive in firm ways. In truth, the average person in a community may have a distorted view of what courses are even in the school curriculum. Therefore, if we want the general public's support, we must come to terms with the fact that we have to give community members something they can support. This means information. But before we impart this information we have to be very clear ourselves about what we *are*, what we *believe*, and what we *do*.

Later in our discussion with the XYZ Hearing School administrators, we asked them to name their largest competitor. The administrators revealed the name of a much larger, more well-known institution in the same community. Then we asked an essential question: "What is it that they do that you don't do?"

They replied, "Our competitor believes in a practice called 'total communication.' That means that along with teaching students how to speak, they teach them how to use sign language."

"And you don't believe in 'total communication,' we gather. Why not?" we asked.

They replied, "Well, when children learn to sign at the same time they are learning to speak, they handicap themselves from ever becoming normally speaking adults. That's because as the child progresses through school, the learning concepts become more difficult. As this occurs, deaf children automatically revert to the signing to help themselves communicate. Eventually, the children use speech less and less and rely exclusively on sign language to communicate."

"Then without a doubt, you are convinced that your way is better. And you believe that your teaching method is absolutely necessary to meet the needs of deaf children?" we asked.

"Yes," they replied.

"You're not going to change your minds?" we questioned again.

"No," they replied emphatically.

"You're sure?" we asked one last time.

"Absolutely."

"If this is your belief and stance," we said, "then magnify it, glorify it, do everything you can to perpetuate it—and never, under any circumstances, apologize for it again."

It was in that spirit of conviction and purpose that the administrators of the XYZ Hearing School were able to begin to lay out a course of action that would help them create the kind of image that the school needed to prosper and thrive both internally and externally.

First, the administrators decided to change the name of the school to the XYZ Speech and Hearing School. Then they decided to fire a secretary who was conveying just the opposite of the image that they wanted to convey. They got board permission to refurbish the rather dull, conventional school entrance so that it communicated excitement, activity, and what the school was all about. They decided to start a preschool for children who could hear so that the deaf children would have daily experiences with speaking children. They started a bimonthly newsletter to doctors' offices, schools, churches, and social service agencies in the area. The newsletter was designed to communicate the different aspects of the school and to give useful tips for detecting hearing problems early. And finally, the staff became recommitted to making regular calls on doctors and hospitals to seek out referrals and meet the needs of their community.

All this happened as a result of planning a comprehensive, cohesive public relations program based upon the three "what's." First, what the school *is*. Second, what it *believes*. Third, what it *does*. And every decision met the needs, not only of students, parents, and the community, but of the organization from top to bottom.

SOME DEFINITIONS WE SHOULD KNOW

Without doubt, words such as promotion, publicity, and public relations are disturbing to many educators. In fact, many words in advertising and selling are complete turn-offs to some of us who work in schools. Maybe they're turn-offs because we automatically associate public relations with business, and we don't want education to be like any business. Or, we might just distrust these terms and practices because we view them as efforts or proclamations without substance or honesty. Thus, we want to convince ourselves that public relations efforts simply are not for schools. And yet, we are reminded daily that part of our job as administrators requires us to be very skillful in communicating with others—both face-to-face and in writing. We are also reminded by experience that we need to have communication skills when dealing with individuals as well as with small and large groups—if we expect to be successful in our jobs. And when we are reminded of the precise and disciplined skills needed to communicate with groups and individuals—skills we often lack—then our interest in acquiring public relations skills is rekindled.

We know that acquiring such skills is not easy. Fortunately, however, it may not be nearly as difficult or confusing as we might think. And once we come to the conclusion that we are in the work of enriching life, we will have an easier time with the whole area of public relations. For in reality, people want and need to know what we have to tell them about schools. All we really need to develop are more effective ways to get our vital messages across. To do so, we first need to examine the distinct differences between publicity, promotion, and public relations in order to deepen our understanding of these subjects and to see how each of these three functions can and does serve our needs and purposes well.

Promotion: Promotion is the activity that one pursues in order to seek or attract attention on behalf of a program or project. It includes efforts which precede the actual event. In schools, we promote continually to create interest in concerts, plays, athletic events, dances, back-to-school nights, and PTA meetings. Usually, promotion does not contain *hard* news nor does it contain a "peg" or "hook" for what could be considered a news story. Rather, promotional information merely communicates the what, where, and when of an activity. Good promotional efforts always reflect a desire to *sell* the benefits of a specific project, program, or activity. Promotional efforts that don't try to sell benefits won't compel people to take the action we want them to take. The rule for promotion is this: Don't just tell about the activity. Sell the *benefits* of the activity to the buyer.

Publicity: Publicity is the effort which occurs *after* an event. Its purpose is to inform or to impart information about something that *has already happened*. To be effective, publicity must have some *immediate news value*. Therefore, in order for an event to receive publicity, it must have a newsworthy "peg" or "hook" on which to hang a story. We can usually gain publicity when an athletic team wins or loses, when a teacher is given a special award, when our students participate in some special event, or when we are announcing honor rolls.

Public Relations: Public relations includes both publicity and promotion, but it also includes much more. Public relations includes communication about the day-to-day activities as well as the ongoing work and mission of the schools. Public relations involves describing the functions of the schools and of the people who work to fulfill the purpose of the schools. And it involves describing how students benefit from this work and mission. Its messages always revolve around the foundations upon which our educational institutions were created and the reason those institutions are maintained. Therefore, public relations is often educational or informational in nature. Good and effective public relations communications are designed to build and develop understanding and confidence in the whole of a community on behalf of the schools in a system. One of the tasks of public relations efforts is to enhance the schools, and establish a reputation of service and benefit to the whole community.

There are two other terms which are vital to your understanding of public relations: marketing and advertising.

Marketing: This is the science that precedes product or service development and advertising. Marketing includes gathering information about one's prospective clients. With this marketing information, an organization or business can make the determination about what needs it can fill, how its products and services can and will be distributed, and what methods it will use to let people know about those products and services.

Advertising: Webster defines advertising this way:

> "to publish a notice of; to give conspicuous notice or information of to the public through newspapers, signs, circulars, posters, periodical publications, radio, television, etc.; especially, to praise publicly in this way to encourage buying; as, to *advertise* goods for sale, entertainments to occur, etc."

In the business world, advertising is the most inexpensive way for manufacturers, jobbers, retailers, and others to communicate to the consumer about their products. On the flip side, advertising is also a very useful and necessary tool for the consumer. It is advertising which usually informs him or her about products and services that will make life easier or better in some way. Advertising also helps the customer expand as well as narrow the selection process when buying. This is a point that is often missed by advertising critics. However, the vast majority of people become educated or knowledgeable about products and services *only* because of advertising. Without advertising, people might know very little about the products and services available to them.

WHAT SCHOOL PUBLIC RELATIONS IS AND IS NOT

● **School public relations *IS...effective communication between schools and public*.** Good school public relations seeks to gain the public's favorable attention by building goodwill and understanding about the work, mission, and activities of the school. In the process of seeking such attention and reputation, educators must remember that a school has many publics. These publics include students, parents, and the community. They also include business people, doctors, lawyers, and laborers. Too, these publics include young, middle-aged, and senior citizens as well as marrieds, singles, and others of different races, cultures, and socioeconomic groups. Remember, your publics include all the individuals and groups in your district—including those citizens who have children in school and those who don't. They also include those who pay high taxes, low taxes, or no taxes at all. In parochial schools, they also include those who support the church, but don't want to support the school. In fact, if the parochial school is concerned about enrollments the public includes all the people in the community, even if they aren't of the same religious preference. They are still affected by the schools and may even consider sending their children to the schools if the education is noted to be of high quality.

- **School public relations *IS NOT...a precise science*.** Though there are some vital fundamental management and communication techniques that facilitate successful public relations, there are no sure-fire ways, means, slogans, events, programs, or ideas that will work in *every* instance, *every* time. In truth, good public relations can make a good school or system appear as good as it is, but it cannot turn a bad school into a good one. Image must match reality for public relations to work. And it needs mentioning that public relations efforts can be prime motivators in helping all who are engaged in the educational process create bigger dreams, make better promises, work harder to keep those promises, and find more recognition and satisfaction in the process.

- **School public relations *IS NOT...handshaking, glad-handing, or employing gimmicks*.** Such actions may even do more harm than good because they are complete turn-offs to many people. In fact, people who rely on these three techniques usually don't survive for the long term. Unfortunately, one of the things that has given public relations a bad name among educators is our mistaken stereotype of a public relations representative. This stereotype consists of a person who smiles without thinking, talks without sincerity, hobnobs with important and influential people, and has a knack for manipulating people as well as the media to achieve his or her own ends. This false concept keeps many educators from wanting to acquire public relations abilities. However, we should be aware that this type of person has nothing to do with *effective* public relations programs or practices—nor will such misdirected efforts survive for the long term. Remember, good public relations is based upon truth and substance, not deception and fluff.

- **School public relations *IS NOT...motivated by self-interest*.** It must be motivated by public interest. Self-interested public relations people frequently subscribe to the philosophy that the public only needs to know what *they*—the public relations people—want the public to know. These public relations people believe that the best way to achieve persuasion is by overwhelming the public with pressure, with force, or by "dazzling." They also hold a supercilious attitude toward the public that is damaging beyond measure. They perpetuate beliefs such as: "They (the public) don't want to know that," "Who do they think they are?" or "They don't care," or "They'll never understand the complexity of this issue." "They" is always the reference given to the public. Unfortunately, such public relations people actually look down on the public as being "common and dumb." This disrespect for the public is certain to result in a public relations effort that is empty, insignificant, synthetic, and disrespected.

Worse, such efforts are seldom rewarding and uplifting to the person who has the task of creating a public relations program. Instead of using truth and persuasion in an attempt to court the public or win the public's favor, such a public relations campaign is obsessed with its own smartness, smugness, and superiority. Public relations efforts that are truly memorable always grow out of *humility, sincerity,* and *respectful consideration* for the public—and for the public's viewpoint.

Unfortunately, there are many ways for public relations efforts to be or to become self-serving. They can become efforts to glorify a person rather than the school. We may even start believing and proclaiming that we, ourselves—rather than the entire staff—have created a good school. And such misdirected thinking and efforts often occur at the expense of the school. We've all known administrators, coaches, choral directors, classroom teachers, and student council sponsors who became "stars" for their involvement in a particular event or cause. Though they may, indeed, have had the ability to make things happen for their particular interest, they may have also lost sight of the whole mission of the school in the process. As a result, parents and community members knew who the "stars" were, as well as the significance of their efforts, but knew nothing about the contributions of others to the achievement being proclaimed or even to other achievements. This is not public relations. This is individual promotion. The educator with good public relations sense will always position himself or herself, as well as his or her special activity, as being a part of the whole—and as having a place in the total education of children. He or she never becomes bigger or more important than other colleagues, other activities, or the institution he or she is serving.

● **School public relations *IS...substance, benefits, and rewards that create interest*.** It involves persuading and convincing people to support the ways and means used to get the work of the school accomplished for the benefit of children. The primary goal of public relations is to communicate the work of students, educators, and the mission of the schools so that people know and understand what they are buying and the benefits of their purchase. This task is vitally important because the majority of people who pay for the schools do not have children in schools. Yet, all of society benefits in a direct way from the work and mission of educational institutions. Herein lies the reason a public relations program is important. After all, you can have the best product or have the best service in the world, but if you can't sell it, it is worthless. Worse, if you can't sell it, you may not survive.

Chrysler is testimony to this fact. Although Chrysler made a good car, the company couldn't sell it until Lee Iacocca arrived on the scene. It was his ability to rekindle the knowledge of the benefits of owning a Chrysler automobile in the minds of the public that turned the company around. There is a parallel in this Chrysler story for schools. The schools of this nation have done a tremendous job of educating children, but they aren't receiving the number of dollars they need to prosper and thrive. This takes selling and persuading.

The first principle of persuasion is this: Individual thought governs individual action. We only have to go to the classroom to learn this public relations principle. A teacher does not teach a class. Rather, a teacher teaches students in a class. The minute a teacher starts to teach a class rather than individual students, trouble can be expected. Therefore, to influence the public's decision to accept our messages, persuasion efforts must be designed to influence the thoughts of individual members of the public. This also means we must appeal to what's important to our public, not what's important to us as educators—or what's important to the school or district. That's why every message to the public must convey personal benefits to each individual with the welfare of children being the fundamental value in every message or decision.

- **School public relations *IS NOT...just information; it is quality information*.** Public relations people often talk about "quality of information." We need to learn exactly what this phrase means. The quality of information is determined and judged by its accuracy, completeness, clearness, and conciseness. If any of these factors is missing, we need to know that misunderstandings can be *expected*.

- **School public relations *IS...inclusive rather than exclusive*.** Good public relations doesn't just "tell" the public information. Rather, it tries to involve community members in their schools with the information being presented. Public relations is communication that appeals to the public's desire to identify with the schools, be a part of the schools, and dream with the schools' teachers, children, and administrators. It also strives to create in the public the desire to have a sense or feeling of ownership in the schools. So many times, we as educators want our work to be admired from a distance, but we don't want outsiders coming in and "mucking it up." We want public support, but we don't want public involvement. Yet, the professional attitude which lies at the foundation of a good public relations program is one that thinks of the public as an *inherent part* of the day-to-day operations of the schools—on the *inside*, not on the *outside*. After all, the schools belong to the public. They do not belong to us. Therefore, any actions which indicate that we believe that the schools belong to us will not find success.

- **School public relations *IS...motivated by a serving interest*.** Those educators who are most effective in their public relations communication hold the belief that their own personal satisfaction occurs in direct proportion to their ability to help others and meet the needs of the school. That's why their every communication holds to the value of serving the welfare of students.

- **School public relations *IS...polite*.** According to public relations expert Alfred M. Cooper, politeness is a vital element in public contact. He defines politeness as those manners or gestures which are essential to human contact. However, he warns that politeness which is not accompanied by an expression of interest in the public's problem may actually antagonize. Therefore, we must not forget to express interest when we are being polite. This action will serve our public relations effort well.

THE BENEFITS OF A STRONG, WELL-PLANNED PUBLIC RELATIONS PROGRAM

The benefits to our public of better, clearer, as well as more continuous and comprehensive information from us are obvious. Yet, some exploration is needed to determine how a strong, well-planned program of public relations benefits administrators, staff, and schools in general. For it is the administrators and staff who will have to expend the effort to formulate and deliver such a program. So let's explore the benefits.

A well-planned public relations program:

1. Helps you establish objectives, procedures, and practices that meet the needs of the organization from the top to the bottom. The example of the XYZ Hearing School illustrated this point very effectively. The administrators of the school decided what the school was, what it believed, and what it did. Determining the three "what's" allowed them to make decisions with conviction about the name, the physical plant, the personnel, the curriculum, the activities of their staff, and the vehicles they would use to communicate the messages of the school. Indeed, the needs of the organization were fulfilled in ways that made sense and ways that were tied together. More than once in the course of our careers we have probably felt that we were making decisions that lacked cohesiveness for the schools and the staff. Not deciding how we wanted to appear and what we stood for may have been the reason.

2. Allows you to explain to people facts they don't know about your school and services that they might not even be aware are available. Make no mistake: There are vast numbers of people who really think schools teach only reading, writing, and arithmetic. They have no idea of the extensiveness of the average curriculum. In fact, you'd be surprised to learn the number of people who don't know what the word "curriculum" means. Nor are most people the least bit knowledgeable about the extracurricular activities the school provides—except the athletic teams or those in which their children participate. A planned program of public relations allows you to inform the public, on an ongoing basis, about all the different facets of school life.

3. Allows people to see all educators as serving functions rather than simply holding positions. Not only do people not know about all the activities of school life, but they don't understand the various tasks performed by paid personnel of the school district. Although most people have had the experience of sitting in a classroom and they know what a teacher does, very few people really know what an administrator does. And even fewer know what a superintendent, media specialist, or curriculum director does. If you were to ask the average kindergartner or first-grader who the superintendent is, the child might tell you he or she is the principal's mother or father. As you make the effort to inform the public in a planned public relations program, people begin to get the idea that all the workers in the school are indispensable, beneficial, and functional parts of the whole system—whatever their positions.

4. *Allows people to see the schools in your district as more than activities-dominated institutions.* As a rule, people don't hear about what goes on in the classrooms. But they do hear about sports events, dances, plays, musicals, and a variety of other activities. This is due to the power of publicity and promotion for these events. However, an overemphasis on publicity for these kinds of events is likely to lead the public into developing images of schools which have nothing to do with academics. And such publicity can turn parents and the public off—just as it can turn them on. After all, there are only eleven players on an offense and eleven on a defense in a football game. If some parent's child is sitting on the bench—or didn't make the team at all—that parent may be very unhappy. The same is true for students who don't make the band, student council, or the spring musical.

On the other hand, every child is in a classroom every day, and every child has a chance to participate—even excel—in particular areas. If we have a plan and execute it properly, we can cover all the classrooms in our school every year with our public relations efforts. Indeed, information about academics is what will give us the image we desire—and it's also the kind of information which parents and public alike want and need to hear.

5. *Helps provide constant staff direction for maintaining a student-centered school— as long as the program is shared with the other school staff members.* A good public relations program begins by asking teachers and support staff how they would like to appear in the minds of the public (See *PUBLIC RELATIONS IDEA #42).* Adjectives such as caring, competent, knowledgeable, fair, loving, sincere, friendly, motivating, and professional will invariably surface. Make no mistake: The achievement of these image goals is impossible if a school is not student-centered. And once staff members know that you are going to magnify and glorify what they are doing, the vast majority will become very careful not to do anything to contradict this image—or do anything about which they wouldn't want others to know. They become very concerned that the reality of what they are doing as professionals matches the image you are trying to create for them and the school or district. This makes the task of improving schools easier because most people will work to stay in the limelight once they experience a little of it. Remember, achievement without recognition renders the achievement less significant in any worker's eyes. Unfortunately, too many administrators expect teachers to maintain a high level of productivity without any recognition for their efforts. And a lack of recognition can also be interpreted as a lack of appreciation.

In essence, an ongoing emphasis on public relations contains the side benefit to staff members of being recognized, appreciated, and rewarded for doing their jobs well. Staff members know that their efforts won't be overlooked or minimized—and that they will count in somebody's eyes other than their own. As a result, such an emphasis helps to sustain a good, hard-working, and continually improving staff.

6. Has a cumulative effect. Unlike publicity and promotion which have their effects and then die after the event is over, good public relations *builds*—as long as the image created matches the reality of what's happening. Good public relations efforts actually help a school or system gain credibility over time. And that's why such efforts are so important.

A
STANCE
FOR SUCCESS

Ideas on public relations, publicity, promotion, marketing, and advertising will be offered throughout this book. We will even number them for you, but by no means do they need to be used in any order. Likewise, it is not implied that you need to use all of the ideas offered. And it needs to be said that you can add to these ideas. Too, you will generate more ideas and will acquire more skills and expertise by practicing the ideas offered, consistently and frequently.

For those educators who really wish to become more knowledgeable about selling themselves, their schools, and their profession, we advise that they adopt this stance: "I may not know much about public relations right now, but six months from now I'm going to know a great deal more than I know today—and a year from now, I'll know even more. In five years, few are going to be able to rival my knowledge." Remember, improvement is the only reasonable management goal for all educators—staff and administrators alike. It is also the only reasonable goal for an organization. Therefore, the most professional and success-producing attitude you can have in learning to use promotion, publicity, and public relations is to strive for continuous improvement. If you take this stance, you'll be a more influential administrator in many ways. But, please don't get discouraged by what you don't know today. We were all novices at some point in our careers in all the areas in which we now have considerable expertise. You'll find the same is true of public relations.

CHAPTER

II

TWO

STEP ONE: DECIDE HOW YOU WANT TO APPEAR

"It is not enough to understand what we ought to be, unless we know what we are; and we do not understand what we are, unless we know what we ought to be."
—T.S. Eliot

We have said it before and we'll say it again. There is much we can learn from the world of business about getting our school message across to the public. After all, businesses invest capital and open their doors—then they prosper or die in direct proportion to their ability to relate the benefits of their goods and services to their customers and potential customers. And make no mistake, we too are a business. We are vying for our share of the private and tax dollars available—and there are only so many dollars in our community. These dollars will be used for education—or to fund roads, bridges, or new agencies. These dollars will be used to buy cars, rings, hamburgers, clothes, shoes, or something else. In fact, everyone in the community is competing for these dollars.

Jewelers, for instance, are not competing only with other jewelers. Rather, they are competing with everyone for a share of the dollars available. They are trying to get people to buy rings instead of cars as well as get people who are buying rings to purchase rings at their store. As educators, we don't like to think in terms of competing for money. Yet, these are the realities we must deal with in getting more money to do the quality job we want to do for children.

That's why it would be wise for each of us to study the communication devices that successful businesses use to create value, tell their stories, and sell their goods and services. Such study is not difficult. And it is very easy to begin. Tonight, for instance, when you read the newspaper concentrate on the advertisements as well as the news. When you turn on the radio or television, pay closer attention to the commercials. You may acquire a great deal of valuable information about advertising which can be applied to schools and the profession of education. Without question, applying what you learn from the various media may have benefits ranging from happier, more productive students to increased satisfaction and higher salaries for teachers and administrators.

Regardless of the number of advertisements you *read, hear,* or *see*, be aware that all the good ones will have some common features. You won't have to observe closely to note that none of the advertisements will tell you to buy because their employees want or need more money. None will say you aren't treating them right or that you don't appreciate their company products enough. *Absolutely* none will tell you what their company can't or won't do for you unless you support them or buy from them.

All the commercials *will* try to inform. And as they do, they will talk about the special values and benefits of their companies, products, and services. They will all try to convince and persuade you to act. Many will even talk about the expertise of their people. Most will make you a promise as well as give you a guarantee. Some will even promise you satisfaction—ranging from convenience to status*—if you'll buy their products or services.

Your public relations efforts should do the same. And they can, if you'll think in terms of values and benefits to the community you serve. It all begins with meeting the needs of students—something which you are already trying to do. Therefore, you have nothing new to develop. You don't have to create any new services in beginning. All you need to do is develop and create a program to tell people *what* you are doing.

THE THREE
MOST IMPORTANT DECISIONS
WE WILL MAKE AS EDUCATORS

So, how do major manufacturers arrive at the lists of benefits that eventually come to us via the media concerning their products and services? The answer is both interesting and thought-provoking. Every year the best companies worldwide outline strategies to increase the public's awareness of their individual products. The foundation of these strategies begins with three basic decisions. They are the same three decisions you must make in order to begin building a positive image for your schools.

---

*See Chapter III, "THE INDIVIDUAL PEOPLE MOTIVATORS AND HOW THEY AFFECT PUBLIC RELATIONS."

DECISION NUMBER ONE: HOW WILL YOU POSITION YOURSELF?

The first decision you must make is to choose how you are going to position yourself, your school, or your system in the community. This means deciding that you are purposely going to build an image for your school instead of just "letting things take their own course." *How* you position yourself and your school is vital. For instance, you can position yourself as one who is approachable or one who is perpetually defensive and close-minded. You can position yourself as progressive or conservative. You can position yourself as one who makes decisions and takes actions which are designed to be in the best interests of students, or as a school or district which is blown in one direction and then another depending upon who is applying the pressure. You can position yourself and your staff as professionals who love children and teaching— or as educators who can't wait for Saturday and Sunday, as well as June, July, and August. You can position yourself as a college prep school or a comprehensive school, an athletic school or an academic one, as a school that cares about *all* students or one that places more value on the "good" students or those who are college bound.

Positioning is everything in building a public image, as well as building a good school. One thing is certain: A superintendent, principal, or teacher who isn't positioned to build the public trust will never acquire the freedom necessary to give the best possible education to students. The simple truth is that you already have a position in the minds of students, parents, and the community. And it's either one that you have effectively implanted or one that the community has developed without input from you. But you have a position nonetheless. You may cherish this position you have. If you do, then magnify it, glorify it, and perpetuate it in a planned way. If you don't like your image, set out to change it in a planned way.

Often, because we haven't decided *how* we wish to position ourselves, we send mixed messages to our public. One day our decisions appear student-centered, the next day they appear teacher-centered or athletic-program-centered. The day after that our decision may seem bus-driver-centered, religious-program-centered, or money-centered. When this is the case, our public is confused—consciously or subconsciously—over *our* confusion and people can't support our actions because they can't follow them. Worse, the staff of the school or district suffers from the same confusion.

Example 1: *A Positioning Error*

    Years ago, a young nun who was new in administration came to us about the problem of declining enrollment in her school. When we asked her what she thought the problem was, it didn't take long for her to offer a reply. It had been the practice of the staff to meet every morning before school for five minutes of prayer. Then, because the school started employing more and more lay teachers—some Catholic and some not—the daily practice was questioned by the staff. So, the sister put the question of daily staff prayer to a staff vote. The teachers voted to abandon the daily prayer practice, but compromised by saying they would agree to meet once a week for prayer. It wasn't long before the school started to have problems with lay teachers not wanting to conduct daily prayer in the classrooms. When this happened, parents became concerned. Some became angry. The next school year, parents began withdrawing their children from the school. Enrollment declined dramatically. And, of course, the school began to have financial problems as the result.

As the young sister talked, she realized that the enrollment problems arose as the result of a basic positioning error. Her school was a Catholic school. It was founded for the purpose of teaching academics along with teaching Christian values— one of which is prayer. When the administration allowed itself to wander from its basic position with the staff, the school began to have problems everywhere.

Example 2: *A Positioning Error*

Attendance at faculty meetings has been a concern for ages. That's why we should be able to relate to the following example. A public high school administrator took a strong position with his staff that *everyone* had to attend faculty meetings. "There will be no exceptions," he said. Then, as is frequently the case when a blanket "no exceptions" rule is made, people came to ask that they be the only exceptions to the rule. The coaches asked to be excused because they had to hold practice. So exceptions were made. Next, certain teachers asked to be excused due to conflicting doctors' appointments, club meetings, and personal commitments. Again, exceptions were made. The effect was that the administrator had taken virtually no position at all regarding attendance at faculty meetings. And as a result, everyone who wanted to be an exception started lining up at his door. As you can well imagine, attendance at the faculty meetings was erratic—and the principal was criticized every time someone was excused.

The mistake was a basic error in positioning. The principal knew what he desired, but didn't have a plan to get it. The principal could have held to his original position *and* taken into account personal commitments, conflicts, and emergencies by holding two identical faculty meetings—one in the morning and one in the afternoon. Then, everyone could attend. But by choosing the course he did, the administrator devalued his original decision, jeopardized staff morale—as well as the efficient functioning of the entire school—and created a credibility gap to boot.

When it comes to image as well as management, positioning is vital. In a public relations program, we first need to decide *what* we want. Second, we must decide *how* we want to position ourselves to get what we want. Third, we must never take action which will conflict with the image or goals we desire.

The most sound professional position we can take is one in which we do everything we can to create and maintain a student-centered philosophy in our schools. As long as every decision has the welfare of students as its foundation, we are on defensible ground—even when we err. A close look will reveal that it's only when we are not student-centered that problems occur. Worse, we can't justify our actions when problems do occur—if we are not student-centered.

It's easy to make a similar parallel in the business world. Businesses that are customer-centered are the ones which are thriving and prospering. And those that are business-centered, employee-centered, or directed in any other way are the ones that are dying—or merely existing from one month to the next.

In this vein, once we are positioned appropriately, we need to consider our second most important decision: making a promise.

DECISION NUMBER TWO: MAKE YOUR STUDENTS/COMMUNITY A PROMISE

In 1977, when a group of leading Americans were asked by *U.S. News and World Report* to rate the influence of major institutions in the United States, these were the results. (See Figure 2-1.)

Organized religion came in twenty-sixth. Educational institutions came in a weak fifteenth behind Wall Street and the Democratic Party. But the real shocker is who came in third: labor unions.

In retrospect, it should be easy to see why labor unions were near the top of the list. They made their members a promise. They said they would elevate the quality of life for their members—and what's more, they delivered. As management, we may not like unions. We may not want to give them credit for anything. However, the truth of the matter is that if we had been thinking in terms of making our employees various kinds of promises to improve the quality of their lives—and delivering—it's doubtful that many unions would have become so powerful.

That's why the second most important thing we must do to establish a powerful public image is to make our students and our communities a promise—and then

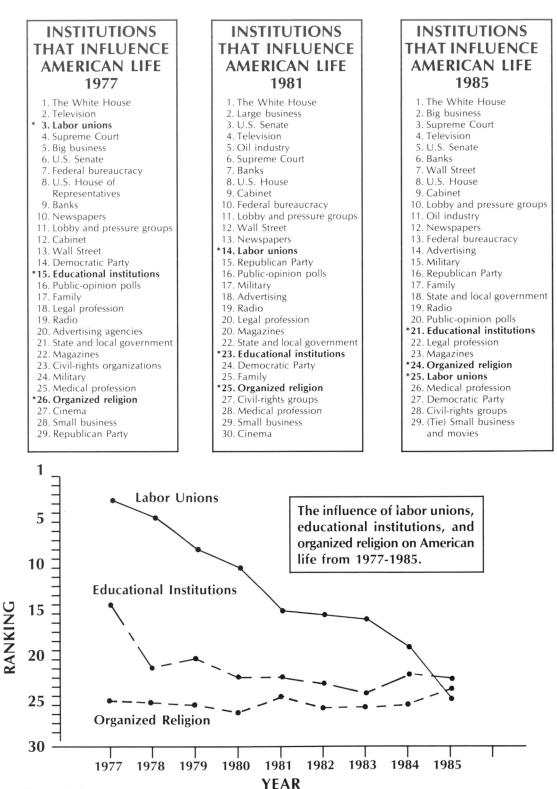

INSTITUTIONS THAT INFLUENCE AMERICAN LIFE 1977

1. The White House
2. Television
* 3. **Labor unions**
4. Supreme Court
5. Big business
6. U.S. Senate
7. Federal bureaucracy
8. U.S. House of Representatives
9. Banks
10. Newspapers
11. Lobby and pressure groups
12. Cabinet
13. Wall Street
14. Democratic Party
*15. **Educational institutions**
16. Public-opinion polls
17. Family
18. Legal profession
19. Radio
20. Advertising agencies
21. State and local government
22. Magazines
23. Civil-rights organizations
24. Military
25. Medical profession
*26. **Organized religion**
27. Cinema
28. Small business
29. Republican Party

INSTITUTIONS THAT INFLUENCE AMERICAN LIFE 1981

1. The White House
2. Large business
3. U.S. Senate
4. Television
5. Oil industry
6. Supreme Court
7. Banks
8. U.S. House
9. Cabinet
10. Federal bureaucracy
11. Lobby and pressure groups
12. Wall Street
13. Newspapers
*14. **Labor unions**
15. Republican Party
16. Public-opinion polls
17. Military
18. Advertising
19. Radio
20. Legal profession
20. Magazines
22. State and local government
*23. **Educational institutions**
24. Democratic Party
25. Family
*25. **Organized religion**
27. Civil-rights groups
28. Medical profession
29. Small business
30. Cinema

INSTITUTIONS THAT INFLUENCE AMERICAN LIFE 1985

1. The White House
2. Big business
3. Supreme Court
4. Television
5. U.S. Senate
6. Banks
7. Wall Street
8. U.S. House
9. Cabinet
10. Lobby and pressure groups
11. Oil industry
12. Newspapers
13. Federal bureaucracy
14. Advertising
15. Military
16. Republican Party
17. Family
18. State and local government
19. Radio
20. Public-opinion polls
*21. **Educational institutions**
22. Legal profession
23. Magazines
*24. **Organized religion**
*25. **Labor unions**
26. Medical profession
27. Democratic Party
28. Civil-rights groups
29. (Tie) Small business and movies

Labor Unions

The influence of labor unions, educational institutions, and organized religion on American life from 1977-1985.

Educational Institutions

Organized Religion

RANKING

YEAR

Figure 2-1

26

deliver. The most desirable promise we can make is that we will give each and every child a great education. It's the best promise we can make to *gain* and *keep* a position of trust, respect, influence, and leadership. But without a plan for *continuous communication* of this stance to our communities, we must realize that people will never know we are making any promises, much less believe that we are keeping the promises we make.

There is a management law called the Law of Positive Reinforcement. We will be discussing this law in depth in Chapter IV. This law relates, *In the absence of positive reinforcement from appointed leaders, negative human attitudes and behaviors are most likely to emerge from the group being led.* In a nutshell, this means that not only do we have to make our students and our communities positive promises, but we have to repeat those promises over and over again in a variety of ways to prevent the negative from emerging and dominating. That's why companies run the same commercials over and over again. And it's the reason that they repeat identical messages in all the media. And they deliver on the promises they make. If we don't take similar action in presenting the work, mission, and benefits of our schools to students and the community, we'll have to learn a public relations lesson the hard way. That lesson is that in the absence of positive communication, the public may believe the worst about us and our schools—especially when a crisis hits.

When we cease to make promises which are in agreement with the reason for our organization's existence (see the Law of Origin, Chapter IV p. 46), and we cease to communicate the benefits of these promises to those that we serve, a predictable thing happens. We fail. By 1980, labor unions had dropped in the influence rating to number ten. Educational institutions had dropped to number twenty-three, and organized religion to number twenty-eight. By 1985, labor unions dropped further. They were now twenty-fifth behind organized religion (24) and educational institutions (21).*

The question is, "Why?" We believe the answer is a very simple one. The promises of labor unions, while good for the worker in 1977, by 1985 had become unwieldy for the companies that had the employees on their payrolls. The promises and demands of the unions became union-centered instead of in the best interests of each organization as a whole. The unions also lost sight of the greater mission of the organizations at which workers were employed—to meet the needs of customers. They began to say, "What's good for the employee is good for the company and its customers," instead of, "What's good for the company and its customers is good for the employee." When foreign competition became a formidable force in the marketplace, the unions, which had kept wages and benefits of workers at a noncompetitive rate, predictably fell from power.

A similar parallel can be made in education. As society changed from a manual labor society to an industrial based society to a high tech, information based society, there

---

*Charts used with permission from *U.S. News & World Report*.

was a greater need for more of our population to be highly educated. Suddenly, the emphasis of the nation had shifted away from the top 50 percent of the students—whom the nation knew it could count on to be productive members of society—to the bottom 50 percent of students whom the nation needed to operate more highly sophisticated equipment. Now, the nation also needed students with increased abilities to reason, communicate, and make good decisions. To compound the problem, for the longest time, educators had been what we call "process" oriented. They executed the "process" of teaching to the best of their ability. The thinking was, "It's my responsibility to teach. It's students' responsibility to learn." As long as the act of learning was a student's responsibility, educators didn't have to be accountable—if they were using all the "right" processes. As the needs of society became even greater, society insisted that educators become accountable. And it's a fact that until we become "results oriented" and see ourselves as accountable, we will continue to get a very low rating among institutions that influence people's lives.

Unfortunately, of all the things we advise administrators to do, the thing that many have the hardest time with is the idea of making promises—to anyone. The fear of not being able to deliver what they promise seems to paralyze them and keep them from making any promise at all. And some will only make conditional promises—which are really no promises at all. And yet, most administrators are already delivering much in the way of benefits—to students, teachers, support staff, and parents—that they should be able to promise up front, and gain the rewards for doing so.

At the Master Teacher Leadership Conference held in Manhattan, Kansas, each summer, we once had an administrator stand up and say vehemently: "Baloney! I don't buy this idea of making promises! I have two sexually abused girls in my school this year. How am I going to promise them that they'll have a great school year?"

In reply, we offered the following: "You're right. You can't promise them that they'll have a great school year. But what *can* you promise them?"

The principal was a very good man, and although he hemmed and hawed, looked down, and shuffled his feet, it didn't take him long to come up with an answer. "Well, I suppose I can promise them that if they ever need anyone to talk to, I'll be there for them...and I know I can promise to arrange special help for them in their studies...and I can also promise that this information will remain absolutely confidential."

"Are you going to do those things anyway?" we asked.

"Yes, of course," he replied.

"Well, why don't you promise the girls those things up front, and help relieve their worry?" we suggested.

The central issue is this: All of us have the opportunity every day to take some of the worry, concern, and fear out of other people's lives and to create the positive image we want and need to function effectively—just by making promises. This doesn't mean far out or pie-in-the-sky types of promises. We should never make promises that we couldn't possibly fulfill. However, there are promises we *can* make for those things we already know we are going to do. Remember, people who position themselves and their organizations as worry-relievers and helpers are always considered valuable and enjoy the best reputations.

We have a colleague at The Master Teacher who went from secretary to office manager in a matter of two years. In looking back, we realize that her advancement was probably due to a very effective technique of hers. Every time someone asked her to do something, she replied, "No problem. You'll have it," or, "I promise I'll have it on your desk in twenty minutes." When there was something she was really going to have to work hard to accomplish, she'd say, "It looks like this might take me a while, but I can promise it by Wednesday morning." She never let anyone worry about when or if she could get something done. She made those decisions—and she always delivered on her promises. Everyone came to rely on her. There's no doubt she wouldn't have been nearly as effective if she had just delivered without relieving the worry by making a promise—up front.

Conversely, we have all known teachers or support staff who just didn't know if they could manage to do something in the time we needed it done. Yet, most of the time they *do* come through. But they let us worry about it until they deliver. When they do deliver, we may be relieved, but we aren't particularly grateful. The reason is that they let us hang out to dry—and never appear to be the least bit concerned about *our* welfare or *our* worry in the process.

That's why if we want to be valued and appreciated by others, we have to learn to make promises to our students and public and help our staffs do the same. After all, it's only by the promises we make—and deliver—that we can convince anyone to trust us to do what we say we can do.

DECISION NUMBER THREE: BUILD YOUR IMAGE ON POSITIVE IDEAS

Along with positioning and promises, the third dimension needed for a public relations program is positive ideas. In truth, unless we build our image on positive ideas for helping students and teachers find success in school, what we are saying about the merits of our schools is unlikely to match reality. We simply must have the constructive ideas which contribute to the makings of a first-rate school so that we can deliver a first-rate image. It takes positive and enthusiastic ideas to make people notice what we are doing for children—and to cause them to develop good feelings about us as well as take the action we want them to take to support us. Furthermore, our ideas must contain benefits for everyone. A close look will tell you that banks don't say they exist only for people with a lot of money. Likewise, retail clothing stores have different lines of apparel for different kinds of people. They don't sell clothes just for people who are a perfect size 10. In schools, we must have ideas for meeting the needs of all students: the average, the gifted, the college bound, the noncollege bound, male, female, English speaking, and non-English speaking. We must have positive ideas about showing *all* students how to be successful in school. And we must realize that many students don't think they can be successful without our help. Therefore, our ideas must involve *more* than merely showing off our schools—they must create in students a desire to use the schools to the fullest.

The fact is this: The ideas we need are already there. We already have much teaching expertise and we are already employing many techniques which are helping children find success. We're doing fantastic things with and for children. But if these methods, techniques, and successes are not known to anyone, they have little value insofar as a public relations effort is concerned. The truth is that we bus children to school and give them more class and extraclass choices than schools anywhere else on earth. We feed them, provide social activities, explore career choices, give health care and counseling services as well as provide books, libraries, gyms, playgrounds, and lounges. The list goes on and on. We often forget about communicating these facts to students, parents, and the public.

Why do you think the people at Coca-Cola® spend millions of dollars each year to keep the name of their product in front of the world public? Don't they really believe that Coke® ("the real thing") is as firmly entrenched in the minds of the average consumer as apple pie and the American flag? Are they really afraid we'll forget?

The answer is *yes*. The history of marketing tells them of an undeniable truth: "Out of sight—out of business." That's why year after year the researchers, chemists, product developers, marketing specialists, and distributors of Coke® think of more and better ideas to captivate the public. New Coke®, Classic Coke®, Cherry Coke®, Diet Coke®, and Caffeine-Free Coke® are just some of the positive ideas that have emerged. They are the products of a company that knows the truth of building an image on positive and beneficial ideas—and that also knows what will happen when a company fails to do so.

As educators, do we really believe that there will ever be a time when our services are not needed? Perhaps not. But maybe if we were afraid that such a time might come, we would take a stronger position, be willing to make some promises, and be dedicated to developing more new ideas which help students and teachers be more successful. Likewise, we might avoid some of the image mistakes we make. Our image mistakes don't lie with the failure to teach and care for children. In truth, educators have probably executed more good ideas more effectively than any other professionals in the world. Our real failure often comes in our inability to formulate and communicate our veritable plethora of ideas for teaching children to the public at large who pay us to do this task.

The following chapters of this book are full of tips that should help you be a more effective public relations communicator of the ideas that already exist in your schools, classrooms, and district. If you don't agree that we have given you more ideas than you can use and if you are not a more effective public relations agent for education after reading this book—return it to us and we will send you a complete refund. That's a promise.

PEOPLE BUY WHAT YOU BUY— BENEFITS

"...No one can long make a profit producing anything unless the customer makes a profit using it."
—Samuel B. Pettengill

As educators, we are first human beings, just like all other professional people. And as human beings, we are prone to cite all kinds of external reasons for the neutral or poor public image we may hold and the public relations problems we face—if our public image is, indeed, a problem. Lack of money is the most common reason given by most of us. But we also cite lack of adequate personnel and time, the interest or noninterest of parents, our inability to attract teachers, and the reputations of competitive schools. Likewise, workload, physical location or condition of the building, our powerless position, and even our sex are the rationalizations we use for not being able to sell our ideas within our schools to those we work with and manage each day. This is normal human thinking. If we aren't familiar with and don't know how to use the motivators which influence buying and the acceptance of ideas—what else is there to blame? Nevertheless, we must know and accept that these rationalizations—from lack of time to the condition of our buildings—are just that: rationalizations.

THE INDIVIDUAL PEOPLE MOTIVATORS AND HOW THEY AFFECT PUBLIC RELATIONS EFFORTS

Once we come to know, come to understand, and are able to employ the nine motivators that influence all people, we will never again seriously consider using our old justifications for lack of success. A close look at these nine motivators will reveal that the overwhelming number of public relations problems, whether internal or external, are usually problems concerning benefits. That's because people don't buy into ideas, plans, programs, decisions, or actions. Rather, they buy into *benefits*—the benefits that these ideas, plans, programs, decisions, or actions will produce or provide for them. If this weren't true, we wouldn't have such a wide variety of products and services to choose from in this country. For example, instead of the hundreds of makes, models, and colors of automobiles on the market, there would be just one. And yet we know that millions of people every year buy, trade, rent, and lease cars of different makes and models, in different price ranges, for different degrees of comfort, convenience, and reliability. They have been compelled to do so by one or more of the following nine motivators. It stands to reason that we, too, can use these same motivators individually and in combination to compel people both inside and outside our schools to be greatly interested in the services and benefits we provide. Let's explore these motivators.

1. PERSONAL GAIN

This is the strongest of all motivators. The need for personal gain is inherent in all decisions to buy—or do anything—and is expressed by what we call the primary question: "What's in it for me?" People ask themselves this question before they bank at a particular bank, eat at a particular restaurant, or send their children to piano lessons. Therefore, if our community asks, "What's in our schools for me?" and the answer is "Nothing" our schools are in trouble. If we want to raise taxes for schools, for instance, people will automatically ask, "What do I get out of it?" If we can't provide the answers, we shouldn't be upset when the public doesn't vote overwhelmingly in favor of the increase we ask for.

Remember, the question, "What's in it for me?" is asked by every human being at every level. Teachers are asking it on a daily basis. "What's in it for me to work on this committee or take on this extra duty?" "What's in it for me to attend staff meetings, work with slow students, do as my principal asks, or be evaluated by my administrator?" Students are asking, "What's in it for me to be taught by this teacher, to do my homework, or to show up for class every day?" Principals, superintendents, and boards of education ask their own primary questions too. And in each case, we are searching for one thing: benefits—personal ones.

When an administrator is having difficulty getting along with a teacher, for instance, knowledge of this motivator will reveal immediately that it would be wise to ask these questions: "What's in it for this teacher to work with me?" "What's in it for him or her to trust me?" "What's in it for him or her to believe in my ideas and put them into practice?" Once we apply these questions about benefits to our personal and professional interactions, we will often realize where our difficulties lie—and where our opportunities and advantages lie as well. We should also be aware that it's an error to assume that each teacher knows the answers to these questions—or that each teacher will always comply with our requests simply because we're administrators. The answers to these questions must be taught.

The foundation of every school public relations program should be to answer the primary question for every segment of the community. "What's in the schools for me?" "How do schools help me *directly*?" These are the questions every community member is asking whether that person is a parent, doctor, lawyer, secretary, store clerk, or store owner. These questions are also being asked by senior citizens, students, teachers, administrators, and school board members. In the end, it is the answers to these questions—in terms of personal benefits—that determine community support as well as involvement in school activities. For instance, senior citizens might consider it a personal benefit to see children being cared for properly or receiving opportunities that were not available to them when they were children. That's why effective public relations programs concentrate on educating the public on the values that the schools offer the community. Such programs do so by using a series of strategic management techniques geared toward reaching the various individuals and groups that make up a community. In the process, the effort is conducted knowing it is *impossible* to reach every person every time, and with every issue. And it is impossible to win everyone to our side all the time. But it is likely that we can reach and persuade the majority of people on the majority of issues most of the time—if we use the student-centered strategy. For when we are student-centered, we are in the best position to answer the primary question satisfactorily for the most people.

2. PRESTIGE

Everyone has the need to feel important. There are no exceptions to this reality. As people, we are motivated by what helps us win approval, by what makes us feel powerful, and by what gives us a good reputation. Many people win prestige by proclaiming all the good things they are doing and by revealing the awards and honors they have received. Some people obtain prestige by revealing which clubs they are asked to join, by bragging about the important telephone calls they have received, or by naming the influential people whom they have assisted. Prestige is a strong motivator. The way we dress, the car we drive, and the neighborhood we live in, all contain a prestige factor. Likewise, whether or not a person graduated from college, or what college or university his or her degree came from, contains prestigious elements. In school, students wear certain shoes, belong to certain groups, and run for certain offices to gain prestige. Athletes will make certain that everyone knows who they are—and, conversely, some students will make sure that everyone knows they *aren't* athletic. Both types of students are trying to attain different kinds of prestigious status. So it is with teachers. Some want you to know they are coaches, so they never appear out of uniform—while others avoid athletics like a plague. This is the prestige motivator at work. The public relations rule of thumb is this: If you can make people feel important and necessary, they will think you are intelligent and perceptive. This includes all of the people you come in contact with daily—children, teachers, support staff, and community members.

We all know that people respond in more positive ways when we address them by name, return their telephone calls quickly, answer their correspondence immediately, and take time to brief them on what we are doing and to hear out their questions, concerns, and suggestions. School employees and the public alike respond to all of the above considerations in similar ways. We can very quickly improve our public relations efforts with students, parents, employees, and the public, by going out of our way to have meaningful interactions with as many individuals as possible—with the intent of making people feel important—and by never doing anything which makes people feel insignificant. Likewise, we can share information on a mass basis to make the community knowledgeable and proud of its schools. On the other hand, anything done to make people—individually or as a group—feel powerless is counterproductive to meeting the need for status. In a bureaucracy, it is easy to make rules, procedures, and requirements which are void of personal status. Rather than treating people as unique and important individuals, we may have a tendency to make sweeping generalizations and rules that penalize the majority for the actions of the minority. This will always work against our ability to use the motivator of prestige to the hilt.

Here are some key questions we can ask ourselves regarding prestige that will help us make maximum use of this important motivator:

• *How can we make each child feel individual and special?* In most schools, educators have been successful in awarding prestige to high profile students—monitors, cheerleaders, student council members, athletes, and scholars. The question remains: What have we done for children who haven't attained this status? The lack of prestige is one of the chief reasons we are failing to reach some students. Some of our students are saying to themselves, "I don't count," "I don't belong," or "I don't fit in or have any ability." Remember, it's hard to be a good student if you don't count. It's hard to be a good citizen if you don't count. It's difficult to believe that the opportunities available at school are for you—if you don't count. In all kinds of ways, students tell us, "If you make me feel important, I will think you are important too. But every time I'm in your class you make me feel dumb. I don't like this feeling, and therefore, I don't like you or what you are teaching." To the public relations practitioner, it should be increasingly clear that we have to be able to find more and better ways to make students feel important, not only for their achievements, but for just being. We can't reserve prestige just for those who have managed to achieve something. Why? Because if we wait for achievement before giving prestige, some students may go their whole young lives feeling very unimportant, indeed.

• *How can we give more prestige to parents?* Unfortunately, in many schools parents feel as if they are uninvited guests. It's really easy to see why. After all, not very many schools have "Parents Welcome" signs outside the office door or "Parents'

Parking" signs outside the school. Likewise, where are the adult-sized chairs which should be in our offices for parents who must wait to see or work with us? And signs that direct parents to different parts of the building may be nonexistent. The truth is that many schools aren't set up to entertain and counsel visitors seriously—even if those visitors are the parents of our students. Yet, they should be. Parents and community members are the very people who fund our work. They are the people most likely to be interested in how we're accomplishing it. And they are the people who must come to our schools and use our services. We ought to make them feel better and more prestigious when they do.

• *How many community members know anything about the academic achievements of students, administrators, and staff? Is the community aware of awards that have been won by staff members?* You and your staff members meet the need for prestige through various professional achievements. If community members are aware of these achievements, they will feel a certain amount of prestige just by associating with you and your staff. That's why you should display your diplomas and awards in your office and you should encourage staff members to display theirs. After all, is it prestigious to follow your leadership? Are you somebody who is recognized as important in the profession? Or, should people in your community look outside the district for a prestigious educator to whom they can listen?

3. PLEASURE

This is the need for joy, happiness, fun, amusement, and satisfaction. There is a need in everyone to have pleasurable experiences rather than unpleasant, difficult, or neutral ones. The more pleasant the experience the greater the chances are that people will want to repeat it. Therefore, to motivate others, we must ask ourselves these questions:

• *How can we make it more pleasurable for the public to support the schools and interact with us?*

• *How can I, as a professional educator, make it more pleasurable for my colleagues to interact with me?*

• *How can we make it more pleasurable for students to attend this school?*

As we consider these questions, for example, we shouldn't overlook the aspect of *fun.* And we should never, under any circumstances, go out of our way to take the joy and fun out of schools. Unfortunately, sometimes we do. Remember, one of the reasons people put off going to the doctor or the dentist is that it's an unpleasant experience. The same is true of banking, buying insurance, and meeting with some salespeople. Children play hooky for similar reasons. Being out of school is more pleasurable than being in it. Certainly schools can't and should not be all fun and games. Yet, there's no reason that schools have to be totally serious places void of pleasure in order to have much learning and achievement going on within them. In fact, research indicates that learning is retained longer through the use of games and exercises that heighten interest. Therefore, we would do well to think up ways that pleasure can be incorporated into the services we provide—and not work to take the pleasure out of schools.

Does this mean that it's our function to entertain children day in and day out? No, of course not. But, we need only to be aware of how we ourselves respond to things that are pleasurable—to know that pleasure is a very successful motivator. Whether passing a bond issue or adding a new rule or requirement, the task must be more pleasant than unpleasant, or it will not be accepted by the people we are trying to influence. Sometimes, all we need to do is state our rule or procedure as a positive instead of a negative. In addition, all we may need to do to get the desired results is reveal the benefits of following the rule rather than focusing on and proclaiming only the punishment for breaking the rule.

In incorporating pleasure into school life, don't let sophistication fool you. Some years back Bernard Neary, a very enthusiastic elementary principal in Iowa, shared with us some of the things he and his staff were doing in their school. Without reservation, this school is an exciting place to visit—and to have a child attend. They have Dress-Up and Dress-Down Days, Teacher Appreciation Days, Reading Days, and Pride Days. In fact, they have special days for all conceivable events. They also have notes, badges, signs, and bulletin boards for every possible learning situation to recognize children's achievements and to motivate both staff and students.

However, while sharing these ideas with fellow administrators at The Master Teacher Leadership Conference, principal Neary almost apologized for the fact that the events and tools used were not very sophisticated. And he noted that other elementary—and most certainly junior high, middle, and high school—educators might be turned off by many of the ideas the staff members were using to make their school a productive and satisfying place for students and educators.

Certainly, the ideas and tools he had designed didn't look sophisticated—because they weren't. And yet excitement, not sophistication, was the primary aim. The ideas of this staff worked. As educators, we would all be wise to think very hard before we reject something just because it appears unsophisticated. Simply looking around the town where you live might show precisely why.

Sometimes we forget that when merchants want to increase traffic and sales, they stage a special event. They have a "Whale of a Sale," "Dog Days" sale, "Crazy Days" sale, "Two for One" sale, "Moonlight Madness" sale, or "One-Cent" sale. It's these kinds of *unsophisticated* events that people can relate to—and that create pleasurable experiences. They excite people, draw the big crowds, gain participation, and motivate people into a desired action. Why? Because they give pleasure. They're fun. They're enjoyable. They meet a big need that we all have as human beings.

Some of the best devices for motivating students, creating a positive classroom climate, and making the school exciting are often used primarily in elementary schools. In middle school, the use of such special events decreases. In high school, such events may be limited or nonexistent. Too often, in our search for sophistication, we become quite dull—and our classrooms or schools become places of routine rather than places filled with pleasure and excitement. In an effort to be more adult-like, we lose our creative imaginations. Yet, if we turn class or school motivational plans over to student or parent committees, they often come up with the kinds of suggestions we regard as "hokey." They suggest Speak-Up Days, Reading Marathons, Note Days, Praise Days, No-Fail Assignments, and Double-or-Nothing Days. They suggest ideas which involve everyone and which jolt people out of their indifference, and make them notice that something is going on which will benefit them and be pleasurable at the same time.

The goal of such activities is not just fun and games. Rather, it's to create a pleasurable climate conducive to work, study, learning, and achievement. After all, the goals of climate—productivity and satisfaction—don't apply just to students. They apply to teachers, cooks, custodians, media specialists, nurses, secretaries, and administrators, too. Remember, teacher productivity and satisfaction have a great deal to do with the productivity and satisfaction of young people. That's why a little *unsophisticated* stimulation which is pleasurable can be productive for all who reside in a school.

4. IMITATION

This is the need to follow a crowd. It's the need to do what the majority or minority is doing, as well as the need to model successful behavior. People have a need to associate themselves with those they admire. Little polo players and alligators have been responsible for selling millions of dollars in sportswear—just out of this need. Likewise, leaders who understand the vital link between modeling and imitation are better equipped to develop strong professional and support staffs. Managers who strive to show their employees the values of hard work, enthusiasm, curiosity, and a professional appearance tend to develop employees who try to imitate these same behaviors.

The motivator of imitation should show us how important it is for educators to look and act successful inside as well as outside the school. If students and the public are to admire and respect us—as well as want to be like us—we must be admirable. This trait has many dimensions.

The questions which need answers relative to imitation and our public relations efforts include these:

- *Do you see yourself as a model for (students) (teachers) (parents)?*
- *What can you do to make people want to imitate your excellence?*
- *Do you try to take other people into your sphere of influence?*
- *Are your standards worthwhile for others to imitate?*
- *How can we make more students imitate those classmates who study hard and who are involved in the activities of the school?*

- *How can we help more students want to give respect?*
- *How can we make the community follow our educational leadership?*

Remember, imitation can be a positive or a negative. Some students are following a street gang, those who drink, those who use drugs, or those who do not study. They admire and are accepted by these people. Likewise, some adults are following the critics of education. The question is *why?* One reason is that they identify more readily with these groups—and do not identify with good students or with educators. This condition will never change until *we* take certain actions.

Most certainly, we must make the values we cherish clear to everyone. Then, we should do everything possible to perpetuate these values as well as recognize and acclaim those students and parents who uphold them. For instance, if we say that we cherish scholarship, we must ask ourselves, "What are we doing to recognize good students—or those students who are showing academic improvement?" If we aren't giving any recognition for academic achievement or improvement, we should not be surprised if the majority of students imitate our apparent lack of enthusiasm for the value.

5. SECURITY

This is a desire for safety. It's a need which includes a concern for being both physically and psychologically safe. This is one of the reasons people are concerned with rules and want to make sure they are doing the right thing always. It's also the reason some people fight change or never offer an idea or endorse one—and won't even offer opinions when asked. They want to be safe.

Millions of dollars worth of life insurance is bought each year out of this need. People also have regular physical examinations, purchase countless burglar alarm systems, and buy credit card protection services—all out of the need for security. When we accept how important the need for security is to people, we will begin asking ourselves how we can give the public as well as students, colleagues, subordinates, and superiors a greater security and peace of mind in trusting us, following us, or accepting our plan to get a job done.

As educators, we should always be asking ourselves what we are doing to make students and parents secure. Often, instead, we *create* fears and insecurity. When we say, "This is going to be a hard course—many will fail," we arouse fears in all. Sometimes we do so in order to gain control. We may even do so in order to dominate. Regardless, there are many such school realities which make students insecure. After all, students can't choose teachers, bring forth complaints, automatically make A's, or automatically get on the teams for which they try out. All of these realities point out the need to work at ways to offer students physical and psychological safeguards which reduce fears.

The questions concerning the motivator of security that must be employed in any

public relations effort include the following:
- *How can you make the school psychologically safe for (employees) (students) (parents)?*
- *Do you motivate by (pressure) (fear)?*
- *Do you feel any obligation to your (teachers) (students) (parents)?*
- *Do people work for you, or do you work with people?*
- *What security do you offer other people?*
- *Is it safe for (students) (staff) to make mistakes in your school?*

6. CONVENIENCE

This is the need to make things easy, quick, and trouble free. People are always looking for an easy way. This is not abnormal. Neither is it wrong. In addition, people are more likely to approve anything that does not involve more work for them. They may vote for anything that relieves them of some duty. And they will usually accept any easy task before they accept a difficult one. Drive-up windows for banking, convenience stores, and fast food restaurants all meet this convenience need. So do catalog shopping, toll-free numbers, and credit cards.

The Book of the Month Club wasn't successful until it added the convenience factor and made buying easy. In the beginning, when you joined the club, you weren't sent the selection of the month. Instead, you received a description of the book. If you wanted the book, you made out an order form and mailed in your request. As a consequence, the club didn't sell many books. Then the club changed the procedure. Members were required to mail back their response cards only if they *didn't* want the book. And if they failed to do so, they received a book. In essence, the club made it easier to accept the monthly selection than to reject it. The club became an instant success.

The need for convenience is a strong one indeed. That's why we need to ask ourselves continually whether we are making it convenient for students to learn, participate in extracurricular activities, and function on a day-to-day basis in our school—and we need to be honest with ourselves about the ways in which we make these things convenient.

Some questions we might ask ourselves concerning convenience and our public relations efforts are as follows:
- *Do we make instructions long or short?*
- *How easy is it for a student to find out about a course or a teacher?*
- *Do we make it convenient for community members to obtain information about us, to get messages to their children at school, and to call us with their questions and concerns?*

Remember, our colleagues and students aren't going to continue to use us as resources if we don't make ourselves available to them or if we make every interaction a huge production.

7. DESIRE TO AVOID FEAR

This is a much stronger need than we may suspect. Fear dominates the lives of many, many people. It controls their every move and keeps them from making changes.

Many people are afraid and will refuse to be involved in anything outside their jobs. They worry about everything, and they often reject new concepts. Many are reluctant to serve in leadership capacities—because of fear.

People also fear being intimidated, being forced to reveal their financial situations, or having to reveal their lack of knowledge about a particular subject. Many of these fears are irrational. But the truth is that for many people, parents and students alike, school is a fearful place. For students the fears include fear of other classmates, students of the opposite sex, students that are older and physically dominating, as well as adults—both male and female.

Parents have a multitude of fears about school, many of which are being carried over from the days when they were in school. That's why identifying these fears and the times of year they are apt to surface, as well as finding ways to help the public overcome them, is a public relations must. And never, under any circumstances, should we make the public fearful by saying, "If you don't give us the money, we won't...." Rather, we should say, "We need money so that we can provide these benefits." Remember, when aroused by fear, tiny kittens can become tigers.

The questions we need to ask ourselves concerning people's desire to avoid fear include these:
- *Am I intimidating?*
- *Are staff members afraid of what my reaction will be if they make a mistake?*
- *Is my word good?*
- *If others agree with me initially, is it possible for them to change their minds later—and stay in my good graces?*
- *Do I motivate people with fear?*
- *Am I a "pay the price" leader?*

8. NEW EXPERIENCES

This is the need felt by many people to do, see, or participate in something new or different. New experiences provide the change of pace many need to maintain their interest. To some people, new means good, progressive, modern, and up-to-date. Doing things the same way all the time is boring.

Every year the fashion industry capitalizes on this overwhelming need. We can too. Experiences that are slightly different from the regular routine can enhance motivation to become involved for students, teachers, and the public alike. That's why new ideas, new achievements, new practices, and new services give the public a reason to continue their interest in us and the work of the schools. These same things keep school employees stimulated, interested, and growing. The same can be said for our own attitudes and actions. When we are open to new ideas and ways—and aren't stubbornly tied to old ones—we can earn a reputation for being forward looking, easy to work with, and invigorating to be around.

Dress-up/dress-down days, carnivals, fairs, changing the furniture in the room, an unscheduled assembly, tours, field trips, and inviting parents to eat lunch with their children on birthdays are all ideas that offer people chances for new experiences.

The questions we need to ask ourselves regarding the need for new experiences are these:

- *What new dimension can we add to a program or service that will make it more interesting?*
- *Are we keeping pace with the community we live in, or are we behind the times?*
- *What is our attitude toward change?*
- *Are we comfortable with our routine?*
- *List the new professional experiences you have had (in the district) (out of the district) in the last three years.*

9. LOVE/CARING

This is an extremely effective motivator—because love is the only emotion that we cannot live without. Indeed, love is important to all of us. In recent polls, appreciation is ranked as the number one reward employees want from their jobs. There is also no doubt that this is the motivator upon which student and parent loyalties are built.

When we accept people for *just being*, we give love. Likewise, when we honor achievement, we give love. When we recognize the birthdays of our staff and students, we show our love. When we acknowledge that a tragedy has befallen a student or a student's family, we teach the meaning of love. This is a most important teaching, because in truth, many of our actions can be seen as manipulative without love. When people see our public relations efforts as manipulations they think they are being used. Then, building a solid public relations program is impossible.

Educators are in the business of teaching students *how* "to walk." But we are in the business of teaching them *where* "to walk" as well. And if all of our love is for books, buildings, desks, and chairs—we have shown that we don't love people, we love things. No doubt, students and parents who feel that we truly love and appreciate them are more apt to love and appreciate us. Those who don't feel loved and appreciated may find it difficult to be able to give love or appreciation. A good rule to follow is this: Put love and caring in everything you do—and take any hate and rejection out, or everyone loses.

Think for a moment about the students who are disinterested, who reject us, and who hate school. These are the students some educators may resent having to handle. In fact, some educators believe such students don't belong in our schools. Yet, the vast majority of these students will be successful in the years ahead. Some will become extremely wealthy and will be able to buy and sell us in ten years. If these students feel that they made it in spite of us—rather than because of us—they may be very reluctant to support us when we need them. But if they are able to come back and say, "Gee, thanks for hanging in there with me. I know I was tough, but you cared enough not to give up on me," we may have their unconditional support all the years of their lives.

The questions we need to ask ourselves concerning the need for love are these:

- *Where do we spend our time—on things or on people?*
- *Where do we put our attention?*
- *Where do we focus our love—on things or on people?*
- *How do we show our special concern for our students, our teachers, our support staff, and the public?*
- *What do we do for people that makes them feel appreciated?*

Truly, it isn't the best and the brightest students who come back to thank us years later. Those former students who meet us on the street and say "thank you" are often those who didn't do very well when we had them in class. And rarely do the doctors, accountants, scientists, bankers, and successful business people who were our gifted students come back to lend a hand when the school needs equipment built on the playground or the fundraising barbecue needs a cook. Rather, the students who return are the ones who needed us the most and to whom we gave special love and concern. Remember this fact the next time you are exasperated and fed up with a student. For these are the times when judgments are made about us—and these impressions will last a lifetime.

WE MUST FOCUS ON DELIVERING BENEFITS

As administrators, we must understand the importance of continually searching for new ways to motivate students, teachers, and the public to buy into what we are doing in both encouraging and supportive ways. And this can't be achieved by just telling. It can only be achieved by adding a little selling too—in terms of values and benefits. Administrators must know that we can't assume that people will want us running their schools in the years to come—unless we are meeting needs. That's why we must take an honest look at how we might be turning away certain children, staff members, and citizens through a lack of concern for our public communications methods as well as for the nine people motivators.

Advertising experts have concluded that if businesses are successful in incorporating just two of these nine motivators into the benefits of a product or service, then that product or service will be successful. And we can conclude that any educator who wants to be successful with colleagues, parents, and children can increase his or her chances of doing so by incorporating two or more of these motivators into each of the services he or she is providing. No longer can we sit back and say, "But we aren't a business" and ignore these motivators. The reason is a simple, but profound one. We live in this world with our community members. They, like us, have been conditioned to buy based on these nine motivators, because these are motivators which have value to them. Therefore, we can't motivate community members with a different set of rules and expect to prosper and thrive. Rather, we must adapt these motivators to the work of the schools and use them to stress the value of education to everyone. It won't be hard when we begin to think in terms of delivering *benefits, benefits, benefits* to all the people with whom we interact—students, colleagues, staff, parents, and citizens alike. This, in the final analysis, is the mind-set that will help people believe that we are valuable and trustworthy, and that we are delivering a vital service.

PUBLIC RELATIONS IDEA

It is surprising how many good teachers have no practice at all in talking about their specific grade level or subject matter. Few second grade teachers, for example, can tell new students what the benefits are of second grade as compared to first grade. Therefore, few make "hay" by allowing students to anticipate and savor the possibilities of what they will learn and the new skills they will acquire.

A great way to help teachers come up with creative ways to teach their subject matter, or just talk about their subject matter in terms of benefits, is to have them do the following exercise.

First, hand out a sheet similar to Figure 3-1. Have teachers in the same grade level or

What Promise Can I Make To Students Using The Nine People Motivators?					
Personal Gain	1. 2.	3. 4.	5. 6.	7. 8.	9. 10.
Pleasure	1. 2.	3. 4.	5. 6.	7. 8.	9. 10.
Prestige	1. 2.	3. 4.	5. 6.	7. 8.	9. 10.
Imitation	1. 2.	3. 4.	5. 6.	7. 8.	9. 10.
Security	1. 2.	3. 4.	5. 6.	7. 8.	9. 10.
Convenience	1. 2.	3. 4.	5. 6.	7. 8.	9. 10.
Desire to Avoid Fear	1. 2.	3. 4.	5. 6.	7. 8.	9. 10.
New Experiences	1. 2.	3. 4.	5. 6.	7. 8.	9. 10.
Love	1. 2.	3. 4.	5. 6.	7. 8.	9. 10.

FIGURE 3-1

teachers who teach the same subject area brainstorm ways in which they will promise students that the grade or subject area they teach will satisfy the specific individual motivators. Then they can use these lists of benefits to talk to students, talk to parents at back-to-school nights, or talk to parents at individual conferences. Figures 3-2 and 3-3 offer other possibilities for you to use this exercise with new programs or at faculty planning meetings.

How To Make These Areas In Our School Come Alive Using The Nine People Motivators							
	Library	Cafeteria	Gym	Restrooms	Hallways	Principal's Office	Counselor's Office
Personal Gain	*Have an advisory board from each grade level for selecting new resources for the library.						
Pleasure	*Will change displays of books on a weekly basis.						
Prestige	*Will allow certain students to be library helpers.						
Imitation	*Will point out special books that every student at a certain grade level seems to enjoy.						
Security	*Offer research help.						
Convenience	*Library will be open before and after school.						
Desire To Avoid Fear	*No question will be considered dumb or unimportant.						
New Experiences	*We will help you develop new interests in new subjects.						
Love	*We will help you develop your love of reading by helping you find reading materials you will enjoy.						

FIGURE 3-2

How To Use The Nine People Motivators To Improve Our Relationships With:				
	Students	Teachers	Administrators	Support Staff	Parents
Personal Gain				
Pleasure				
Prestige				
Imitation				
Security				
Convenience				
Desire To Avoid Fear				
New Experiences				
Love				

FIGURE 3-3

44

CHAPTER

IV

FOUR

THE LAWS AND PRINCIPLES OF MANAGEMENT AS THEY APPLY TO SCHOOL PUBLIC RELATIONS

> *"...while the principles of management are undoubtedly the same throughout business, the applications differ of necessity, and it is in the application of principles which anyone can understand that management proves itself good or bad."*
> *—Herman Nelson*

There are certain rules which govern the science of public relations. They are not rules or laws that we have created or manufactured. Rather, they are natural laws. We have simply observed how things work in this world of ours, and then we have put these realities into identifiable rationale and put names on them. Needless to say, they are extremely important because skillful use of these laws will determine our success. Without knowledge of these laws, we have no guideposts for our public relations efforts. We have nothing that we can refer to when all is going well—and nothing to refer to when the chips are down.

The following paragraphs in this chapter contain these nine laws* as well as nine formal public relations understandings. It's our hope that with these guideposts, you will have a firm foundation upon which your public relations efforts can rest.

---

*These laws first appeared in *Causing Others To Want Your Leadership* by Robert L. DeBruyn, 1976. They are explained here in terms of their specific application to public relations.

THE
LAW OF
ORIGIN

Rationale: *Institutions—and the people who work in them—must operate in agreement with the reason for their origin and existence, or failure rather than success becomes the probability.*

When it comes to promotion, publicity, or public relations, what is inferred, said, or done in our schools must be in agreement with the reason for the schools' existence. This means that what we say we are doing must have the best interests of students at the heart of every message. This is the only position we can take or promote that is 100 percent defensible, 100 percent of the time.

Even when we err, we can defend actions which are student-centered—or which we intended to be student-centered. We cannot, however, defend actions which are teacher-centered, administrator-centered, or focused in any other direction. The Law of Origin tells us that what we are doing, want to do, or intend to do must benefit children, not us. Therefore, our rules, regulations, enrollment practices, and services offered can only be justified if they are student-centered. When they are, we can anticipate support from the staff and the entire community that we serve. When they are not, we should anticipate opposition on any or all fronts.

The reason that many of our public relations efforts fail is that we vary from a student-centered position. Remember, schools do not exist to employ administrators, teachers, counselors, aides, cooks, custodians, secretaries, bus drivers, or anyone else. But sometimes we act as if they do. Often, the only time the community hears anything from us about the schools is when we want more money. Sometimes, we even say that we will not perform well if *we* don't see more money. Then, we wonder why we don't enjoy our community's respect—or the same level of respect that other professions enjoy.

Unfortunately, there is evidence that citizens view many governmental agencies, including some schools, as cold and uncaring bureaucracies. Often, this results from proclamations as well as procedures which are viewed to be self-centered rather than student-centered. It makes little difference whether a school is large or small, or in a rural or urban area. This is because a school is sometimes perceived as being removed from the people it is designed to serve. The news media find this public belief a tempting topic. The issue of school red tape is a particularly popular topic for the media. You don't have to go to many meetings in a school or district to realize that even teachers and administrators often view the school as a bureaucracy. Certainly, more than one teacher has written a letter to a professional publication or a local newspaper complaining that the bureaucracy was interfering with his or her work. That's why bureaucracy is an issue which deserves professional discussion.

Unfortunately, some people see educators and schools as placing their own needs above the needs and concerns of ordinary citizens and average students. They see haughty attitudes rather than helping actions. We may have resigned ourselves to living with such criticism. More than likely, however, we believe that this situation does not exist in *our* schools. Rather, we see it as an affliction of neighboring schools or perhaps of those in other cities or states.

Bureaucracy—and its evils—is a part of all organizations. Make no mistake regarding this fact. It exists in business, government, religion, and education. It even exists in families. That's why we need to pay some attention to the bureaucracy that can develop in our classrooms and our schools—or we violate the Law of Origin inadvertently. While we may not always be successful in creating a classroom or school system free of bureaucracy, we should recognize those factors that lead people to believe a bureaucracy exists—and take action designed to eliminate those factors.

A bureaucracy is present when people see inflexibility. And it's always present when people cannot get answers to their questions within a reasonable period of time. For example, students and parents may make a simple request for information or consideration. When they are put off with the promise that they will be contacted—and the call never comes—they have had an unfortunate brush with school bureaucracy. Students and parents also see bureaucracy when they approach one educator for information and are referred to another person or office for the answer. Sometimes, they may be referred even further—and they may give up before they find the answer. Every time people feel "passed along," they also feel they have encountered an inefficient and impersonal bureaucracy. None of these realities make it possible to have a student-centered school.

It's not possible, of course, for each of us to have the answer to every question at the tip of the tongue. Yet, there are three simple techniques that every teacher and administrator should make a part of his or her standard operating procedure, or good public relations is almost impossible.

2	PUBLIC RELATIONS IDEA

First, any time we or members of our staff are asked a question, we should resolve to give a complete and correct answer. Second, if we don't have the answer, we should say so immediately. Finally, we should suggest to citizens where they are likely to find the answer—and then offer to get the information for them.

A good rule to follow is one we might think impossible: Make sure any student or parent asking a question receives a satisfactory answer or some explanatory assistance in finding the answer from the first educator he or she asks. Hard as this might be, it is the *very best way* to avoid a bureaucratic reputation. Actually, helping people obtain answers to their questions builds confidence in the competencies of our schools. After all, offering to get information and then doing it amounts to saying, "I care, I want to help, I can help, and I will help." This stance makes us and schools seem more caring, flexible, responsive, and competent. In addition, we must recognize and teach our staff to recognize that students and parents should be able to seek help anywhere. And they should be able to seek help from anyone without fear of offending the rest of us. Indeed, if we are offended because a colleague was sought out rather than us, then we should realize that we work in a bureaucracy—and we are part of its perpetuation.

In addition, we must always openly tell questioners *where* requested information *was obtained*. For instance, we must freely relate that we sought out the information from administrators, the math department, the central office, or English teachers. We must give credit where credit is due, rather than acting as if *we* are the ones who "always get things done" or as if *we* are the purveyors of all knowledge about the schools.

When it is appropriate, also proceed beyond the question asked. We need to tell many questioners what our fellow educators are doing in the area about which they are inquiring, what is being taught in that area, and what plans are being made for the future. Then, students and parents alike will be able to relate to us as well as to what we and the institution are doing. Finally, we must act like part of the team and mission rather than the whole of it if we want to project the image of service. Serving, after all, is the only way to avoid bureaucratic practices—and to guarantee adherence to the Law of Origin. It all begins, of course, with knowing that we exist to meet the needs of students and with carrying out this reality in the operation of the schools as well as in our programs of promotion, publicity, and public relations.

3 PUBLIC RELATIONS IDEA

It's one thing to have a sophisticated book of board policies—and quite another to effect policies in the school district. Therefore, it is imperative that citizens know whom they can go to with questions about district policies. After all, job titles and descriptions do not always describe job functions accurately. If community members understand the policies which the board hands down, they are more likely to conform to those policies, and administrators will find it easier to implement the policies. Here is a way we can get the job done.

First, direct the administrative staff to develop procedures for those policies which directly affect the operation and management of the school district. Since administrators develop policy procedures themselves, they are more likely to see that the policies are implemented consistently.

Second, communicate to the professional and support staff and to the public the names of the administrative officers who can answer questions about policies or procedures in various areas. These areas might include boundaries, transportation, food service, and curriculum.

This information can be communicated through the mail in either the district calendar or individual school newsletters. The public should expect direct access to these administrators.

Third, each area should be assigned to the appropriate person based upon that person's expertise, experience, and availability. This will ensure that the public receives clear, knowledgeable answers to its inquiries.

Try these techniques. They help make policies practical and workable solutions in a school district.

THE
LAW OF
POSITIVE REINFORCEMENT

Rationale: *In the absence of positive reinforcement from appointed leaders, negative human attitudes and behaviors are most likely to emerge from the group being led—internally and externally.*

If we want to have effective public relations in schools, it is important that the positive aspects of the school and the district overshadow the negative. The truth of this law tells us that not allowing the negative to dominate is virtually impossible without a specific strategy for communicating the positive. The truth is that the positive already exists. It outweighs the negative significantly in every school. This fact should give us some pause as administrators. Though we are well aware that there are many positive things going on in our schools, few of us have a comprehensive plan for communicating them to people. Unfortunately, this means we are "sitting ducks" for that one unanticipated negative incident to happen and put our schools and our competency into question. That's why we need to be aware that the Law of Positive Reinforcement tells us that if we are not proclaiming the positive, the negative will win. It doesn't mean we should skirt the truth. We must be truthful always. Truth is not the problem. The problem is this: We often don't have a plan to deliver the good news. All this law does is remind us that we must deliver good news consistently or the only side people will hear is the negative. That's why the relationship between positive and negative needs our very close attention.

Dr. Al Wilson is a professor who serves as the liaison between The Master Teacher and Kansas State University, in Manhattan, Kansas. In this role, he participates in sessions of The Master Teacher Academy* for which the university grants graduate credit. Dr. Wilson is nationally known because of his work pertaining to the relationship between climate and effective leadership in the classroom. He has been called many times to situations where

*The Master Teacher Academy is a curriculum designed to help educators find success in their profession. For more information contact The Master Teacher, Leadership Lane, P.O. Box 1207, Manhattan, Kansas 66502; (913) 539-0555.

relationships have deteriorated to near zero. His concern deals with restoring an environment in which teachers and students can function successfully. His conclusions can prove highly beneficial to all of us who work in the school as well as to those who guide a public relations program for a school or district. Here are his conclusions.

We Need To Create Positives
Because The Negatives
Will Always Be Present

Dr. Wilson firmly believes that unless six positives are given for every negative, the environment will fall apart. This is true for a friendship, a marriage, a business, or a school. Therefore, when positives aren't dominant, the only way to control the situation is via two extremes—force or permissiveness, depending upon who is involved. Regardless, neither choice is a good one for an educator to make.

Unfortunately, negatives will always exist in any place. In a school, however, where adherence to rules is absolutely necessary, where students are being taught and evaluated constantly, where performance standards must be met to achieve satisfactorily, and where parents and citizens are not daily visitors to schools, the task of decreasing negatives is made more difficult. Reducing negatives for students who are failing as well as parents who operate with limited information is doubly difficult. Yet, the problem remains: If there aren't six positives for every negative, the environment may disintegrate.

As educators, we have a practical need to search out the positives. The only way we're ever going to have a six-to-one ratio, however, is to create positives. If we don't create or manufacture positives whenever possible, we have little chance of getting the ratio needed to function successfully. Yet, this task may be difficult for a very natural reason: Many people, including ourselves, seem to see what's wrong first, rather than what's right. For instance, we may function as teachers or administrators from a negative base because our task is to look for what's wrong and correct it quickly. And yet, we know the more positives that exist in the environment, the easier it is to resolve problems. Indeed, this ratio is vital to our corrective efforts with students, staff, and the public alike. Fortunately, there are some understandings and actions which can put the six-to-one ratio in our classrooms and schools quickly.

We
Should Take
A Personal Inventory

First, we need to realize that just as negatives come in many forms, so do positives. Neither is confined only to what we say or do. Both can be found in the whole of the school. Our task is to identify positives, point them out, and build up a reservoir to counter the negatives. Remember, the negatives will always exist. Yet, positives can be found in everything from the comfortable temperature of our rooms, to good light, to plentiful resources, to beautiful bulletin boards, to sensible procedures, to fun activities, and to welcomed opportunities. Therefore, we can begin by making a list of every positive in our school or district.

Second, we can check ourselves out. We need to know whether we tend to be positive, negative, or neutral relative to the various conditions which exist in school. Then, we need to know that being habitually neutral or negative can hinder our ability to build a reservoir of positives. For instance, do teachers begin test days or do we begin faculty meetings on a negative note? Likewise, do we state rules both verbally and in the student handbook by telling students what they *can't* do—or what they *can* do? In the morning, do we convey a neutral stance by staying in the office and ignoring students and teachers? Do we leave school in the evening or at the close of a staff meeting by offering pleasant words to teachers—or by criticizing and complaining?

Third, we can begin pointing out the positives in our school and district. We can't just hope they are seen, appreciated, and known to all. We can also urge teachers and students to look for the positives. After all, it takes no talent to see the negative. But it takes intelligence to see strengths and capitalize upon them.

Fourth, we can try to run a positive-dominated operation. We can start by being ready for school, planning positive activities, and seeking out and proclaiming the positive talents and strengths of each teacher and student. We can make good questions out of poor ones in the classroom and the office. And, we can respond in caring ways—even when we have to say no to students, staff members, or parents. And, of course, we can hold our tongues and eliminate some of our criticism. All these acts will help us create a strong foundation of positives which will help us run a better school as well as give us a better school to proclaim.

THE LAW OF TRUST

Rationale: *Trust is a necessary ingredient in the school-public relationship which emerges from positive educator input—not from exclusive relationships, special privilege, title, or appointment—and requires a mutuality of dependence between all parties: students, staff, parents, and the public.*

Positive input by educators means we speak the truth. It means we take the right actions, in the right ways, for the right reasons. This requires that we invite the public to be a part of the school, and never exclude them, deceive them, or consider them in any way other than a partner. We need them—and they need us. This is the mutuality of dependence.

Our public relations effort involves giving people the truth about our strengths and weaknesses. If we don't, we set ourselves up for the big fall. For instance, we may keep telling people all is well. We may keep relating how great we are and what a wonderful job we are doing. Then, test scores fall and we suddenly want to say, "Things have been bad for a long time because we haven't had what we needed to get the job done." This is a contradiction. And it causes distrust. For instance, a chief executive in one school hedged on maintenance of school facilities for twenty-five years while telling the public how great he was for saving them money. He was fired when the state fire marshal closed the high school building.

Trust and distrust can weigh strongly on the public's emotions, and emotions are a vital part of good public relations. Trust should be used to eliminate barriers between the schools and the public. But trust is not an automatic condition.

Knowledge is a building block of trust. People cannot trust what has been untrustworthy. Neither can they trust people or things about which they know nothing. Therefore, public relations efforts must seek to educate students, parents, and other community members—as completely as possible—about the inner workings of the schools, the people who work in them, the mission of the schools, the schools' strengths and weaknesses, and the schools' successes and failures. However, we must be aware that trust is not a one-way street.

In order for trust to be established, the communication must be two-way. This requires that we involve students, parents, and the public in schools as well as ask questions of these publics to determine what their concerns are about us. It is from this point that the Law of Trust either makes or breaks us. That's because it's at this point that we operate truthfully or untruthfully.

For instance, we are going to receive and deliver bad news occasionally. Whenever large numbers of people gather in one place, problems and bad news will be experienced. This condition is normal and it should be expected in our schools. But, how we handle bad news and whether we trust people to handle the truth will, in large measure, determine how much they come to trust us.

Here are some guidelines that comply with the Law of Trust which can be helpful.

First, never try to hide bad news. Doing so is a form of dishonesty. Remember, people cannot accept dishonesty or exaggeration in either direction when it comes to handling bad news. And hiding bad news will only make things worse—and guarantee that the problem will remain, perhaps with destructive side effects. Instead, quickly identify what you can do about the bad news. Ask yourself: Can I change the situation? Can I accept it? With whom should I share the information? Keep in mind that the purpose of sharing bad news can be positive or negative. For instance, exaggeration as well as "telling tales" are both forms of dishonesty that only serve to misguide the people who are trying to solve the problem. And the results of exaggeration and "telling tales" are rarely positive.

Second, at this point you must make sure that you have accepted and resolved the bad news in your own mind. This step must precede any action. That's because you have a choice to make: to handle the news in a professional way or to react to it in a personal and self-serving way. Regardless of whether the news is correct or incorrect, if you react personally you'll almost certainly make a bad situation worse. That's because handling bad news always requires a prudent attitude and perspective. After all, the amount of bad news seldom outweighs the amount of good news in a school. And if we lose our perspective our poor responses can turn short-term negatives into long-term ones.

In the process of handling bad news we also need to be aware that "this too will pass."

That's why we need objectivity as well as perspective. When we don't have either—and there will be times when we don't—we must seek the help of colleagues. Finally, we need to know ourselves and remember what we have learned from the experience of handling bad news. This is a must—because it allows us to take the necessary steps to ensure that we handle bad news better in the future.

The staff of a school in New York made some very interesting discoveries about themselves regarding the way they handled bad news. They knew that bad news was normal—and that it was their responsibility to handle it. However, they realized that bad news at 8:00 a.m. did not make for a good beginning to their day. It didn't create positive and constructive thoughts about people or work. And neither did it enhance productivity at their school. In fact, handling problems and bad news wore them out before the first bell rang. And this situation made for long days and even longer weeks.

They were able to establish some guidelines because they learned something about themselves: They handled problems and bad news best if the news came *during* the school day rather than before it. In fact, they found they could handle anything if it came after they started their day productively. However, if they didn't do anything except handle problems for the first thirty minutes each day they got behind and felt frustrated the entire day. With this one insight, they established a single rule that ensured consideration and guaranteed that they would operate more effectively.

Faculty and students jointly adopted a "no bad news until 10:00 a.m." rule. Bad news, except messages that absolutely had to be conveyed immediately, was to be withheld until people had settled in and started working. Specific guidelines were set up that applied to students and staff alike, in the classroom as well as in the office. The bad news rule has been working effectively for years. Kids love the rule. Teachers love the rule. Administrators love the rule. And all agree that even emergency problems that occur at the beginning of the day are handled more efficiently and effectively.

THE THEORY OF GROUP COMMUNICATION

Rationale: *Management communication must be arranged and presented in such a manner that messages offered contain personal impact upon the life style of the listener, or only partial listening and involvement will result.*

Good public relations involves making the public want to listen to and understand the messages we are trying to get across. People won't listen to what they're not interested in hearing and, therefore, will not retain the information—much less allow it to impact upon them. The public can't be forced to listen, of course. Therefore, a school or district must have effective, inventive, interacting, and workable communication approaches and techniques to create the desire to listen in the minds of the public. The techniques and media employed must also vary so that you can reach as many of your publics as possible, not just the segment that will be affected by the *media* you want to use.

We know, for instance, that with only one medium you can't reach all people. In fact, any media effort will reach, at best, only 42 percent of the people to whom it goes. With this statistic in mind, you'll know that only 42 percent of the parents may read the newsletter you send home. Likewise, only 42 percent will hear your story on the radio or read it in the newspaper. That's why an effective public relations program must use a wide variety of media methods to get its message to a targeted public. Nonetheless, you must know that it's virtually impossible to reach all the people all the time with all your messages. This will be true even if you have an unlimited budget.

To increase readership and effectiveness, a school must also help the public believe that what's being discussed *does* affect them. Therefore, every message must be expressed so that it has a personal impact on the public and so that it shows concern and respect for their time and their special interests. Remember, whenever people read or listen to anything, they ask the question known as the primary question, "What's in it for me?" If their answer is "Nothing," they won't be interested.

Fortunately, we can increase readership for our newsletters, notes home, posters, and newspaper articles by adhering to some tried and tested communication techniques. We can do the same for our messages that are delivered over the radio, in our speeches, and in our public service announcements. We will be discussing these techniques in depth in Chapter VI.

THE LAW OF PLANNING

Rationale: *In achieving objectives, success is dependent upon the means, the tools, and the measurement of the plan established prior to the beginning of the task.*

For all the planning we do in school, public relations is rarely a part of it. We plan curriculum, athletic schedules, music programs, debate tournaments, parties, dances, and countless other special events. And if we want or need attendance at these events, both staff and students may plan a promotion for them. If something special or significant happens at school, we may be the lucky recipients of some publicity regarding the event after the fact. But public relations efforts are often just "happenstance." They are not planned activities with the means, tools, and measurements of success established before the effort begins. Yet, they should be.

It's been said time and time again, "Positive programs and successful public relations efforts are those which are planned. Negative public relations is that which just happens." We must realize that a public relations plan is essential if we are going to do a good job of letting the community know what's going on in our school—and gain constructive benefits when we do. And we must know in advance what we will regard as a successful effort. If not, we and others will not know when we have succeeded. For instance, let's say we want to increase attendance at back-to-school night. First, we need to know how many parents came last year. Second, we need to determine how many we are trying to attract this year. Third, we have to ask ourselves, "What will we do differently this year to get more parents to attend?" Consequently, we can't just send notes home with students as we did last year, and increase attendance. Finally, when the event is over we must analyze how successful we were at attracting parents this year. And this will help us in our planning for next year's events.

Unfortunately, many administrators make a mistake by thinking that they alone have to be the sole originator of the plan, the means, and the tools for public relations efforts. This is not only a false notion, but a management mistake as well. When the administrator makes this mistake, he or she becomes the sole public relations contact for the school. Such public relations efforts are doomed to fail.

5 | PUBLIC RELATIONS IDEA

There are often several teachers in our schools who are or would be much better public relations facilitators than we are. These teachers may have a gift for writing. They may have an artistic bent. They may have many contacts in the community or may have a need to coordinate or be "in charge" of such a project in your school. Seek out this talent or this need among your staff members. Then, ask these individuals if they would help you make public relations a priority. In the process, don't overlook some of the secretaries and other support personnel on your staff. There is often at least one person in these positions who has a real gift for public relations.

Once you have identified your key public relations priorities (see *Public Relations Idea #42*) ask every staff member to be responsible for helping in some capacity. Depending on the size of your staff, ask each teacher to be responsible for at least one article a year for the newsletter to parents. Brainstorm ideas for inclusion in the local newspaper at least once a month. Have your key staff public relations contacts make up a calendar of possible public relations activities for the year. The calendar should also include all the special events which will need promotion and publicity. This calendar can and should be sent to the education editors of the local newspaper and radio station. (See also, *"Tips For Working With Media Representatives Or*

Reporters," Chapter VI, p. 143.) Your initial plan can be used from year to year. You can make additions and deletions, of course. However, the plan should emphasize telling the story of life in your school, grade by grade or class by class. And your first concern should be for academics, not extraclass activities. Above all, be aware that public relations is not a task that can be turned over to anyone without administrative involvement. Public relations must have administrative input, direction, influence, and approval to make sure the parts fit with the whole.

THE
LAW OF
REAL TRUTH AND TIME

Rationale: ***In a problem situation, during the process of discovering and sorting out the real truth regarding the attitudes, opinions, and beliefs of staff, students, and community members, the passage of time can magnify the problem.***

This law makes us aware of the fact that a problem can and will grow if there is a time lag between the time the problem is identified and the time at which something can be done about it. This time lag lends itself to people forming opinions when they don't know all the facts. These opinions or beliefs can be very difficult to change. Remember, a time lag also lends itself to rumor, and rumor tends to cause the formation of irrational, improper, and incorrect opinions, beliefs, and attitudes. Worse, these problems may eventually cause reactions from those who are affected by them as well as those who are not.

Once people are committed to certain beliefs and actions, we all know it's very difficult to change those beliefs—even when they are given the real facts. Therefore, every public relations program should address the urgent issues which concern people. And provisions should be made so that we answer problems truthfully and as quickly as possible.

Sometimes the reason we fail to take swift action as leaders is that we, too, are at a loss for a solution. Rather than admit this fact, we may try to "buy time" or try to ignore the problem. Yet, this law reminds us that ignoring the problem will almost always cause the issue to escalate. When we find ourselves in this position, the quick action we should take is to bring together the key people with the key issues. We must get all of the concerned parties together to brainstorm a solution.

For example, a group of high school seniors planned a week long "drink-till-you-puke" party off the school campus at a nearby lake. It was planned to last every evening for the week after graduation. The rumor was that hundreds of seniors were going to participate. Parents were up in arms about it. The outcry from the public was, "Why doesn't the school *do* something?"

The truth of the matter was that this was not a school problem. The seniors would be graduated and the party was not going to be held on school grounds. But instead of ignoring the problem, the school administration held a public forum to discuss the issue. This swift action confirmed that the administration was concerned, competent, and caring. The action gave parents the opportunity to solve *their* problem. And they did. Parents organized an alternate party. And the school held to the Law of Origin—acting in behalf of the welfare of students. As far as parents, community, educators, and many members of the senior class were concerned, the forum was the solution—and rightfully so. Make no mistake: If the school had decided that the issue was none of its business or responsibility and had taken no action, the school would have violated the Law of Origin. And the school would have been blamed by students, parents, and the community for the entire event. As a result of the forum, however, both administrators and teachers were lauded in the school by concerned students, and in the media as well as by parents.

This example also brings up another important rule of thumb. The principal of the high school held a forum for interested and concerned parents of the senior class. He didn't encourage or even invite all the parents in the community to attend—especially those parents who didn't have a child attending high school. Remember, when an urgent issue arises, we usually have to address our attention to only a specific target group. We should never try to include more people than are necessary, or we may only facilitate the spreading of our problems. In this case, the principal confined the problem to the group of people best able to solve it. The application of this management strategy presents itself often. For instance, if we have fighting on a school bus or in the cafeteria, we need not have a school assembly to talk about the problem. If we do, we have only apprised all students and staff members of an issue about which they knew nothing. We need only, therefore, to unite the key culprits with the key issues.

THE PRINCIPLE OF OWNERSHIP

Rationale: ***People work for and support their own goals or goals which they set when they recognize a problem and have input for both solution and implementation. They don't work for and support the goals formed or mandated by others.***

This principle relates that one of the most important steps a leader can take whenever he or she is trying to have a staff adopt a new attitude or stance, or solve a problem, is to ask them how *they* propose to solve this problem, or to ask them how they would like to be viewed in this particular situation. Once they answer one or both of these questions, people are much more likely to work for the plan as *they* have expressed it.

For example, take the issue of professional dress, which is discussed in depth in Chapter XI. Administrators repeatedly ask us, "How do I get my staff to dress more professionally? I can't mandate it. What's the solution?"

Our answer is always the same, "Ask them how they *want* to appear." Few educators would ever respond with adjectives such as unprofessional, untrustworthy, casual, unintelligent, or second-class. Most want just the opposite. They want to appear intelligent, competent, professional, and first-class. They want to be respected and they want to be appreciated. When teachers are presented with the research on what would make them appear as *they say* they want to appear—they are much more likely to work for a plan that gives them what they want.

As Leon Lessinger stated so well, "People need three things to be successful. First, they must feel successful. Second, others must feel they are successful. Third, they must have ownership." Never forget, unless people buy into a problem, they seldom buy into a solution. This was pointed out most clearly with the 55 mph speed limit. People didn't buy into the problem, so they didn't buy into the solution. Rather, they bought "fuzz busters" for the sole purpose of breaking the law. Whether we are dealing with students, staff, parents, or community, it is vital that we involve people in both identifying the problem and finding a solution. If we are wondering, for instance, what we should tell the community about our math program, we should ask students and staff what *they* think we should say.

In schools, we are prone to do a good job regarding Leon Lessinger's first two success requirements: helping students feel successful and helping others see them as successful. But we don't fare as well on trying to give students a sense of *ownership*. Maybe that's because we haven't thought about ownership insofar as students are concerned. Or, it might be that we have reservations about giving students feelings of ownership in classrooms or schools because we view ownership as power—and we don't want to give up power. We shouldn't feel this way, however. When young people develop a sense of ownership toward their school, the benefits to staff and students alike are tremendous.

We don't have to look far to see how much people want ownership. There's a company that's sold a lot of insurance by selling people "a piece of the rock." Indeed, ownership is also one of the primary reasons behind teacher negotiation committees. This movement resulted, in part, because teachers wanted to feel ownership.

Ownership is a strong motivator because it has a lot to do with a primary human need: *security*. As educators, we need to look at how ownership really motivates people in our society—and see how we can adapt it to our classrooms and schools at large. Certainly, we may be motivated to mow our own lawn every week, but we may not be motivated to mow our neighbor's. And we don't see students tearing up *their own* cars in the parking lot. Rather, they're polishing them. That's because they *own* them.

Young people who break windows or vandalize auditoriums, cafeterias, and restrooms don't feel as if they are wrecking *their school*. They're wrecking *our* school. The question is this: What can we do to create schools where children feel successful, where others feel they're successful, and most important, where they have a sense of ownership? Our public relations goal should be to help students feel that it is *their* school, *their* curriculum, *their* cafeteria, *their* halls, *their* activities, *their* library, and so forth. But we may not be able to do so because of our own needs for security.

No doubt, giving children a true sense of ownership means giving them a degree of power.

And in giving them power, we also give them the power to fail. However, we can give students a degree of ownership with a minimum of risk by involving them in the creation of class rules and regulations. We can also realize that involving them in what's happening to them in classrooms is vital. Giving students a measure of control over their lives is the biggest key. When it comes to academics, we can seek student input before and after lessons. We can ask students what interested them the most or least. We can ask them how they would like to tackle a project, and then respond accordingly.

Great things can happen when schools belong to children. Students come to feel responsibility rather than a need to blame. They accept responsibility for their own academic condition and behavior. And when they do, the lives of educators are greatly improved—automatically.

That's why we must give more than lip service to creating a school where students feel successful, others think they are successful, and they feel ownership. We must have a plan to help young people gain all three—in our classrooms and in the school. When we do, students will get what we intended them to get from school. Discipline will improve and we'll see quicker solutions to problems. There will be fewer crises—and students will get more rewards. This shouldn't surprise us. After all, schools weren't created to provide an ownership sanctuary for adults. Rather, schools were created to meet students' needs. Indeed, the schools belong to them. If we instill this sense of ownership, we may produce students who do better personally as well as academically in our classes.

THE
LAW OF
BLAME AND CREDIT

The first part of the law states the following:

> *In any situation, if you try to take all the blame, people won't let you. If you try to blame others for the whole problem, they may not accept any of the blame.*

Examine your own response when someone has tried to blame you *totally* for an error or a problem—even when you were the primary culprit. Then you'll see why this law works so consistently. Further examination may lead you to the conclusion that when a teacher handles a situation poorly with a parent, for instance, you might do well to accept all the blame openly for not being with that teacher and guiding him or her. Don't be surprised if the immediate teacher response is, "No, it was my fault."

The same is true when we are dealing with our community. If we try to blame them for all our woes, including not funding the school adequately, we may find ourselves between a rock and a hard place. They may even claim we have more money than we need. In fact, they may say we're not competent managers. This is the law of blame and credit at work. Yet, if we try to take the blame, they won't let us.

Know that there's a reason for this reaction. It's the need for autonomy. We all have a need to have control of our own lives. Only the degree of the need varies among us. Therefore, when someone tries to take total blame for something that is partly our responsibility, we won't let him or her. To do so would be tantamount to giving away our ownership and control over that responsibility.

Coaches are highly skilled in this area. If they weren't they would be fired. When a team loses, does the coach say to the press, "We lost because we don't have any talent," "We lost because our kids are dumb," or "We lost because the players didn't do what I told them"? When questioned by the press, does the coach say, "Don't ask me. They lost it, not me"? No, the good coach takes *all* the blame. Even if a player dropped a touchdown pass in the last second, the coach tells the press, "Games are not won or lost on one play." This law also teaches us that if the coach would blame the players, they wouldn't take the blame—nor would anyone else. In truth, the coach who blames the players will lose his or her job quickly. Likewise, if the coach tries to take all the blame, parents and players alike will come to his or her defense right away by saying, "We didn't do what we were told to do," or "We just got beat by a better team."

The second part of this law teaches us about taking credit.

> *If you do something extremely well or experience a big success and you try to take all the credit, people may deny you any credit. On the other hand, if you give away all the credit for an obvious success, people will insist that you take some or all of the credit for the success.*

In the process, people may even diminish the contributions of others, including themselves. Human nature is often a predictable contradiction. Remember this law in your next interaction with teachers, parents, students, superiors, or the media. It can serve you well. Looking again to the example of the coach can show us how the law works.

If, following a victory, the best coach in the world said, "We won because of me. We won because I outcoached the other coach, had a superior game plan, and taught these student athletes everything they know about the game," what would people's response be? It's guaranteed—people would be upset. Students would be angry. Worse, people would try to take *all* the credit away from such a coach. They might even fire him or her. Yet, when this same coach gives *all* the credit to the players, fans, parents, assistant coaches, and even the administration, what happens? We force credit upon the coach, some of which is not his or hers. The public relations rule that needs remembering is this: Take the blame and give the credit, and you'll win almost *every time*. Give the blame and take the credit, however, and you'll lose in almost every situation. Unfortunately, we often have a hard time practicing this law. And when we do, the law tells us why we have failed to get the response that we desired.

THE
LAW OF
TOP-DOWN MANAGEMENT

Rationale: *Public relations is a management responsibility and should be effected from the top down in any organization.*

As we all know well, good management is probably the single most important factor in determining the effectiveness and success of any institution. More than anything else—finances included—it is management that initiates and maintains the tone and direction as well as the moral and professional ethics of an institution. With good management, you can sustain an institution which is financially deprived. However, you cannot sustain an institution with poor management no matter how much money you have. Management competency, more than any other factor, determines the success or failure of any effort. And this reality pertains to promotion, publicity, and public relations as well.

Certainly, good public relations and image-building ideas and their implementation can and should come from the various teachers and support staff as well as the classes and activities within the school or district. However, good public relations and image building *must* be initiated at the top. This means the principal and superintendent must have a program which is whole and vigorous in nature—or only parts of the school or district will be presented. And the results of such partiality are obvious. Some teachers and activities will enjoy a good reputation and some will not, and the school or district will not be perceived as balanced or comprehensive.

As difficult as achieving effective and competent public relations leadership may seem, it is not. And its attainment is one of the most rewarding and satisfying experiences one can earn. The benefits extend beyond us to students, staff, and community. However, this fulfillment can never be realized without meeting and relating to the challenges which are inherent in the basic leadership responsibilities of an administrator. Such administrator attitudes as, "I can't help what people think," or "It's the people's responsibility to find out," or "What we are doing will speak for itself," will not get the job done. These attitudes simply reveal that the person who has been appointed leader does not have the attitude, ability, or understanding required to master the art of public relations—and is an inactive leader.

Administrators who do not adhere to the Law of Top-Down Management will experience continuous failure relative to image and telling the ongoing story of the work and mission of the schools. Quite frankly, some will fail because they are confused by the authoritative nature of this principle. They believe that it conflicts with their beliefs regarding staff input and participation. It does not. The principle of top-down management responsibility does not discourage staff input or individual action relative to the public relations effort of any school or district. However, it does fix responsibility for coordination and comprehensive public relations leadership rather than allow it to be delegated or disseminated to others.

Grassroots
Doesn't Produce
Good Public Relations

When it comes to promotion, publicity, and public relations we cannot "wait and watch" the staff or confer continually on everything and with everyone before initiating a directive or action. Nothing will ever happen or get done with such a stance. Neither can we *expect* ideas and plans to come from the staff always. And we can't mistakenly believe that group suggestion is a prerequisite for public relations efforts. Hard as it is to convince some administrators, this is a management misconception.

Many good public relations ideas *can* and *do* come from within an organization. Many such ideas even work their way to the top—as they should. Grassroots is a great source of ideas, opinions, needs, and even action. However, grassroots is the *result* of good leadership, but it is not leadership.

An administrator should promote and encourage—but he or she must never expect or demand—public relations action to come from the staff of the organization. School and district leadership is a management responsibility—and public relations is not the exception to this management truth. It is not the duty or responsibility of the teaching staff. Therefore, always keep in mind that public relations leadership not only comes from within the organization—but it must always come from the top of one. In every institution, be it a business, school, or church, the initiation of a public relations program must come from where the authority is and cover all aspects of the organization.

When grassroots is the expected source of all public relations efforts, then management becomes a position rather than a function. In truth, in institutions where public relations is effected primarily through grassroots efforts, conflict and confusion become the rules of the day. Too, some teachers and departments enjoy great reputations, and some have no reputation at all. Worse, administrators will still be blamed for any poor image or communication voids and be seen as obstacles in telling the story of our schools. Amazingly, administrators are usually bewildered, hurt, and disappointed because teachers and superiors are critical of their leadership when this is the case.

Not
Truly
Democratic

It is simply impossible to be completely democratic in planning and carrying out a public relations program. Common sense should reveal that no one expects you to involve everyone in this function. In truth, many don't want to be involved. Remember, the fact that staff members would like to be informed of the public relations plan does not mean that they want or expect to make the final decisions regarding the plan or its implementation. And we also need to be aware that democracy would end the first time an administrator had to say no to anything a staff member suggested or wanted.

An administrator cannot delegate to others any leadership responsibility that is inherent in a principalship or superintendency. This is no more possible than it is for teachers to delegate the responsibilities inherent in teaching to students. If a teacher puts a student "in charge" and goes to the lounge for coffee and something happens, who is at fault? The student? No. Likewise, if administrators pass their public relations responsibilities to teachers and something happens or nothing happens, who is responsible?

The administrator who does not recognize that leadership is the function of administration is in trouble. So it is with the public relations effort. This is exactly what happens when the Law of Top-Down Management is ignored, forgotten, or rationalized away. We become "hopers that all is well" or "seekers of approval" rather than agents of action. And it all results because we expected every new idea, plan, or innovation to come from within the institution rather than from the top—where both the authority and responsibility lie.

ADMINISTRATIVE UNDERSTANDINGS THAT PROMOTE SOUND PROFESSIONAL RELATIONSHIPS

Along with the laws we have just discussed, some understandings that promote sound professional and public relationships need our attention. Let's discuss some of these understandings. They are vital to our personal and professional public relations program both internally and externally. These understandings are part of the basis of knowledge we must have to make public relations work. Remember, these understandings are not tricks or gimmicks. They are necessary motivational concepts that we need in order to do the right things, in the right ways, for the right reasons. The first two understandings are related to fear.

UNDERSTANDING #1: FEAR IS A POWERFUL EMOTION WHICH HAS A DIRECT IMPACT ON INTELLECT AND ACHIEVEMENT.

UNDERSTANDING #2: THE POWER OF FEAR IS ULTIMATELY DESTRUCTIVE, WHEREAS THE POWER OF JOY IS A POSITIVE AND CONSTRUCTIVE FORCE.

We all know fear. We know its benefits and detriments. We may, however, see more merit in fear when it's used against others than when it's used against us. And we may even be hostile if someone suggests that we should never use fear tactics with children or the public. Though we may think we know fear well, we may not really understand fear as it relates to intellect and achievement, as well as to our public image. We may not really understand how it motivates or demotivates people in learning or decision-making situations, much less in our public relations efforts. As educators, we should understand fear and its effects—for good reason. Fear is an ever-present condition in the school for some pupils, parents, and teachers. And this reality diminishes all our public relations efforts as long as the fear remains.

Yet, fear has good and bad sides. It *is* a powerful motivator. Certainly, a lot of insurance is sold to us, even when we can't afford it, to protect our families and reduce our fears. In fact, the number of products we buy because of fear is staggering. We buy safety belts, smoke detectors, burglar alarms, locks, and other protective devices because of our fears. We support police departments and promote neighborhood watch programs because of fear. And without a sense of fear which causes us to be careful and look both ways before crossing a street, we might get hit by a car tonight after school.

Fear, without question, is our warning system. It also causes us a lot of pain. In truth, the desire to avoid that which we fear dominates the lives of many, many people. If you think not, reflect on the people who have told you they wouldn't do something they really wanted to do—because they were afraid. They were afraid to go on vacation, buy a car, wear a certain dress, participate in a meeting, change jobs, or go out after dark. That's the extensive power of fear revealed. We all see it—and experience it—daily. But, when it comes to learning and to promoting our schools, we would be wise to use every motivator in the book except fear—for two vitally important reasons.

First, we must be constantly aware that fear is an ever-present, negative, and dominant condition in the world today. It will exist whether *we* use it or not. And none of us, including children or parents, need any more of it. Fear diminishes risk-taking, desires for involvement, and feelings of self-worth. It affects both attitude and behavior. We all know that many children won't speak up in class because they fear appearing dumb. Many students fear that their ability is limited and they can't perform satisfactorily. Thus, children put limits on their efforts out of fear. They fear losing their friends, the approval of teachers, and the love of their parents. Fear can cancel a teacher's efforts to motivate children to study, work hard, and learn. It doesn't make sense to tell children it's silly to be afraid—and then use fear as a motivator or club in the classroom. Too, we know parents who are afraid of teachers, administrators, and schools. Worse, we know parents who have a fear that neither they nor their children "have a chance" to be successful in school.

Second, when we are using fear as a motivator in the classroom or the school, it's not always easy to know when to stop. This is important in a learning situation because, in truth, there is a point at which fear ceases to be of value. There is a point at which it becomes a detriment to student effort, thinking, and action. Experience should tell us that once fear enters the picture, it almost always wins over all else.

Fear motivation would be a teacher's asset if we could use it to get students to a point of action, and then cancel all fears so they could act without fear. So it is with parents and public alike. That's because we know that even intellect yields to fear. Fear overpowers our intelligence. We've all been in a situation in which we've asked someone, "How could you do something so stupid?" and he or she replied, "Because I was afraid." It's not difficult for us as educators to see how vitally important this insight is in our efforts to get children to achieve or to get people to support schools.

If we continually remember the impact fear has on intellect, we can be more effective motivators. Never forget, when people are afraid they do things that they wouldn't normally do. We don't think straight when we're scared. Decision-making ability is almost always impaired by fear. We may not be able to think of anything except getting away from the fear. Then, the end rather than the means becomes the point of our focus. And we may do something foolish—like lie or cheat. So it is with children and parents. Fear simply cancels their intellect momentarily. And children need to have every element of their intellect functioning unimpaired if they're to achieve in the classroom. The public needs the same to support schools.

We will always have fear in schools. Some children will always fear tests. Some will be afraid of other students, of losing possessions, or of failing class. We'll even have teachers and administrators who will be afraid that they are going to lose their jobs. And, occasionally, we will find ourselves in a position in which we may have to make a student or parent fearful. After all, we can't tell a student or parents that "everything is fine and there's no need to worry" when such is not the case.

However, we need to understand the power that fear has over intellect. If we don't, the fear we project may be our biggest obstacle to teaching effectiveness—and public relations. Remember, fear may make people move. But *how* it makes them move is the real issue when it comes to achieving in the classroom. So it is with parents and other members of the community.

These understandings are vital to public relations. Without these understandings entrenched like a rock, we may opt for the wrong choice and our public relations efforts will rest on foundations of sand.

In Contrast With Fear, Joy Is Totally Positive

Joy is a totally positive emotion which has the best chance to cause people—students, staff, and community—to further involve themselves with both the people and the activities of the school. For instance, current research indicates that the amount of significant work accomplished in an organization is directly proportionate to the feelings of rich job challenge and joy that exist therein. When we experience joy, we tend to be openly accepting as well as curious in positive and constructive ways. While fear causes people to withdraw, protect themselves, and become callous against further pain, people who experience joy seem to be able to face difficulties more easily in open and nondestructive ways and turn them into advantages and even opportunities. As administrators we need to be aware of this human condition of responsiveness to joy. It can help us make motivational choices when trying to stimulate employees, young people, and the citizens in our community.

Statements such as "Do it or else!" or "If we don't get more money, we'll have to cut programs," can be very effective, indeed. The threat of the "or else" will propel many dutiful people to action. Although in most cases the threat is short lived, the resulting resentment remains. And the more such approaches are used, the less they may be believed and the more resentment may grow. In truth, such public feelings may turn into a doubt of our competency. What's more, a person, adult or child, who has been threatened will seldom become *self-motivated* as long as the resentment and the fear persist.

In contrast, people who find joy in their work and accomplishments and who are rewarded and appreciated by their administrator, teacher, or school will work to achieve more of the same. They will even become self-motivated simply to obtain more of the rewards of joy.

An added benefit of joy is that those teachers, support staff, and parents who experience joy are more able to be tolerant of others. But employees who are fearful cannot afford to be tolerant of themselves, their peers, or their bosses. Rather, they must build defenses or withdraw because both seem to be easier moves than facing the fear. And any new failure seems to bring on fear of further failure rather than a possibility of success. Thus, fear is debilitating in both the short- and long-term public relations effort.

As administrators, we must promote joy in the classroom, the school, and the mission of education. If we don't, it's unlikely that joy will become a common condition throughout the entire school. When joy is present, however, a whole new dimension is added.

It doesn't make sense not to enjoy children and the things they do. Whether we teach first-graders or high school seniors, we all could tell stories about the funny and delightful things our students have done in class. Indeed, many of these incidents are seen as annoying or frustrating at times. This may be because we have been taught or programmed to see them in such a light. In truth, if we're really going to enjoy being in this business, we must like children—and enjoy the things they do. Without question, this can and will be difficult—until we can teach all to accept young people for "just being."

Such acceptance is called "unconditional acceptance." That means no strings and no demands that students prove anything to us before we begin accepting. After all, each child comes to us with some degree of imperfection. And unless parents can believe that we accept their children for "just being," our public relations efforts will not be believable to parents.

Humor:
A Key To Unconditional Acceptance

A sense of humor can go a long way in helping us accept, unconditionally, all who are involved in the education process. If we can laugh and enjoy people in the present, we'll add a new dimension to teaching and working in the school. Certainly, it doesn't make much sense to laugh when we tell the story to colleagues later—and be mad and miss the joy today.

Laughter in a school has countless benefits. It's a great equalizer. It annihilates feelings of ill will. When people are laughing, they can't frown, be angry, or feel sorry for themselves. Laughter is a positive force beyond compare. It should be heard in every classroom—from teachers as well as from students.

Many teachers avoid and discourage laughter in the classroom. Certainly, many "shy away" from introducing humor because they fear a "loss of control." And though none can deny that humor can be inappropriate, teachers who fear humor must be helped to realize that it has benefits when it is used wisely and when it occurs naturally. We must also help teachers be aware of classroom situations in which words and actions used to produce laughter are appropriate and motivating. And we must help the entire staff recognize that establishing a good climate for learning is almost impossible without laughter because laughter produces joy.

Today's world needs humor much more than we might suspect. It's a very serious world for the most part. Once we begin enjoying children, however, we'll begin to look at them and their world differently. We won't look at dress habits and fads as odd or bad. In fact, we may see strong parallels between their childhoods and our own. After all, children have always had customs, preferences, and dress habits distinctly different from those of adults of the time.

We ought to concentrate on helping the staff enjoy students and colleagues in every way. We should help teachers take pleasure in what children say and do, and in how they act. When we do, we will help the staff gain a new appreciation of young people and vice versa. Most certainly, we will help teachers as well as students find a new source of enjoyment in their lives. And all will find new joy in being in school.

UNDERSTANDING #3: WHEN YOU LOOK DOWN ON JOBS, YOU LOOK DOWN ON THE PEOPLE WHO HAVE THEM.

A school or school district is no better than the sum of its parts. Yet, every school system has a varied number of job positions and functions from custodian to superintendent to the president of the board, which must be occupied by able individuals of varying skills and educational levels. As we all know, each individual provides an important service for the organization, though each does not contribute in the same way to the school's overall success. Nevertheless, it is the combination of these parts that make up the whole.

Now, it stands to reason that if you are the superintendent, you may not value a custodian's work as highly as you value the efforts of your best building principal. However, if you begin to look down on some jobs in your school—by word or action—because of the degree of skill required or their significance to you personally, you are looking down on the *people* who do those jobs. This one attitude is more damaging to internal public relations than any other. In some schools, cooks, custodians, and others are not allowed in faculty meetings because teachers say, "They are staff, not teachers." Make no mistake: These attitudes and actions lie at the root of destroying a public relations effort from the inside out—even before it is off the ground.

Looking down on jobs is a serious management and public relations error and one which other school employees will detect easily. Soon employees will begin to say, "If he doesn't respect them, I wonder if he respects me." Or worse, they will begin to model the administrator's disrespect of certain positions and people. Remember, we are all on the same team with the same mission. Only our functions differ—and this stance should be at the philosophical and practical base of every public relations program. Indeed, it is a stance that needs constant and emphatic teaching within the whole of the school and district.

Rule Of Thumb:
No Disrespect For Property Or People

There's a rule of thumb that every administrator would do well to institute. It's actually the only major rule an organization needs to have. It's a philosophical foundation as well as a practical guideline which is all inclusive. It states: "There shall be no disrespect for property or people, including yourself." This rule should apply to everybody in the organization. Adherence to it means that showing respect to all people equally—even people whom you don't like—is necessary. The reason for this rule is simple. People *must* feel respected and valued in order to respect and value the work they are asked to do, as well as the people with or for whom they must work.

For people to feel that their work is important, *we* must convey to them that it's important as well as why it's important. And they need to know how their individual parts fit in with and contribute to the success of the whole. In addition, others need to be taught these realities. No matter what the job, if it needs to be done, it's important—regardless of the level of brainpower or brawn it might require. The only way to have employees take all aspects of their jobs seriously is for us to treat every task in a serious and important way. When we ignore, overlook, play-down, or belittle even one task that any employee has to do, we belittle that person. We also undervalue the significance of both the task and the person to the whole organization. This is where administrator-employee problems begin and internal public relations efforts break down completely. The attitude that employees begin to convey is "She doesn't know what it takes to keep this school running smoothly," or "He doesn't even know we exist," or "He thinks he's too good for us," or "She wanders out of the office once in a while...to mingle with us peasants." The basic principle is this: Inclusion of people and the tasks they perform is a prerequisite for any internal public relations effort—and exclusion always destroys public relations efforts.

We need to teach, expand, and magnify continually the value of the diverse skills needed to get the work of the organization accomplished. It isn't an impossibility to have a cafeteria worker perform his or her job more skillfully than a member of the administrative team performs his or hers. The fact is that unless people at all levels do their jobs with skill, the work of the entire organization fails to get accomplished. All you have to do to realize this fact is to lose a person in your organization who does a simple job extraordinarily well and note the resulting inconvenience to people at all levels. If, for instance, custodians didn't clean chalkboards for just one night, teachers might go crazy. And if we went to the cafeteria and nothing was prepared for the noon meal, the school day would come to an abrupt halt. What's more, the quality of the tasks performed by custodians and cooks has a bearing on how others do their jobs.

Excellence at any level is a quality that is very rare. When it is evident it should be rewarded, not overlooked because someone may judge a task unimportant or insignificant. Therefore, to establish a good internal public relations program, the administrator must learn to recognize, acknowledge, and reward excellence. And that means we can't overlook the people who are at the entry levels of work. A secretary may be responsible for the good feelings parents have about our school. A nurse may be giving extraordinary care which a child and parents need. An aide may be giving extra help to a student which makes the difference between passing and failing. A bus driver may be establishing the safe and friendly atmosphere we want before children arrive at school.

Fortunately, whatever the degree of responsibility, excellence is possible. It is up to you to decide whether your other employees will learn from the excellence that is demonstrated by their colleagues, or will simply dismiss excellence because of how they feel about the importance of the task. Remember, once disrespect becomes a condition, excellence will decrease automatically. People will rationalize away their shortcomings with one sentence, "I could do better, but nobody cares."

The effective public relations program begins internally. And it includes respecting people and the jobs they do—all of them!

UNDERSTANDING #4: PEOPLE ARE MORE IMPORTANT THAN THINGS.

This understanding may seem to parrot the obvious. Yet, we often need to remind ourselves of the obvious to avoid sliding in the wrong direction. If we don't, our actions may contradict our beliefs.

That's why we need to look closely at our priorities—especially with the passage of time. It's easy enough for us to enter administration full of concern for students and teachers. We can be eager to demonstrate our commitment with every word and action. Yet, after a few years, we may show more concern for books, supplies, chairs, restrooms, football fields, and equipment than we do for children and staff. Few of us can deny that we have seen administrators and teachers alike shift and become more caring of *things* than people.

Remember, there are two sides to being a teacher or an administrator. One side involves *things*. It is called the technical or academic side of teaching and administration. The technical aspect of teaching involves books, desks, equipment, supplies, materials, buildings, and other *things*. The other side of being a teacher or an administrator involves people. This is the difficult side—for *things* are always more easily managed than people. After all, *things* don't have to be motivated. *Things* aren't capable of monopolizing, criticizing, and ignoring either. Only people are capable of these things. Likewise, *things* can't plot, scheme, backbite, or condemn—people can. The fact that we have to be good managers with so many people so much of the time—from students to colleagues—places a great deal of pressure on us as educators. This may be one of the reasons we become *thing* oriented. *Things* are easy to manage in comparison to people. We can put things in their place, and they stay there. We can count them, measure their effectiveness, and make them do what we want them to do. We can depend upon them. We can make *things* look perfect. *Things* don't talk back or disagree with us. They can make us feel good and give us security. This may be one of the reasons we can fall into the "I-need-this-and-I-need that" trap so easily and truly feel that if we had certain *things,* we could be better at our jobs. It would be great if this were so—but it isn't.

People are the primary source of the happiness and the success as well as the frustrations we will experience in administration. We may blame *things* for our failures, but people are behind most of our difficulties. We may feel that if we had new books, more supplies, a bigger room, more equipment, or a bigger budget, we could teach in and administrate our schools more completely and effectively. But that's not really true. These tools help a teacher or administrator. But the most beneficial learning and teaching aid is the quality of the teacher-student, teacher-administrator, or administrator-student relationship. What students need most in order to excel is a good teacher. Teachers need a good administrator. When we allow *things* to gain priority over people, our attitudes and actions contradict our beliefs. We start acting in ways we shouldn't.

Things rather than students and teachers may become our fundamental value. We can treat *things* with great care—but people with no care at all. We may begin believing that an overhead projector is more effective than a teacher. We may show outrage when we see a book or piece of equipment used carelessly, and no emotion at all when a child is mistreated or hurt, when a teacher is discouraged, or when a parent is upset. We may scold students for wasting materials—but think nothing of our proclamations that "certain students, teachers, and parents aren't worth the effort." We may not even see the contradiction in the notion that we need every available tool to have a good school, but we don't necessarily need students and teachers. All these actions should serve as warnings that we are becoming more concerned with *things* than with people. The rule is this: People, not *things*, get the work done in schools. People, not *things*, are the fundamental value in schools. And all of our things are operated by people. *Things* are simply the tools made for us to use. We manage things—and lead people. It is these kinds of beliefs that allow us to keep both the technical and human sides of teaching and administering in proper perspective and put our public relations effort on solid footing.

UNDERSTANDING #5: DON'T TAKE YOUR PERSONAL LIFE OR YOUR PERSONAL TROUBLES TO SCHOOL—AND DON'T PROCLAIM ALL YOUR PROFESSIONAL PROBLEMS IN SCHOOL.

There are some rules for human behavior, standards of professional conduct, and common-sense actions of which we are very much aware when talking about relationships of any kind. Yet, as human beings, we find it extremely difficult to practice them. When it comes to effective management as well as effective public relations, we must. One such rule is this: Don't take your problems to school.

Every administrator is aware of this standard for professional conduct. We are even aware of the consequences when it is violated. We realize, for instance, that when we express personal problems at school or talk continually about the personal side of our lives, we steal professional time from people and alter their productivity. In the process, we gather an audience to which we have no right. And if we talk about our personal problems, we can infect the whole professional staff and cause them to be less positive and effective— all because of us.

We should also be aware that our professional dispositions can render us less competent in the eyes of others—and can cause us to hurt colleagues and students alike by both word and action. And if we "bite someone's head off" for any reason—justified in our minds or not—or react negatively to any suggestion; become catty, sarcastic, or picky; or buttonhole our friends for lengthy discussions of our problems, we detract from ourselves as well as from what the school is and should be. We know we shouldn't. We don't want to be this way, of course. Yet, what course can we take when periods of trouble enter our lives?

Some Things You Can Do...
And Teach Others To Do

■ *First, make yourself aware that the problems you have are contributing to the foul mood you are in.* If you don't arrive at such an awareness you usually can't compensate for your troubled state of mind. Tell yourself before you walk through the school doors that your mood is not the best, and that you must counteract it today. When you arrive at school, make it a point to see the positive people on the staff and avoid those who you can predict will be in the same mood you're in. Remind yourself that you are not at your mental best today and resolve to try not to offend anyone. People who don't have these conversations with themselves not only miss a sure way to professional growth, but also overlook their best problem-solver—themselves.

■ *Second, create a symbol in your mind that signals you to shift gears.* Tell yourself that the door to the school or the office means that you are entering another world and that your mood and your thinking need to change. This symbol could be your way of making yourself conscious of the needed change. However, *don't* put a sign up in your office which tells you to take such a stance. Such a move will only tell the world that you have such a problem.

■ *Third, change your starting time.* Though you and your staff may find it difficult to believe, the vast majority of people who take their troubles to work can directly relate their moods to the time they get up in the morning. Morning is a bad time for some people. This can be especially true for the employee with children. He or she can't get his or her spouse awake or the children off to school or to the baby-sitter—and no one eats an adequate breakfast. If the employee is a mother, she might feel that she is not caring for her children properly. A man might feel that he is a good provider but a poor father and husband because of the things that happen in the morning at home—all because of twenty or thirty minutes' extra sleep. These employees don't even have time in the morning to right their wrongs before leaving for work. They feel the pressure of time too heavily and this results in poor or inadequate treatment of those they love the most. Yet, you will find that rising thirty minutes earlier in the morning can literally change your entire outlook each day. It is, at least, worth your consideration.

■ *Fourth, try to become completely absorbed in your work.* This can be difficult when personal problems are being experienced. But it is possible, with awareness and persistence. Discipline yourself to remember that fretting about personal problems during a time when you can't do anything about them is pointless and can, without reservation, create professional problems as well. Instead, decide you are going to do something useful and productive. You'll find that if you do, your troubles will soon seem less severe—or at least more manageable.

■ *Fifth, realize that everyone has personal problems and often, they will seem big. Too, be aware that we all have professional problems at times.* Above all, know that even though we can expect problems, we can never be totally prepared for them. But we can know that it is never appropriate to vent our personal or professional problems at school to whoever will listen. No matter how trusted our associates, we weaken ourselves in their eyes when we burden them with our personal problems. And whether we think so or not, teachers and colleagues will soon begin avoiding us because they can predict that we will exhaust their time or their emotions, or both. In addition, no professional can ever tell the public about his or her problems. If, for instance, a parent comes to school with a problem and we tell that parent our own problems, we have violated every rule in the book.

Those who eventually conquer their problems begin by employing their own personal strength and determination. They don't impose on their colleagues repeatedly for help. Rather, they divert their energy from worrying and use it to accomplish professional goals. The rule is this: Personal and professional problems can be a setback to the individual administrator as well as to those he or she is trying to lead. This rule applies to teachers and support staff as well. Therefore, such problems need stowing rather than proclaiming. This may seem too obvious even to mention. Yet, bringing problems to school as well as imposing school problems on all is one of the biggest destroyers of professional image in and out of the workplace. In truth, this venting of problems too often by too many people is not uncommon. And it will completely destroy image, excellence, work, and the perception that *all the various* publics have of us and of the school. This is a reality of working with people that we need to teach all who work in the school—teachers, coaches, secretaries, media specialists, aides, and others.

UNDERSTANDING #6: STRIVE FOR ESTEEM, NOT ENVY

As an administrator, you know right now just how good you are and how good you want or intend to be. You know whether you're striving to be the best or whether you're willing to settle for something less. You also know how good you want your school to be as well as what you are willing to do to reach your expectations. While you may want to be well thought of, like most of us, you may or may not have thought about whether you are really going to strive for those characteristics that will give you what you want. For instance, do you want respect? Do you want admiration? These are important intangibles when it comes to public relations. For whether you end up creating esteem or envy can determine whether you get what you want—and others get what they need.

So what makes the difference? A close examination will reveal that esteem is an emotion that grows out of admiration for what someone is, has become, or has built. Envy, on the other hand, is superficial in nature. It's an emotion born out of a desire to possess the things, situations, achievements, or title that another possesses. It has nothing to do with the other person.

Harder To Attain...

Esteem, far and away, is harder to earn than envy. That's because the qualities that inspire esteem can't be "hung on" from the outside. Esteem is not a natural consequence of the size of buildings, number of students, number of programs, or the level of position. Those qualities which can be esteemed are born from within and come to fruition slowly. They are usually tempered through much struggle, reflection, and self-doubt. In fact, to be esteemed usually comes as a surprise to those who are, for it is not the result of any overt contrivance. Envy is.

Unfortunately, many who are not esteemed settle for envy. So it is with some organizations. Rather than delve deeper, it is easier to dress oneself with superficialities that receive a fleeting kind of admiration. Subconsciously, the train of thought and action follows the pattern: "If I can't receive admiration for what I am, I'll opt for admiration for what I have." Many organizations and the people in them do precisely the same thing.

Educators who wish to be envied wear a look which says, "See what I have," not "Come know who I am." In fact, they almost need to hold others at bay in order to preserve their own glamour and prestige. This is in contrast to those who are esteemed and whose whole being invites others to know them better and enter their orbit. Schools may attempt to win envy with fancy athletic and band uniforms, special elective courses, long distance trips, and other showpieces. These things are intended to attract the envy of other schools rather than to capture the esteem of the community. This is not to say that any of these activities or actions are wrong or bad—unless they are the focal point or sole dimensions of a public relations effort.

Short Term
vs.
Long Term

Those who wish to be envied will settle for short-term wins without a long-term future. Those who wish to be envied are only as strong as their last win or their most current conquest. They are usually short-sighted individuals or organizations with little regard for lasting values.

In contrast, those who are esteemed have become thus because they have weathered the test of time and have maintained their values and their vision. Harvard and Yale are two institutions that have opted for esteem rather than envy. Esteemed people and organizations endure because their values have always been more important than any individual win or short-term trapping. Therefore, they can't be "done in" by a failure or short-term loss.

Every public relations effort must take into account the difference between the fleeting compliment of envy and the lasting value of esteem. We must also be well aware that many times, in building a career or a school of significance, choices have to be made. Does one follow a path of high visibility that's enviable—or one which may have lower visibility but higher quality? Esteem of both self and others is earned by choosing paths of quality—no matter what the visibility. Without question, public relations efforts that have substance rather than fluff give the best results. If we want to have careers and schools that we will be able to look to and be proud of in the future, we have to learn to make such choices. This is a foundation belief that will affect the type, style, and direction of our public relations efforts and keep us on course.

UNDERSTANDING #7: AVOID THE "I, ME, AND MY" SYNDROME.

Most administrators who are guilty of lapsing into an "I, me, and my" pattern are surrounded by others who continually tell such administrators what they want to hear—or by those who *refuse* to recognize the power that goes with the administrative position. In either extreme, such administrators try to communicate a sense of power through possessive language in order to impress others—usually those who they know are not familiar with how things really are. "My school," "my teachers," and "my students" are typical phrases used by such administrators. The same can be said of teachers.

The use of "I," "me," and "my" is a tip-off that an administrator or teacher may be operating alone and not using colleagues for advice on matters both large and small. Certainly, it's clear that the team approach is not present and that such administrators are not giving credit where credit is due. Psychologically, such administrators think of themselves as being superior and/or being alone, and thus refer to people and property in exclusive terms. Because they have been acting alone, they often feel both insecure and fearful that if they allow others to become involved in their work, their methods and decisions will be questioned.

Astute administrators know that "I, me, and my" people are turn-offs to almost everyone in a school or district. Therefore, it's to an administrator's advantage to teach all staff members the value of using language that fosters a work climate of community and mutuality of dependence. At the same time, staff members need to be reminded that they will never achieve their personal goals or the school's goals alone.

Phrases such as "my work," "my equipment," "my opinion," and "my achievements" alienate other people and perpetuate a work pattern that excludes the talents of co-workers. Believe it or not, gearing one's language to an inclusive "we, us, and our" position is the first step in positioning oneself to receive the ideas and energies of others as well as make certain that our image matches reality.

Staff members should also be reminded that references such as "my department," "my people," and "my Xerox machine" will cause colleagues and outsiders to mock them. Possessive language pertaining to a school simply isn't acceptable. Neither is it believable. People who use possessive "I" and "me" language are always opening themselves up to criticism. "Hey, when did you buy the place?" is a back-handed comment just waiting to be delivered to them or said to others in their absence.

A
Self-Centered Attitude
Destroys Public Relations

Teachers and administrators who let the "I, me, and my" attitude work against them are those who display to both students and colleagues a detrimental, but not uncommon, personal and professional philosophy. They operate on the assumption that "What's good for me is good for everyone." *Everyone* includes *my* class, *my* colleagues, *my* schedule, *my* workload, *my* ideas, *my* needs, and *my* school. Worse, such educators justify this philosophy in their own minds—morally and educationally. As a result, everything these teachers and administrators do is self-centered. Yet, they turn every situation around and rationalize it to be student-centered. It is not. Their foundation remains: "What's good for me as a teacher or an administrator, is good—and good for everyone else too." This stance comes before everything else. Although they would be the last to admit it, these teachers give assignments when they want to keep students busy and don't give assignments when they want to save themselves some work. Discipline rules are established totally for the benefit of these teachers—to facilitate accomplishing their teaching objectives. When students from these teachers' classes are excused for an hour or a day because the opportunity arises to participate in a music program or take a field trip, it's impossible for one of these teachers to express joy that such an opportunity awaited a student. Rather, their reaction is, "Why would you take one of *my* students out of *my* class?" Even here, their self-centeredness holds steady. In reality, these teachers feel that the school revolves around them, or should, and that if decisions are made which run counter to their best interests, the school is wrong—without question.

Self-Concept
As An Asset

The educator who is happy as well as successful in this profession firmly believes that "What's good for *students* and the *school* is good for me." In theory as well as in practice, this is the only ideology a professional person can assume—regardless of the title under which he or she operates. For both short- and long-term rewards, this is the only attitude that will fulfill the needs of "me, myself, and I." This is often a hard point to prove to a person. Yet, one can ask a happy and successful person in any field—and the theory will not be denied.

It is this belief in practice that allows a teacher to give students and learning priority as an extension of self—and allows administrators to make the same extensions toward both teachers and students. The goals for student assignments are student-centered rather than teacher-centered. Discipline standards are not established for the teacher's benefit but in order to help students achieve self-discipline. Nor does this teacher react negatively to administrative decisions which might result in readjustment—if such decisions are good for students. He or she maintains the opinion that if something is good for the students, then at least we ought to try to meet the need. Too, opportunity is opportunity—and the student-centered teacher realizes that students find benefits in the total school structure and not just in his or her classroom.

As tactfully as possible, correct the speech patterns of teachers and support staff when they begin to speak in terms of "I, me, and my." This speech pattern must be broken. Employees may be irritated at first, but they'll get the point. Soon they'll be aware of it themselves, and slowly you'll see a change in attitudes and actions. Remember, habits are hard to break, and developing new habits requires a great deal of patience.

Reinforce this lesson by teaching staff members that when approaching people, they should always keep tomorrow in mind—and should never be misled by the egotistical moment of today. Teach them to think about *how* they want to appear in the eyes of students, parents, and other staff members. Make them aware that being someone who is believable and someone others would like to know is key, and that speaking in inclusive terms about our schools and our mission is absolutely vital. You might even wish to say, "Remember, today you might be the most important person in the organization in the eyes of a single student, but tomorrow he or she might meet someone else who is more instrumental to his or her success. Referring to your position and influence in terms that reflect joint ownership and joint responsibility is far more credible and a far safer position in the long term." Remember, it's vital that students not change their minds about us as they progress down the road of school life, and life itself. But this is exactly what will happen if we are self-directed today—no matter how influential we appear to be with students at the present time.

UNDERSTANDING #8: THERE MUST BE ROOM FOR DISAGREEMENT.

There must always be room in our lives for those who disagree with us. If not, a public relations effort cannot and will not survive simply because of the nature of human beings. Therefore, a built-in system for disagreement is needed. We make friends and develop likes and dislikes on the mutuality of agreements. Why shouldn't we? It doesn't make much sense not to. We like sharing the same life styles, views, and dreams. We like basking in the pleasantness of affirmation of those people who agree with us, like what we do, and approve of us in both personal and professional ways. If we don't have people around us with whom we can share mutuality, we may not be very happy people. In fact, we may not feel very good about ourselves or others.

This reality, however, can be the source of our strength as well as our weakness. It can help us to develop strong human relationships. On the other hand, it can also cause us to exclude all who disagree with us in any way. It can even result in our being lulled into an absolute stupor by refusing to give or receive disagreement and refusing to admit to any. We can end up with a quiet, isolated, and agreeable world of nothing.

Our Most Difficult Act...

Administrator and teacher alike must learn quickly that not accepting disagreement is as unhealthy as refusing to admit to any. Business and industry spend a lot of money to find out what people *don't like* about their products or services. They have complaint departments and customer service centers to find and handle disagreement. We should learn early in our careers that out of our disagreeing and being disagreed with comes an awareness of both self and the reacting world. Out of disagreement come change, improvement, and new satisfactions. With it also come new experiences that mold our personal and professional being. So there must be room for disagreement in our schools—from students, staff, parents, and the public. Our task is to make disagreement professional, so that it does not become personal or destructive.

Disagreement is one of the toughest human relationship problems for people to deal with because it is multisided. How disagreement is presented, how it's received, who gives it, and the manner in which it is offered all have a bearing on our feelings, emotions, and responses.

For instance, if the disagreeing person attacks, he or she sets up a reactive condition known as "fight or flight," and encourages defensiveness. Think how different every faculty, parent, or media disagreement could be if attack were void. Anger almost guarantees the omission of constructive discussion and change. It defeats itself.

Likewise, disagreement must find a recipient willing to accept reasonable disagreement as just that—reasonable. If disagreement is translated as a personal affront, the open discussion will be lost again. We remember an incident in which a new teacher was offering a valid point of disagreement in a faculty meeting. The disagreement involved a program developed by one of the most conscientious, hard-working teachers on the staff—one who had, indeed, done much for all students, all teachers, and the school. Immediately, all came to the defense of their admired colleague and "put down" the disagreeing points hard and fast because they took the disagreement as a personal reflection. Result: A valid point of disagreement was not permitted. Worse, something which could have been improved continued with a weakness. Here, the presentation was misinterpreted. Consequently, the faculty response established the fact that there was, indeed, no room for disagreement. Remember, if disagreement is not permitted you don't have a public relations program. You have propaganda.

An Equal · Right

Yet, we all know colleagues, students, interest groups, and some parents who are never in agreement with anything. The question is this: Although we may feel we are dishonoring our own integrity, do we always have to allow them to state irrational and personal disagreements? Yes, we do. Never, under any circumstances, should a statement of disagreement be disallowed in the discourse. The chronic "disagreer" will almost always be in our midst. Regardless, he or she has a right to disagree. However, others have the right to refute the disagreer's destructive contribution. Operating from this stance allows our public relations program to be fruitful and free, rather than deceitful and contrived. Many boards of education, for example, never learn that a 5-2 vote often receives more public support than a 7-0 casting.

Remember, it's the prefix "dis" that specifically sets a negative tone for disagreement. It's too bad that it does, for healthy differences indicate a vitality we need and simply must have in education. Allowing disagreement means we care very much about what is happening. It signals a healthy involvement. Under such conditions, disagreement is a strong and positive force and will actually help our public relations efforts both internally and externally. It also signals the possibility for an exciting and challenging exchange and offers the opportunity to hear and be heard. Among professional educators, it must be promoted rather than declared inadmissible. A classroom without disagreement is not a learning room. A faculty without differences is dead. A public without disagreement is not interested in schools—and will never support them to the degree we desire.

Likewise, learning for student and teacher alike is available through constructive, responsible, and mature disagreement. All we need to do is establish the fact by word and deed that there is room for disagreement in our lives, in the classroom, in the office, and in the community.

Our public relations program can never contradict the promise that education is the primary bastion for free expression and thought in our society. Out of this belief have come ways of life and attitudes toward others that are traditions of free people wherever they might live. But this belief is in jeopardy the moment we do not leave room for disagreement, or when we allow the ways, means, and manner in which we disagree to negate our right to disagree.

In many classrooms, businesses, governments, and families there really isn't any room for disagreement. Instead, we adopt the attitude "either you agree with me or you oppose me. And if you oppose me, then you are against me, and must not like me; therefore, I am against you and don't like you." Similar thinking has resulted in many attitudes and behaviors which are detrimental to education as well as damaging to efforts to create an effective public relations program—a program which carries the message of schools and our need for them to the people.

UNDERSTANDING #9: WE MUST OBSERVE AND TEACH SIX ABSOLUTES OF PROFESSIONAL COURTESY.

If you want your school or district to be a good place to work and project a good image, you have to abide by certain unwritten laws, and encourage staff members to abide by them as well. Although there are no formal penalties for violating them, these absolutes help guarantee that an organization will not be filled with infighting, suspicion, and jealousy. Rather, the organization will attempt to make the desired professional image match the reality. That's why we have included in this chapter the following absolutes of professional courtesy.

1. Never say anything derogatory about a colleague to anyone—inside or outside your school. This is a tough one. Our human need to gossip, let off steam, and let others know that our views—along with our performance—are superior to those of our colleagues is, at times, insatiable. But if we don't want derogatory statements to be made about us behind our backs, we must refrain from making such statements about others.

Likewise, we must never be guilty of calling down a colleague or subordinate in front of fellow staff members, students, or the public. This kind of embarrassment is never forgotten. It almost always triggers a resolution on the part of the wounded victim to "pay back" the offender. What's more, calling down a fellow educator publicly is rarely necessary. Time can always be made to handle such situations in private.

2. Always show respect for the positions held by subordinates, colleagues, and superiors in the school or system. You may not like a teacher in your school, but you are obligated to show respect for his or her position as an educator. You may feel that the work being performed by someone in a certain administrative position is of inferior quality or you may disagree with his or her decisions or actions. And you can try to talk to that person about the matter privately. But any action you take that undermines respect for that person's position also undermines the function of that position in relation to the rest of the staff.

3. Never put down or show inconsideration for the work of another person or department. Statements like "Science and math are what's important to me—I couldn't care less about what they're doing in gym" are completely inappropriate in a school. All the work that's done in a school or school system is important. If you want colleagues, students, parents, and the public to appreciate the work you do, learn to show appreciation for the work of others. The truth of the matter is that without the efforts of people in other positions in your school, your own efforts don't amount to a hill of beans insofar as creating a good school is concerned.

4. Never counter the orders of another administrator to the staff. People in authority positions have a tough job. And because school leaders are human, they may misjudge, make decisions without an understanding of the whole situation, and sometimes just behave poorly. Nevertheless, an administrator can't maintain authority if someone repeatedly undermines his or her decisions. If you disagree with the actions or orders of another administrator, talk to him or her privately, and let that person announce any resulting changes in procedure to his or her own staff. But don't try to enforce your own authority where it isn't wanted or needed. You will only make matters worse. If you doubt this philosophy, just think what a mess you would be facing if someone interfered with your authority where your staff was concerned.

5. Never ask co-workers to lie or cover up for you. Doing so is tantamount to asking them to lay aside their principles for your own personal convenience or protection. Such practices compromise them and you as well as the entire organization. In addition, covering up or lying will cause a chain reaction and you'll find workers on all levels behaving unethically.

6. Never ask for special privileges that can't be extended to the rest of the staff. When we ask for special privileges that can't be extended to everyone, we are asking our superiors to do something that they must feel they have to hide. If they do extend the privileges, they must then worry about other employees finding out and claiming "unfair treatment." If they don't extend the privileges to others after giving them to you, they are left to handle their own feelings about not being able to comply with such requests. This is a bad position to put others in, whatever they decide.

We all complain continually about the apathy, backbiting, politics, and disrespect that exist in our profession. The wise administrator knows that any administrator who wants a climate of professional courtesy in his or her school must be the first to extend that courtesy to his or her colleagues as well as to the student body. Consistently extending such courtesy takes a great deal of personal discipline. But the successful administrator knows that people can extend only those courtesies that they first experience. The strong administrator knows that he or she must lead the way and that professional courtesy lies at the foundation of every public relations effort.

DEFINING YOUR MARKET AND GIVING THE PUBLIC WHAT IT WANTS

"Emotion has taught mankind to reason."
—Vauvenargues

The market area for a school is different from the market for a business. So it is important that we know the difference between the two. A business must ask, "Is our market the city, the whole county, or the entire country?" Businesses must also ask, "Is our market women or men, young people or older people, people from certain ethnic persuasions or all races of people?" Identifying a business market has to do with identifying the wants, needs, and habits of all these different groups of people and deciding whether or not they will have reason to use the products and services of a particular business.

For more and more people in business or industry, a market is even being defined as a single area where people can be reached from a single media source. Therefore, a business market is being defined in terms of ease of reaching people via newspaper, direct mail, radio, television, or outdoor signs, including billboards.

WHAT IS YOUR MARKET?

Unlike retail stores and other businesses, schools have to reach *all* the people in the district. That's because all the people pay for the schools. However, all people in our community do not have children in school. In some communities, only 33 percent of the people have children in school. This is all the more reason we need to reach everyone with our public relations efforts. If we don't, we may find it hard to gain support and almost impossible to pass such things as bond issues for buildings. And tax increases of any kind may turn friends into adversaries. Therefore, very simply...

QUESTION: Who makes up the market for the public relations program in a school district?

ANSWER: All persons living within the borders of the entire district.
1. Students
2. Teachers
3. Administrators
4. Support Staff
5. Parents
6. Nonparents

The market can be broken down further to include different age groups; groups according to marital status; various groups of professional people, such as lawyers, doctors, and laborers; and even retired people and certain ethnic groups.

Once the market has been successfully and clearly defined we must try to reach *everyone* in our market to the best of our ability. That's because people from all these groups pay taxes which support our schools, or they may influence someone who does. In the case of private schools, people from all these groups have the power to influence prospective families to enroll their children as students. Therefore, we must always know whom we are and are not reaching with each of our communication messages.

WHAT THE PUBLIC WANTS AND NEEDS IN ORDER TO BE AN ADVOCATE FOR SCHOOLS

First and foremost, the public wants information about the workings as well as the successes and failures of the schools. Information, or knowledge, is power. And without information the community feels powerless. With powerlessness come feelings of resentment, negativeness, and detachment. In addition, people can identify with that which is familiar. They cannot, however, identify and relate to the unfamiliar. And to support what is not known is almost impossible.

If we want support, we need to help people understand education. After all, many adults have strong opinions but little real knowledge about education and how schools work. Worse, many of their opinions were formed during their childhoods when they attended school, and those opinions have carried over into their adult lives. This is not a condemnation, but a simple statement of fact that we need to recognize and make attempts to alter. Therefore, unless we can give the public a broader understanding of education, they may not think that what we're doing in schools is meaningful.

If we want people to rise above their childhood memories, we must help them gain an understanding of the purposes of education today. They must be taught that schools in our society strive to prepare young people to live successfully—a goal that encompasses more than personal academic success. Students must retain facts and grasp concepts as they learn how to think. Therefore, the purposes of education include—and extend beyond—the successful teaching of the "Three R's." Let's discuss a few of the purposes.

- *We must teach the public that schools make sure that students master basic skills.* This includes the "Three R's." However, the public must be told that schools are also responsible for teaching the practical skills that will help students live successfully today as well as after graduation. Part of this task is to help young people embrace the concepts of craftsmanship and pride in their work. In addition, without learning specific facts, students can't build foundations of usable knowledge that can be applied to daily living. That's why teaching facts and practical knowledge is the primary mission of the school. The public must understand this reality.

- *We must teach the public that schools teach the young how to develop the ability to cope with constant change.* This means refining students' thinking abilities, both logical and creative. Great masses of information constantly bombard students today and will continue to bombard them in the future. Thus, students must develop the skills of choosing, sorting, and arranging quantities of information. Only as students develop these skills can we expect them to think rationally and decide wisely. The real world is composed of many choices. The ability to make wise choices will mean the difference between success and failure for most of our students. When the public understands this mission of the schools, people will be in a better position to support the work of the schools in this regard.

- *We must teach the public that schools are dedicated to helping students embrace ethical standards and to seeing that such standards overlap even the most practical decisions and responsibilities.* As educators, we need to understand these standards as well. There's a common ethical base that holds our democratic society together. Only as students understand this truth can we expect their lives to be both vibrant and free of constant conflict. For example, we can tell the public that we try to teach students that every human being has dignity and worth. If the school ignores its responsibility to teach this standard, all of us are diminished in value and importance.

- *We must teach the public that schools make students aware of their obligation to participate in their community and its governance.* The concepts of good citizenship and public service are essential to the functioning of our society. The parochial schools have an additional responsibility—the teaching of religion.

The public also needs to be reminded of another important fact in our society: Each generation has been committed to helping the young *have* more, *experience* more, and *enjoy* a better life. This is one of the primary reasons our country has prospered. And the technological improvements and scientific breakthroughs that have resulted have given us the means to improve the quality of life for people all over the world.

Citizens across the nation have spent many hours throughout the years developing complex statements about the purposes of education. Without reservation, it has been time well spent. However, most of those statements are essentially expansions of the purposes discussed here. Thus, by keeping these purposes in mind, we'll retain some perspective about schools and how they ought to function. Our task is to make sure students, parents, and the public understand these purposes too. It's important to remember, however, that the purposes listed here are not purposes that belong to the schools alone. They are purposes shared by parents and most of our institutions. It's both comforting and exciting to know that schools aren't alone in their work, but that they share the responsibility with others. And this is a message we must constantly carry in our public relations effort.

We need to remember that schools are best when teachers, parents, and the public share a common vision. If we expect parents and community members alike to share a vision, we must first convey it to them. Only as we do, will we—parents, the school, the community—stay on the intended course.

Sometimes, we feel that it is dangerous to give out *too* much information about our schools. We feel that with too much information we create monsters within our public instead of advocates. Though this is the risk of an "open information" policy, total information is also the only way people who *want* to be friends of the schools can gain the information needed to say good things about us. Hollywood studios have subscribed to this theory for years. They learned that the people who attended movies were actually their best ticket agents. Now, when a new movie is released a large part of the promotion money is spent to give movie goers more "sales" information: how a particular movie was made, how much money was spent, what the difficulties were, what the real personalities of the stars are, and how the special effects were achieved. Hollywood knows that people love passing along these tidbits. It makes them feel like they are on the "inside." We've all been acquainted with people who know everything there is to know about a movie or a particular star. By the time they get through telling us what they know, we would swear they had written the script. Without doubt, these people do exactly what the movie promoters want them to do. They create the interest which motivates us to go and see the movie for ourselves.

There's another very important point that needs to be made about giving out more information concerning schools. And we often forget it. It's the public's *right* to know just about anything that happens unless that information would breach a confidence about a particular student. This is true whether schools are public, private, or parochial. Not only are these schools supported financially by the public at large or by our private public, but parents entrust their most prized possessions to school employees for a considerable portion of each day. And because parents will continue to value their children above all other things, they will demand information concerning every aspect of their children's education. Now, as educators, we can decide to give this information willingly or grudgingly. And how we give it will determine what image we will leave in the minds of community members as well as the extent of the trust they will want to give us.

THE QUESTION OF PARAMOUNT SIGNIFICANCE: DO YOU REALLY WANT PUBLIC INVOLVEMENT?

This is a very good question that requires an honest answer. After all, the issues of parental and public involvement and support for schools are long-standing ones. We must admit that while all educators may want public support, not all want public involvement. Therefore, when it comes to public relations, we must decide what we want: support, involvement, or both. We need to be aware that parents and public alike will have a difficult time supporting something they either know nothing about or are excluded from being a part of in meaningful ways. Therefore, we need to know the rule: It *is possible* to gain support without involvement, *but* this requires giving parents and the public frequent and comprehensive information about what we're doing and why we're doing it. Too, we need to realize that support is easier to acquire if it is linked with involvement because personal investment and hands-on experience help people create or manufacture the desire to give their support. As we decide what we want, we need to be aware that students do better and consider school more important when parents are involved. And schools are more apt to be funded adequately when the public is involved.

If we decide we want community involvement in our schools, two questions must be answered: First, how do we secure parental and public involvement in ways that are meaningful? Second, how do we make certain that involvement results in excellence rather than interference or mediocrity?

■ *First, we can never play games with parents or the community.* For instance, we can't routinely send home a progress report using a mass communication vehicle and expect a telephone call in response without giving parents instructions as well as a specific day and time to call. After all, mimeographed letters seldom get high rates of response. If we feel a meeting is wise, we should ask parents to come on a specific day at a specific time and for a specific reason. Likewise, we can't fail to plan an agenda or prepare a meeting place. Parents must know they are welcome and needed—and must be prompted to respond in the ways we desire. If not, parents may think our "progress report speaks for itself," and they may believe we don't want their involvement. Likewise, we must know that open door policies must have content or they'll be treated like the "we'll have to get together sometime" or "come by and see me anytime" kinds of invitations. Such invitations may be sincere, but few of them will be picked up on or actualized.

■ *Second, we have to decide what type or level of involvement we want—and develop a plan to get it.* There are several levels of involvement. We may merely want periodic individual contact at PTA, PTO, and back-to-school nights. We may want small and select group meetings in which we can offer information. We may want input and involvement in decision making. Or we may want volunteers to help with certain tasks. Each level of involvement requires specific techniques. One of the biggest areas of involvement we desire is helping in the classroom. This includes having parents and members of the community plan school parties, help with field trips, serve as guest speakers, and even teach certain lessons. As we decide what level of involvement we want, however, we need to know that many of the old practices we used in past years may not work any more for large percentages of people.

The traditional ways to involve parents and the public in schools don't seem to attract interest like they used to. The number of people who want to make cookies for school events is diminishing. Yet, the number of adults who not only know how important teachers are, but who recognize good teachers is growing. The number of parents who want to be involved in their child's education is growing in many places as well. We need to understand this reality and plan accordingly—if we really want involvement. If we don't want involvement, we might not act as if we do or criticize parents when we don't get it, especially if we are not taking the kinds of actions necessary to get it.

■ *Third, we can keep parents and community alike well informed about what is happening in our school.* This requires comprehensive reporting through notes, class newsletters, meetings, briefings, telephone calls, and requests for specific kinds of help.

■ *Fourth, we can communicate with parents individually on a regular basis.* Remember, although group communication is important, it's never as successful in generating involvement as individual communication. Therefore, class, school, and district newsletters and bulletins should seek to inform and educate, but should not be relied upon to create a desire for involvement or to draw parental involvement.

■ *Fifth, we can create and implement a consistent plan.* We can make sure we're available at specific times for conferences and we can schedule times for class visits. We can make telephone calls and send notes as well as class, school, and district newsletters at regular and predetermined intervals. And each of our efforts in this regard should have one or more purposes.

■ *Sixth, we can design every meeting to be interesting, enlightening, relevant, and meaningful—and to get and give information, create active participation, and show parents and community alike how to help children learn.* A tone of mutual need, commitment, and shared responsibility is a must. As educators who work with children every day, we know about the ways and habits of children. We have considerable information which could help parents with the tasks of raising, understanding, relating to, and living with children. The question is this: Do we use meetings for giving this kind of information or play it safe by telling parents very little about what we know—and what they need to know to be successful?

■ *Seventh, we can recognize that parents' involvement may pertain only to their child or to their child's class.* In both instances, however, we can teach adults the benefits of involvement to them, their child, and all children. Many parents and community members want to be involved in the school—and probably just as many don't. But even though some adults don't want to be involved, we shouldn't assume they don't trust us or don't hold education in high regard. Most do. We also shouldn't make judgments about what kind of parents they are if they don't want extensive involvement. Some parents can't handle involvement in school activities along with all the other pressures in their lives. In addition, the fact that some parents can't or don't want to be involved today doesn't mean that they never wish to be involved. However, whether or not they feel that they are being judged by us may well determine the extent of their involvement today and in the future.

Remember, parental and community involvement won't just happen. We must create ways to involve adults in specific ways which are meaningful to them. This requires time, effort, and special communication. If we really believe that home-school-community cooperation is of value to children, we will initiate our own plan for gaining the level of involvement we want and need—and with which we are comfortable.

EMOTIONAL INVOLVEMENT

There is no doubt that the public also wants emotional involvement with the schools—in the right kind of way. Please note that we say in the right kind of way—for the public is already emotionally involved when it comes to the education of its young people. And this fact is something that we should see as highly favorable where our publicity, promotion, and public relations efforts are concerned.

The truth is that nobody was ever bored into becoming an advocate for the work of educators or into supporting the schools. Unfortunately, too many public relations messages are impersonal, detached, cold, and dull. It pays to talk to people in a warm, friendly manner. It pays to charm them, to make them hungry to know more about schools. And it pays to cause them to participate by including rather than excluding them as well as by sharing rather than telling, presenting rather than denouncing, convincing rather than talking, and exciting them rather than boring them. And this, of course, is impossible unless we are excited about what we are doing, what they might be doing, and what's happening in positive ways to children while they are in school. Here, our expectations have a great deal to do with what we get. In truth, many of us expect nothing in the way of meaningful involvement, and that's exactly what we get.

Public Relations Messages
Must Encourage The Reader/Viewer/Public
To Participate In The Message

One of the basic tenets of public relations is that to be effective, public relations efforts must get people to *participate* in the messages. According to Dr. Ernist Dichter of the Institute for Motivational Research, more and more public relations messages today are being prepared to be forgotten—instead of remembered. Whether a public relations message is remembered depends largely upon how successful the message is in overcoming apathy and indifference and in making contact with a basic "interest" or "want" of the public so that a "dialogue" can take place.

Recipients of a public relations message should perceive that the message concerns them—*personally*. Since so many public relations messages are unwanted, like so many television commercials, the mind acts to screen out promotional stimuli that do not correspond with its immediate interests. Therefore, in a sense, people become psychologically deaf and blind to those things that fail to interest them. It is not the loudness of the message or its overpowering nature which assures that it will be memorable. Instead, it is whether or not the message stimulus can penetrate a listener's interest screen sufficiently to permit a "dialogue" to take place between the recipient and the public relations message.

A mistaken belief, however, which is dogmatically defended by certain Madison Avenue executives, is that incessant repetition fosters retention of the message. Psychological experiments have demonstrated that, if anything, the very opposite is true. Repetition alone is one of the least effective methods for remembering. It is participation that is necessary to create retention. This means establishing a "dialogue" between the recipient of the message and the message itself. Experiments have shown that retention can be increased by as much as 30 percent when participation is induced.

Therefore, repetition should not be used just to prevent recipients from forgetting the message. Rather, it should be used as a means of inviting the reader/viewer/public to participate by filling in part of the story himself or herself. It is this "filling in" which accounts for increased assimilation and retention of the subject matter. In other words, three messages, each of which invites and encourages *active participation,* may be the equivalent of twenty messages which are largely repetitious.

Although the primary job of school public relations is to reach as many people as possible—and to help them remember the schools and their messages—studies have shown repeatedly that much of modern communication neglects one of the basic tenets of experimental psychology: the process of perception, assimilation, and memory. In creating public relations messages that are remembered it is empathy that holds the key to success.

It is our emotions that help us remember. If you doubt this, think back to a time when you flunked a test in school. The question you could not answer was the one you remembered the longest. It was a traumatic experience in which you were emotionally involved. Thus, one public relations message that *involves the viewer, reader, or listener* may be the equivalent of ten purely rational, unexciting, and repetitious messages. It may serve us well to become familiar with the seven types of emotional involvement so that we can make use of what "turns the public on."

SEVEN TYPES
OF EMOTIONAL INVOLVEMENT TO USE
IN PUBLIC RELATIONS EFFORTS

Vicarious Experience

Here, a person tends to identify with the persons or situations being depicted—and experience the same emotions as well.

Practically everyone has formed an opinion about school from his or her own experience of it. Childhood is an experience we all have in common. Let's not forget that parents and grandparents are "reliving" parts of their own childhood through their children, grandchildren, or the children in the community. Parents of "little leaguers" are a case in point. These adults are swinging the bat and playing first base in their own minds. They cheer the children's wins and wear their disappointments. Likewise, there are few adults who aren't able to understand from experience what a delight chocolate milk, ice cream sandwiches, and flash cards can be to an elementary school student.

The point is this: Adults can relate strongly to the emotions of children—because they've been there. Our public relations messages should capitalize on this reality. We need not and should not talk to the public as if they were *complete* strangers without any emotional knowledge.

Curiosity

It's possible to stretch this characteristic to mean nosiness. Public relations can use the media to create a peephole through which the public can view the details of the activities of students, teachers, and administrators, as well as their work and achievements. A large majority of people turn to the media to satisfy their curiosity. Examples in the media for this common use include gossip columns, obituaries, society pages, letters to the editor, human interest stories, and so forth. The point is this: There are a lot of interesting activities taking place in school. There are many varied and significant achievements on a wide front. Many people are doing many different things. And many of these people or their families are known to our public. All of these people have interests and all of their activities and achievements can be used in our public relations efforts to satisfy or stimulate the curiosity need.

Humor

It's a very serious world. Turn on the news tonight, and you'll see just how serious it is. Yet, people want to laugh. The beauty of the business of education is that the opportunities for humor are everywhere in a school. Children present us with countless opportunities to laugh and to make others laugh as well. There isn't a teacher in the world who doesn't have a bag full of incidents that will make people laugh and remember their own childhoods. All we need to do is relate them in speeches and newsletters as well as calls to parents to help create a better image of school. When we speak publicly we need only to relate the story—without names of course. We should learn to magnify this aspect of our work in order to delight and charm our public. An entertainer named Art Linkletter built a career around the numerous things children do or say.

Aesthetic Pleasure

This type of pleasure comes from experiencing something which the individual considers beautiful. It involves such things as music, colorful settings, and artwork. Indeed, the school has much to offer the public in the area of aesthetic pleasure. If we cultivate the aesthetic aspects of our schools and classrooms, we can help them become more "alive" places in our communities. Aesthetic pleasure is inherent in the arts, and the arts raise the quality of life in a community. That's why knowledge about the arts in our schools should be an integral part of our public relations program. In many communities, the visual and performing arts program is already the school's best public relations effort. In fact, in many communities, if our entire public relations efforts were as good as the efforts on behalf of the visual and performing arts, we would be enjoying unlimited acclaim and support. Again, however, we need to teach people the benefits of involvement in the visual and performing arts—as a participant or as a spectator.* After all, we know there is a direct correlation between the quality of the arts and the quality of life in a place. That's why the arts are one of our most practical public relations tools—internally and externally.

Self-Rating Appeal

Make no mistake: Many individuals enjoy testing their personal knowledge and abilities. People are able to self-rate from working on such activities as crossword puzzles, quiz shows, and audience participation shows and from figuring out mystery stories. All of these things allow people to see themselves as part of the solution to a problem. People also get emotional pleasure from seeing how others are identifying and solving problems. This is the reason that advisory committees made up of teachers, parents, students, and citizens work so well. Remember, sharing the responsibility means giving ownership—a vital part of any public relations effort.

Human Contact

This is the pleasure of spending time with people in the school. There was a time when the school was the social center for the community. In many small towns, it still is. And we meet the human contact need for parents with our PTO's and PTA's, back-to-school nights, parent-teacher conferences, potluck dinners, carnivals, class visitations, school tours, school plays, musicals, and sporting events. We meet this need for children when we acknowledge students as people with interests other than those that pertain to our particular subject matter.

---

*For information on *About the Arts,* a program to enhance the arts in your school and community, write or call The Master Teacher, Leadership Lane, P.O. Box 1207, Manhattan, Kansas 66502; (913) 539-0555.

Many of us can recall a special teacher or principal who did things with us other than "at school activities"—drove us home, took us on field trips or to a museum, took us for a Coke®, or talked to us in restaurants or grocery stores. These educators became real to us—and had a special impact on our lives because of it. Every successful public relations program must include such contact. It cannot be done with the media alone. Staff breakfasts, holiday meals, luncheons at the end of the school year, staff-development days, faculty lounge visits, department and faculty meetings, and room visits need to be included in our internal public relations effort. Externally, school visits, birthday lunches, carnivals, advisory committees, parent days, and other activities have real human contact emotional value.

Friendship

People come to view certain mass communication vehicles and media people as friends. The school newsletter is a case in point. It is a mass communication vehicle that is directed to parents personally. That's why it has such a high readership. People respond to others who approach them in friendship—whether their news is positive or negative. Remembering this one reality about friendship can save us hours of emotional strain. The public is our friend—our best friend—even though it may not seem that way at times. The media can become our friends and help us create more friends if we approach the media and people with trust and friendship.

SIX

DEALING WITH MASS COMMUNICATION VEHICLES

"The daily press has more power in the shaping of public opinion than any other force in America."
—*Jerome D. Barnum*

Every administrator has the responsibility and the challenge of frequently communicating information to large groups of people. We also have the responsibility for increasing the public's emotional involvement with the schools through that information which is given to large groups of people. To do both, administrators must have a skillful grasp of the media: how each medium works and how to use it best. There are few of us who have such knowledge. It isn't something we were taught when we were getting our degrees. But experience in administration has taught us that being skilled in the media would greatly enhance our work.

How People Use The Various Media

By understanding how business, industry, the professions, advertising agencies, and consulting firms use the various mass media, we can help ourselves use the communication vehicles more effectively. There are four basic media that are a part of our everyday living that have applications to schools. These are radio, television, newspaper, and direct mail. Each of these major media has a great deal of value by itself. And each has greater value when used in conjunction with another. That's why our discussion of the media will include these vital relationships. However, before we enter into an in-depth analysis of each medium, we have an important point which needs your consideration.

**You
Can Choose First Class...
Or Second Class**

Because most schools are both public and nonprofit institutions, money seems to be continually in short supply. As a result, the entire focus of our public relations effort can become the *economy* of doing something. Though our training as educators rarely allows us to compromise the *content* of our messages, we do allow ourselves to compromise how our messages are packaged and delivered—in the name of economy. Most of us do not have advertising or public relations dollars in our budgets. Thus, we've adopted a "bargain basement" mentality toward our public relations efforts. We do what we can do—inexpensively. We put out what we can—if it's cheap. In fact, we think of the cost first and the effort second. We have allowed ourselves to compromise the quality of the delivery of our messages and, as a result, we have compromised our entire public relations effort.

The truth of the matter is that it usually isn't any more expensive to do something well and with good taste, than it is to give something a half-hearted effort. For instance, it is no more expensive to put a well-designed, professionally executed nameplate at the top of our newsletters than it is to put a carelessly and poorly designed one. It's also no more expensive to put a well-thought-out, child-centered slogan at the bottom of our letterhead than it is to leave a slogan off. Too, it's no more expensive to make certain our hallways are well decorated with student work, than it is to leave them barren.

Yet, a first-class posture does require extra work, extra vigilance, and a critical eye for whether or not your public relations efforts are representing high standards and the *excellence* of the school. But it is not as hard or as time consuming as it may seem. It all begins with deciding how you are going to do simple tasks in a first-class way. And you will get better and more alert at meeting this standard with time and practice. For instance, when time restraints are propelling you to throw something together, stop. There are very few public relations efforts that can't be delayed a few hours for more careful scrutiny. There's no doubt that you will be happier with the image that you project if you follow this simple rule: *Adhere to maintaining quality rather than saving time and you'll see more positive and successful results.*

Take Inventory

Lack of communication is often singled out as a primary reason for many of the problems that we have in our public and private schools. People say the school board doesn't tell them anything. They say they are never apprised of how much money is spent and they claim that dollars are being wasted. And yet, we know that the legal requirements make all expenditures accessible to the public. If people want the information, they can get it. People also say they don't know about school programs and curriculum. Yet, board meetings are open to the public. People say they aren't consulted. Yet, we know great effort is being expended to increase community involvement in the decision-making process. Still, educators receive complaints about a lack of information and involvement. Often, the board of education points a finger at administrators and demands that they do more in this regard. However, before any commands or demands are made, it's wise to take a close look at school and district communications and keep our perspective in the process.

7 PUBLIC RELATIONS IDEA

Before parent and public complaints about a lack of communication are acted upon, a school board or administrators should do several things. Perhaps the first and most important is to list those communication activities in which the district is currently engaged.

This listing of current communication practices should be divided into several categories. The district should choose its own categories, of course. However, those that might be considered are the following:

A. Communication between the administration and the board.
B. Communication between the board and the employees of the district.
C. Communication between the district and students.
D. Communication between the district and parents.
E. Communication between the district and the community.
F. District communication with the press.
G. Individual school communication with parents, students, and the press.

Even in the smallest district, we will find many communication activities that are an ongoing part of the district's program. And don't forget that financial, curricular, and personal reports made to the board are also communication activities. Minutes of board meetings serve as vehicles for communicating with employees and the community at large. Curriculum committees, councils, citizens' advisory committees, parent-teacher conferences, home-school visits, student publications, and even report cards are all means of communication and involvement between the community and the schools. Likewise, progress reports, letters, notes home, weekly bulletins, intercom announcements, posters, signs, letters, telephone calls, student radio programs, athletic games and results, and handbooks should be included in the list of schools' efforts to communicate with people.

**Evaluate
Your
Efforts**

Once a list of such communication activities is completed in the district, the chances are greater that it will be both extensive and impressive. We should not stop at the point of identifying our current communication practices, however. We should be looking for a solution to the criticism being received as well as for ways to create positive public relations rather than for excuses or rationalizations that allow us to avoid acknowledging the need or the problem. We should be fully aware that the list of communication practices must be examined and evaluated from three different perspectives.

- First, are the communication activities extensive enough with respect to coverage? Is all of the community involved in some way and receiving some form of communication?

- Second, what is the quality of the ongoing communication activities? Are they well done, clear, and concise? Are they planned activities which are delivered on a consistent basis or are they dispatched irregularly?

- Third, do the activities tell a consistent, comprehensive, and related story of the school activities in a meaningful way?

These are the kinds of questions which must be answered regarding school communications. However, we must be aware that there is no way to reach all the people all the time with any or all of the media. Therefore, the objective must be to reach as many people as possible in the most effective way. Likewise, all efforts must be continuous, comprehensive, and consistent. These are reasonable public relations goals.

Then, and only then, should we begin to take a look at the four major media to decide how we can give our schools more coverage, give them better coverage, tell our story more clearly, and get information out faster and in a more interesting fashion. As we decide these things, we should keep in mind that the media are only tools like shovels and rakes. A medium is not an end in itself. We should use the media as much or as sparingly as it takes to get the job done. We should not make the media, themselves, the central focus of our attention.

MEDIUM NUMBER ONE:
DIRECT MAIL

The advantage of direct mail is that it allows you to reach a specific target audience. Readership is high because the interest level of the targeted audience is also usually high. For instance, if you want to send a newsletter to each student's parents, you don't have to send one to every person in the community to get the job done.

Among many others, direct mail communications used in schools include the following important ones:

- Letterheads on stationery and envelopes
- Newsletters
- Staff Bulletins
- Progress Reports
- Grade Cards
- Memos
- Purchase Orders

Let's discuss each in detail.

LETTERHEADS

Letterheads are one of the most important communication tools that almost 90 percent of all schools overlook. We know because we get hundreds of letters from schools daily, many of which ask for critiques of their stationery and envelopes.

Buildings, Bulldogs, And Blahs

In the process of reviewing school letterheads over the years, we have come to categorize letterheads into what we humorously term the "Three B's": Buildings, Bulldogs, and Blahs. Within the school or district letterheads, as in all of our communication efforts, we have the opportunity to state our position, make a promise, and communicate a positive idea and image. Unfortunately, many schools fail to seize this opportunity. Instead, we may plant a big picture of our school buildings on our stationery. Such an image might be fine for an architectural firm, a construction firm, a building-materials firm, or a funeral home—but not for a school. Other letterheads might feature a bulldog, a viking, a wildcat, or another equally vicious symbol. These images are completely inappropriate for a profession which, every day, touches this country's most prized possessions—its children.

Traditionally, because we have used these symbols to denote strength and power in our sports teams, we carry over the symbols as mascots for the entire educational mission of the schools. Unfortunately, there is no reasonable link between a vicious animal and the educational mission of our schools.

Likewise, stationery that features the school district's number is equally destructive to the district's image. In this computerized world of ours, people are turned off by being treated like a number. We are a number to our bank, to the IRS, to the Social

Security Administration, to the stores where we have charge accounts, and to the Office of Motor Vehicles. We certainly don't want our children to spend 180 days at a number— or worse, be considered a number by their teachers and principals. When we feature numbers instead of people, we inadvertently give this impression whether we know it or not.

As educators, it should give us pause that we're surrounded every day by children and yet the first public relations image that comes to mind is a building, an animal, or a number. Putting pictures of buildings on our correspondence is as ludicrous as the Pepsi-Cola® company trying to sell more bottles of their soft drink by showing us pictures of their executive offices. Buildings, animals, and numbers do not create a "thirst" for what we have to tell or sell. Children are the heart of our mission. We need to put them in all our public relations messages.

PUBLIC RELATIONS IDEA

Examine your school logo and letterhead. Ask yourself, "Does our logo tell people that this is a student-centered school, where we are concerned about excellence in education for all students?" If the answer is no, go to your art teacher or a professional artist in your community and ask him or her to submit to you some new designs that would communicate your message more appropriately. Then, once you have something you feel confident in, give all your messages—your letterhead, envelopes, newsletters to parents, and notes home—a unified look.

We have included some examples of logos we think are outstanding.

St. John Elementary School

This logo expresses several key ingredients about St. John's in a simple and beautiful way. The image of two children joining hands at the cross sends the immediate message that the school is both child-centered and Christ-centered. The children also appear to be in a window or a doorway which is a very positive symbol for growth and learning.

EVERETT SCHOOL DISTRICT NO. 2
Educational Service Center

BOARD OF DIRECTORS

ROBERT D. DAGUST
President

BRUCE B. LAMUS, M.D.
Vice President

EARL E. DUTTON

SHIRLEY VANDERMEER

DON A. RIDER

DR. RUDY JOHNSON
Superintendent

DR. ORIN B. FJERAN
Assistant Superintendent
For Business

DR. DON BARBACOVI
Director Of Special
Services

JO LOVE BEACH
Director Of Personnel/
Public Information

BILL DUNN
Director Of Construction

LEONARD QUINN
Director Of Instruction

ELEANOR HORENSKY
Executive Secretary To
The Superintendent

Everett School District

Here is a case in which the *district* has tried to communicate the message that all the schools in the district are child-centered. This abstract logo conveys the message very effectively. On the actual stationery, the doorway where the child is standing is printed in yellow. This creates the impression that light, love, and cheer surround the children who go to Everett Schools.

Anderson County School District No. 4

How will my decision affect the children?
From the: Board of Trustees

Anderson County School District

This logo displays a very effective use of words to communicate a message. Is there any question what the mind-set of the district is?

Niles Adult & Community Education

The message "You Can" is ideal for adult education since the primary fear of many adults may be "I can't."

Dayspring Christian Schools

This school's logo boldly proclaims, "We are a Bible-oriented school. Your children will be taught from this foundation." Here, the message is clear to all regarding what the school stands for—and that it functions out of this belief.

Waterloo County Catholic Schools

This logo is very similar in tone to the St. John logo. The message: "The children attending this school will find friendship, and will be taught with Christian (and Catholic) values."

Holy Family School

This logo, like the St. John logo, beautifully expresses the fact that this school is not only child-centered, but Christ-centered as well.

Steele School

From this logo, even the most casual observer would have to deduce that the staff of this school is interested in developing happy, playful children.

The Davis Joint Unified School District

This fine logo communicates the message that this is a place where both adults and children of all ages, sexes, and ethnic origins work and learn harmoniously together. What a comforting thought to the many different ethnic families in this California community.

Davis Joint Unified School District 526 B Street · Davis, CA 95616

The Mesa Educational Foundation

This beautifully designed logo depicting two children under a tree of knowledge gives the viewer a real sense of the yearning that children have for knowledge and the true joy its attainment brings. It is obvious that continuing to provide fine teaching is the mission of this foundation.

THE MESA EDUCATIONAL FOUNDATION

Church of St. Mary Of The Lake
This simple illustration communicates the message of Christian community and partnership between teachers and students in the school setting.

Church of St. Mary Of The Lake
Elementary School

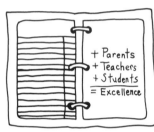

Hutchinson
Public
Schools

Hutchinson Public Schools
Focusing on the partnership between parents, teachers, and students is at the core of this public relations message. Certainly, parents must feel welcome in their schools when they see this message on every piece of stationery.

HILLCREST ELEMENTARY SCHOOL
515 Elizabeth Street
ALMA, MICHIGAN 48801

Hillcrest Elementary School
This logo makes us smile every time we see it. It is joyful and upbeat—just as most of our public relations messages should try to be. In this case, the receiver is positioned to be in a good mood before he or she even opens the envelope.

We have included a few negative examples of logos for your comparison. We think they speak for themselves.

Slogans

School slogans offer a great opportunity to communicate a message to our public. Phrases which interpret goals, objectives, and benefits of the district can be very effective image communicators. In fact, school slogans are an ideal opportunity to communicate a promise.

What we have to keep in mind is that our central focus in our schools is education of students. Therefore, slogans which attempt to communicate athletic team spirit instead of a commitment to the education of the students don't communicate the promise that the majority of our public really wants to hear. Here are some examples of good and bad slogans.

Good Slogans
1. "A Great Place to Learn"
2. "Where Teachers Are Committed to Students"
3. "A School Where Every Mind Is Precious"
4. "Where Every School Is a Child-Centered School"
5. "Excellence with Kindness"
6. "Partners in Educational Excellence"
7. "Where Young People Come First"
8. "Where Futures Begin"
9. "Learning for Today and Tomorrow and to Enrich Life"

Bad Slogans
1. "Wildcats Are Great"
2. "Indians Can't Be Beat"
3. "You Can't Keep a Bulldog Down"
4. "The School in the Valley"
5. "Home of Eagle Pride"

When you come up with an appropriate slogan, don't be bashful about using it. It is appropriate for stationery, envelopes, grade cards, program reports, newsletters, memo pads, outdoor signs, and indoor banners. Remember too that when you have to send a negative message home—such as a poor report card or a note about a behavioral problem—a positive message on the stationery helps to neutralize the devastating effect of the bad news.

Choosing Paper And Inks

The best and most functional stationery is white. Readership is high when white paper is used and white paper is the easiest to correct on a typewriter. Other acceptable colors include ivory, light blue, or very light gray. *There are no other acceptable colors of stationery if you want to create a highly professional image.*

The best ink colors are black, dark gray, dark blue, dark brown, and maroon. Red, green, purple, and orange are difficult ink colors to read and letterheads which use these colors tend to gain less respect from readers than publications which use the other colors listed.

If your school colors are among those not recommended and you have a strong desire to use them on your stationery, make sure you combine the colors with black. Then, use the colors as an accent only and print all words in the black ink.

Gold and silver inks can be used with black for a very rich effect. However, as a general rule, gold and silver are among the most expensive ink colors to use in the printing process. Because they do reflect high cost, you may not wish to use them.

Colors For Logos—
And What Each Color Symbolizes

Yellow: A cheery color which attracts attention. Communicates light, sparkle, and activity. However, it is surprisingly low on the list of people's favorite colors—but it is excellent for highlighting.

Red: Symbolizes warmth, heat, and fire. Attracts a great deal of attention. Can communicate alarm or danger. A powerful color which many advertisers use to sell their products. A favorite color of many people.

Bright Blue: A soothing color. Communicates peace, holiness, and cleanliness. Associated with water and sky. One of people's favorite colors.

Black: Symbolizes death or danger. Also associated with space age and high technology. Has been standard for so long that it has come to be associated with a no-frills, competent, and down-to-business look.

Green: A symbol of growth, life, youth, and nature.

Navy Blue: Symbolizes stability, establishment. A rich and distinguished color.

Orange: A spunky color associated with excitement and warmth. Notice the large number of fast-food restaurants that use orange in their logos.

Purple: A carnival color, often associated with something humorous or crazy. However, in very deep tones, it is associated with royalty, especially when used with gold or red.

Tan: An earth color. Neutral. Also associated with flesh. Rarely the primary color used in a logo. Rather, used as a background color.

Brown: Also an earth color. Considered a less distinguished color than navy or black. A masculine color associated with the outdoors: outdoor cooking, clothing, and sports.

Pink: Always associated with fun: bubble gum, cotton candy, ice cream, and bubble bath. A frivolous and feminine color, long associated with baby girls.

White: A symbol of purity, serenity, magnificence, holiness, cleanliness, sophistication, and age. Also a high-tech color. Associated with cold things—ice, ice cream, and snow.

Gray: Associated with stability, richness, age, sophistication, dependability, and durability. A rich, but highly conservative color.

Logo Shapes
And Their Meaning

Points and Jagged Edges: Masculine, but they have negative connotations for many people, especially women.

Natural Forms, Ovals, Circles: Positive and warm connotations. Always appeal more to women than do jagged edges or points. These are natural forms, and they are friendlier, less threatening to people.

Do's And Don'ts For Logo Designs

1. *Do*...keep your logo simple. Too many elements make a logo harder to read and less versatile.
2. *Do*...use your logo consistently on signs, stationery, envelopes, purchase orders, uniforms, emblems, bags, flags, banners, folders, blazers, etc. In general, use your logo wherever you use your school name. The logo can, however, stand alone.

3. *Don't*...allow your logo to be used in any colors other than the ones you have selected originally. Use it in the colors in which you design it or totally in black. Used in different colors your logo will have an unrecognizable look.

4. *Do*...consider the message of your logo. It sends a message whether you are aware of it or not.

Make Sure All The Schools In The District Are Sending The Same Message

Identity Packages

No matter how many departments there are in a school, it is one organization. Likewise, no matter how many schools are in a district, the district is one organization. For instance, a music department or athletic department is not a different school—and shouldn't be treated as such in the public relations effort. Neither is an elementary school a separate organization from the rest of the district. Remember, all schools in the district are united by purpose. They have the same mission. Certainly, there are a lot of good things that go on in individual school buildings within a district. And when this happens, those good things should be a reflection on the total district—not the individual school. Too often, however, each school thinks of itself as an individual entity. Each has its own logo. Each may have its own slogan—or some may have a slogan and others may not. When this is the case, each school actually competes with the images of the other schools in the district rather than jointly benefiting from the whole. Likewise, departments within individual schools often try to project an image separate from the school's image. This is a mistake.

Often, there are instances in which a school district's central office stationery will be designed to communicate the message of child-centered schools. Then, the high school, because it has the largest physical plant in the district, will decide to place a big picture of its building on its own individual stationery. As a result, the school and the district send mixed messages to the public. While the image of the district appears student-centered, the high school's image appears nonconforming and heretical. The public is left to sort it all out.

A unified image is important for any public relations effort. Suppose the IBM Corporation had one logo for its sales division, a different one for its research and development division, another for the sales force, and still another for its corporate headquarters. The message to the public would be that the left hand had no idea what the right hand was doing. But, in fact, just the opposite is true at IBM. Through effective and cohesive advertising, the consumer can now recognize an IBM advertisement before the name is mentioned or before the logo appears. And when the logo does appear, it stands for a company in which every dimension is synonymous with quality, innovation, and service.

Ideally, all the communications that go out of all the schools in the district should correspond to one another. This means letters, newsletters, grade cards, and notes home. Remember, you have to be very concerned about the total message that is being sent to your public. Scattered identities *will* create an image of nonunity and disorganized management. It's as simple as that.

The problem is that most of us fall into the trap referred to by advertisers as "inside-out thinking." In other words, we're thinking too much like people who work for the institution instead of like the people we are trying to influence. And because we are separate people working in separate buildings, it's easy to forget that families in our district might have children going to the elementary, middle, and high schools, all at the same time. We lose sight of the fact that it's important to these families that they believe their children are receiving the same level of care and nurturing in each grade. We need to give the assurance that they are. Likewise, families need the assurance that if they move within the district and their children change schools, they will be sending their children to schools of equal merit. This is another reason that promoting our buildings or our school mascots works against us. The results of a good education are the products we are selling, and this is the message that ought to ring out loud and clear in all the images and messages that go to the public from any place in a district.

The best stance for a district to take is to develop a letterhead that represents the educational position of the entire district. Then, each of the buildings of the district should use the same design, *changing only the name and address of the school.* This is also the most economical move a district can make. Printers can run all the letterheads at the same time, saving money on plates, press wash-ups, and running time. Paper, when bought in large quantities for all the schools rather than individually for each school, can be purchased at a much lower price. All in all, using the same logo and printing all the letterheads and envelopes at the same time just makes good common sense as well as good public relations sense.

THE NEWSLETTER

Newsletters, as a rule, are particularly well-read publications. Parents are very concerned about their children's education and they want a lot of information about it. In fact, parents get the majority of their information about schools from notes, memos, newsletters, or other publications from the schools. That's because these communication vehicles are personal and impact upon the life of the reader. And unlike a newspaper article, or a radio or television story, the receiver is assured that the newsletter has been prepared by somebody *from the school.* Therefore, newsletters are also considered by the public to be more accurate than the more far-removed media. For this reason, if you ever want to dispel a myth or bring a halt to a rumor, it is best done through your *own* publication.

**One Of Your
Most Influential
Communication Tools**

Radio, newspaper, and television will cover the exceptional occurrences of school life: poor test scores, the results of sporting events, a teacher strike, or a bond issue. But these media will not cover everyday happenings—what's happening in English class, math class, music class, or any other classroom. This is why a newsletter is so valuable. For this reason, and because the newsletter and other forms of communication that go home are unique representations of you and your schools, a large portion of this chapter will be devoted to them.

**Formula
For Developing Newsletters**

The best newsletters do not take on a different character each time they are published. The best newsletters are written by following a prescribed formula that works. The formula allows your content to be the best it can be, while you follow some tried and true rules. Here they are:

1. Establish a purpose for your newsletter. For many administrators, the school newsletter is drudgery because they haven't defined its purpose. For many it's just a monthly or quarterly exercise. It's just a task that must be done, and a paper that must be filled. However, other administrators realize that the school newsletter serves a very important function—for the schools and for parents. It is a vehicle that the administrator can use to inform parents and community members, cause them to take certain actions, and elicit their feedback.

Remember, your primary target audience is parents. Your secondary audience might be other community members, including government officials, staff of feeder schools, other schools in the district, parents of incoming students, and members of the local media.

2. The administrator need not be the sole author, but must be intimately involved with and show great enthusiasm for the school newsletter. He or she is responsible for seeing to it that the content continues to have value, that the material is well presented, that it is representative of the whole school, and that it goes out on time and at regular intervals. Therefore, the principal or superintendent needs to be able to generate enthusiasm from the staff for helping with the newsletter's contents. Remember the Principle of Ownership (p. 57), which states that people work for and support their own goals, not your goals. It's of vital importance that you ask your staff each year how they would like to be represented in the newsletter. Brainstorm these ideas with your staff. Then, with their ideas, ask for their commitment to help in providing useful information on a planned schedule for the year. Explain to the staff how important the school newsletter is to the image of the school and to the knowledge that parents have about what goes on within it. When you do, you will receive greater cooperation from staff members in accomplishing this important job.

3. Make yearly schedules for the types of articles you would like to have staff members write.

4. Ask each teacher what would be the best time for him or her to contribute, and then have each teacher sign up for particular newsletters and dates. This way, every grade or course is covered during the year.

5. Give each staff member several copies of a simple form that has a place for: Who, What, Why, When, Where, and How as well as major points to be made. This will make it easier for teachers to give you the information you need. It also makes it easy for you, or someone you designate, to edit the writings and put them into an interesting format. Make sure you indicate to teachers that all six elements should be contained in their articles.

Tips For Increasing Newsletter Readership

**Layout
And
Word Tools**

• *Establish a nameplate.* This is the artwork that goes at the top of the first page. It should include your school logo so that the reader immediately identifies the newsletter with your school. *The nameplate should never be hand lettered.* This practice may be easy, but it creates a very unprofessional and second-class image for your school. You can have your nameplate professionally typeset at a local printer or a vocational school in your district at a very low cost. Press-type, available at most art supply stores, also provides an inexpensive alternative to hand lettering. You only need to have this nameplate produced one time. This artwork, or a good copy of the artwork, can be pasted on the top of any newsletter every time you wish to reproduce it. If you are laying out the newsletter yourself, paste your nameplate on the top of the page, making sure all your angles and lines are square. Then, apply correction fluid around the edges of the nameplate. This will keep the edges from being detectable on photocopies.

• *Put your most important points/information closest to the opening of the document.* Magazines have utilized this important truth for years as justification for charging the most for advertising space in three locations. The back cover is the most expensive. The inside back cover and the inside front cover come in a close second.

This is due to the fact that people read magazines from the front to the back or from the back to the front, and people usually see what's on the covers. A magazine lies on a table one of two ways—front cover up or back cover up. Advertising on the back cover is likely to be read. These same rules apply to your own publication and should be treated accordingly.

- *Put your most important points in the first paragraphs of each article and first two lines of each paragraph.*

- *Put benefits into all your headlines.* On the average, five times as many people read the headlines as read the body copy in a story. It follows that, if your headlines don't persuade the reader to read your stories, you have wasted valuable time and effort. You have less than five seconds to interest the reader in your content. Therefore, your headlines and subheads must be powerful. They must also contain pertinent information. You can't assume that the reader will read further.

- *Longer headlines are better.* When the New York University School of Retailing ran headline tests with the cooperation of a big department store, they found that headlines of ten words or longer sold more goods than short headlines. This reality can serve us well in our public relations efforts. In terms of recall, according to the school, headlines between eight and ten words are most effective. In direct mail, headlines between six and twelve words get the most coupon returns. On the average, however, long headlines sell more merchandise than short ones.

Examples

INSTEAD OF:	Middle School—Spring Musical
DO THIS:	Tickets for Spring Musical Available at the School Office
INSTEAD OF:	Baseball Registration Information
DO THIS:	Register for Baseball Leagues June 2-9 Between 9:00 a.m. and 2:00 p.m.
INSTEAD OF:	Parent Coffee—Fifth Grade Parents
DO THIS:	Fifth Grade Parents: Come to the Parent Coffee and Get Acquainted with Opportunities Ahead for Your Student

- *Use simple headlines.* Your headlines should telegraph what you want to say—in simple language. Readers do not stop to decipher the meaning of obscure headlines.

- *Break up copy with subheads.* The more body copy you have, the more you must break it up with headlines, subheads, and pictures. (See Figure 6-1.)

- *Use numbers or heavy dots, called bullets, to emphasize specific points.* (See Figure 6-1.)

- *Start a new paragraph every time you use "First," "Second," "Third," and so forth to make a point.*

● *Yes, people read long copy.* Readership does fall off rapidly up to fifty words. However, it drops very little between fifty and five hundred words. Therefore, you can use long copy—with notable success. This is confirmed by the Graduate School of Retailing at New York University. The more facts you tell, the more you persuade, convince, and sell. A public relations message's chance for success increases as the number of pertinent facts included in the message increases.

● *Use figures and charts frequently.* They add credibility and are the first items to be read. Therefore, pack them with information you want the reader to retain. (See Figure 6-2.)

● *Limit building newsletters to four typed pages (back and front of an 11-inch-by-17-inch sheet, folded in half).*

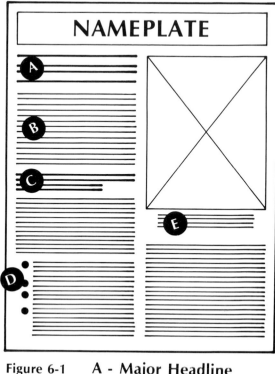

Figure 6-1

A - Major Headline
B - Body Copy
C - Subhead
D - Bullets
E - Caption

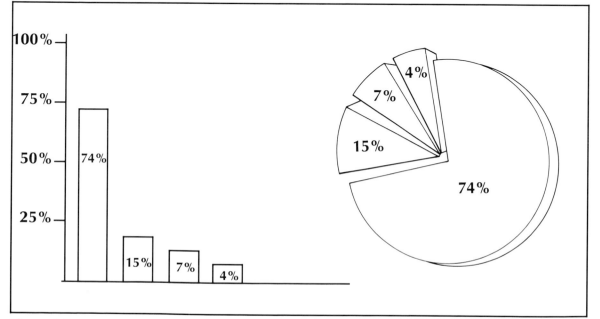

Figure 6-2

- *Frequency is far more important than the amount of material you give all at once.* The newsletter should take only 5 to 8 minutes maximum reading time.

- *Recommendation: Publish at least one newsletter a month.* This is simply our recommendation. We even suggest that you have a newsletter going home during the summer months when school isn't in session. You are still working and parents as well as the community need to know what you're working on and why. In the latter part of the summer, parents are beginning to worry about having their children start school in the fall. This is when a "welcome back" newsletter with all pertinent information regarding the opening of school would be ideal. Remember, many community members honestly don't believe that educators work very hard. We can openly dispel this myth by taking a simple step like this one.

In addition, be sure to send your teachers a copy of the summer newsletter. They too need communication from you during the summer months.

**Pictures
And
Artwork**

- *People want to see pictures of and read about other people.* The success of publications such as *People Magazine* and *The National Enquirer* is a good testimonial to this truth—whether you like them or not. Therefore, use the names of children and teachers frequently and show their pictures.

- *People always read the captions under the pictures before they read the body copy.* Therefore, the more space a picture takes up, the more copy there should be to support it.

- *Photographs should always be printed in black ink.* They are acceptable in dark blue ink, but photographs in any other color discredit the person or thing being photographed.

- *Be careful about the use of too much clip art.* Clip art is artwork that one can buy from a service. It provides the person who lays out the newsletter with funny or serious little figures, arrows, stars, and borders to "jazz up" a newsletter. While clip art can make a newsletter more exciting, a little goes a long way. Remember, you are trying to present a professional image at the same time that you are trying to create interest. Clip art attracts attention, but its overuse tends to detract from image-building appeal, especially if the clip art you choose doesn't "fit" your desired image.

Type

- *Letters should be typed on a typewriter. Professional documents such as brochures, report cards, certain reports, and certain newsletters should be typeset.* This does not mean, of course, that you *cannot* typeset a letter or type a newsletter. It simply means that neither is as effective or as image building if the techniques are reversed.

• *Vary the size, weight, and sometimes the style of type for interest and ease of reading.* This can be done by changing the ball on some typewriters—or by using all capital letters for headlines. Of course, if you have your newsletter professionally typeset by a printer, there are many type styles available from which you may choose. Press-type lettering—available at any art supply store—is a great way to spruce up the headlines of your newsletter.

Computer programs are available for personal computers that allow you to put in borders, symbols, bullets, and other figures wherever you wish. If you should decide to use such a program, make sure your printer prints with *letter quality* and not with a dot-matrix.

• *Never use smaller than 10 point type for body copy.* And to ensure easy readability, make sure that the difference between the type size and the leading, or space between the lines, is no greater than two points. In other words, if the type size is 10 point, the ideal leading is 12. (See Figure 6-3.)

• *Choice of type should be conservative.* There should not be any big flourishes in the type style you choose. (See Figure 6-4.)

9 pt
Excellence in typography is the result of nothing more than an attitude. Its appeal comes from the understanding used in its planning; the designer must care. In con-temporary advertising the perfect integra-tion of design elements often demands unorthodox typography. It may require the use of compact spacing, minus leading,

↑
NO

- -

YES
↑

Excellence in typography is the result of nothing more than an attitude. Its appeal comes from the understanding used in its planning; the designer must care. In contemporary advertising the perfect integration of design elements often demands unorthodox typography. It may require the use of compact spac-
10 pt

Excellence in typography is the result of nothing more than an attitude. Its appeal comes from the understanding used in its planning; the designer must care. In contemporary advertis-ing the perfect integration of design elements often demands
12 pt

Excellence in typography is the result of nothing more than an attitude. Its appeal comes from the understand-ing used in its planning; the designer must care. In con-temporary advertising the perfect integration of de-
14 pt

Figure 6-3   Comparison of type sizes.

113

Figure 6-4

The Family of Type - Helios

ABCDEFGHIJ
LIGHT

ABCDEFGHIJ
LIGHT ITALIC

ABCDEFGHIJ
LIGHT CONDENSED

ABCDEFGHIJ
LIGHT EXTENDED

ABCDEFGHIJ
MEDIUM

ABCDEFGHIJ
MEDIUM ITALIC

ABCDEFGHIJ
MEDIUM CONDENSED

ABCDEFGHIJ
MEDIUM EXTENDED

ABCDEFGHIJ
BOLD

ABCDEFGHIJ
BOLD ITALIC

Figure 6-5

GOUDY	SERIF
ABCDEFGHIJKLMNOPQRSTUVWXYZ& abcdefghijklmnopqrstuvwxyz 1234567890(.,:;!?''—/$-%	

ENGLISH TIMES	
ABCDEFGHIJKLMNOPQRSTUVWXYZ& abcdefghijklmnopqrstuvwxyz 1234567890(.,:;!?''—/$-%	

CASLON	
ABCDEFGHIJKLMNOPQRSTUVWXYZ& abcdefghijklmnopqrstuvwxyz 1234567890(.,:;!?''—/$-%	

AMERICAN TYPEWRITER	
ABCDEFGHIJKLMNOPQRSTUVWXYZ& abcdefghijklmnopqrstuvwxyz 1234567890(.,:;!?''—/$-%	

AVANT GARDE	SANS SERIF
ABCDEFGHIJKLMNOPQRSTUVWXYZ& abcdefghijklmnopqrstuvwxyz 1234567890(.,:;!?''—/$-%	

HELIOS	
ABCDEFGHIJKLMNOPQRSTUVWXYZ& abcdefghijklmnopqrstuvwxyz 1234567890(.,:;!?''—/$-%	

ORACLE	
ABCDEFGHIJKLMNOPQRSTUVWXYZ& abcdefghijklmnopqrstuvwxyz 1234567890(.,:;!?''—/$-%	

Figure 6-6   Examples of serif and sans serif type styles.

115

Figure 6-5 illustrates what is called a family of type. This means that one type style can be used in large or small sizes, thin or fat lettering, and italic or condensed form. It is possible to achieve a good deal of variety in your newsletter by using the many different styles of lettering that exist within the same family.

When choosing a typeface for your newsletter, remember to select one that is easy to read. This is most often accomplished by choosing a type that is simple and has few complicated flourishes. Typefaces fall into two major categories: serif and sans serif. Serif means that the letters have "feet" or end markings which finish each stroke of the letter. Serif faces include: Goudy, English Times, Caslon, and American Typewriter. (See Figure 6-6.)

The images communicated by serif faces tend to be friendly, conservative, rich, established, and inviting.

Sans serif means "without flourish." Such faces have no end markings or "feet." Sans serif faces include: Avant Garde, Helios, and Oracle.

The images communicated by sans serif faces are ones of straightforwardness, modernness, cleanliness, and coldness.

**Paper
And
Ink**

- *Colored ink has 50 percent greater readership than black and white.*
- *The best paper colors are white and ivory.*
- *The highest readership is gained by using white paper with two colors of ink.*
- *Best color combinations of ink are these:*
  —Black and Blue
  —Black and Maroon
  —Black and Brown

- *Avoid using the following ink colors for newsletters* (though they are good for brochures):
  —Purple
  —Orange
  —Green
  —Yellow
  —Red
  —And combinations of these colors other than with black.

- *Full-color printing works for business, but not necessarily for schools.* While full-color printing is beautiful and attracts attention, it is also very expensive. Many people know it is expensive. So when a school uses full-color printing, the public is likely to draw the conclusion that the school district has too much money, or that the money it has is being misused.

● ***The best paper stock for letterhead stationery is a textured, light-weight paper.*** Textured stock adds interest and importance to your letters, while flat stock is boring and looks cheap.

● ***The best paper stock for other printed matter is a medium-weight, nongloss stock.*** Glossy stock says, "This is expensive." In addition, glossy stock adds a glare to the page that makes reading more difficult.

Writing And Proofreading

● ***Use third-person supports—quotations from famous people or community leaders—to draw attention to your major points or to support your messages.*** People usually like short, easy-to-read quotations which contain meaty information. The natural curiosity that people have about their neighbors' opinions also causes quotations to receive high readership.

● ***Keep the text personal—don't be afraid to use "we."*** Use appropriate contractions and occasional fragments just as you would in a personal letter. The writing shouldn't sound as if it were for publication in an educational journal. So keep your messages jargon free. Avoid slipping into the catch words of education. Use common words and simple explanations.

● ***Proofread carefully for spelling errors, typographical errors, and grammatical mistakes.*** English teachers, journalists, or journalism classes are good resources for proofreading.

● ***Use "callouts" to bring readers into copy blocks.*** A callout is a visual technique used by mail-order professionals to draw attention to a specific point in a letter or a body of copy. Callouts are used because they work. An example of a callout is an arrow pointing to a specific copy line. This arrow is usually accompanied by handwriting in the margin which conveys the message, "This is important," or "If you don't read anything else, read this!"

Folding And Mailing Your Newsletter

● ***Ideally, newsletters should be mailed to students' homes—especially if the*** *students are in the senior grades.* It is ludicrous to spend so much time and money on writing, typing, and printing newsletters, only to have 60 percent of the students throw them in the wastebasket or leave them in lockers.

● *All the school mailings—whether letters, newsletters, or notes home—qualify for a very inexpensive nonprofit mailing rate if mailings are done in quantities of 200 identical pieces and are mailed at the same time.* Check with your post office for specifics, including a bulk rate mailing permit.

● *Don't assume that a newsletter must be put in an envelope to be mailed—or that a newsletter must be sealed.* Newsletters which are mailed without an envelope should arrive in very good condition, especially if they are delivered locally. Remember: An envelope, a staple, or a seal is an obstacle which a parent must break through to read what you have to say. However, if you should decide to use a staple, place it where it will be the case in even more areas. Yet, as we have stressed, the money to support the schools must come from every taxpayer. Therefore, everyone in your community has a vested interest in what's going on in your schools.

Who Should Get Your Newsletter?

Obviously, parents aren't the only people who should be receiving your newsletter. Depending upon the demographics of your community, parents with school age children may make up only one-third of your total population. In the years to come this will be the case in even more areas. Yet, as we have stressed, the money to support the schools must come from every taxpayer. Therefore, everyone in your community has a vested interest in what's going on in your schools.

We suggest you consider:

1. Sending your newsletter to everyone who pays a water bill.
2. Putting newsletters at check-out counters at grocery stores.
3. Placing them in barber shops and beauty salons as well as the offices of doctors, lawyers, accountants, and real estate agents—anywhere that people have to wait and need something to read. It doesn't even matter if the copies aren't recent.
4. Sending a copy to the education editors of your local newspaper and radio station. Such editors just might find something of special interest on which to run a full-fledged story.
5. Giving copies to the entire staff of your school.
6. Sending them to administrators in other schools, the central office, and the board of education.

A Word
About Classroom Newsletters
And District-Wide Newsletters

Classroom Newsletters

Just as a letter from a friend has more interest value for you than a newsletter from your alma mater, so does a newsletter from a classroom have more interest for parents than the school newsletter. After all, the information in a classroom newsletter has been narrowed from information that affects the whole student body to information that pertains directly to "my" children in their respective classrooms. The message is more specific and, thus, creates more emotional involvement and more interest.

Parents who receive newsletters from teachers are generally favorably impressed with the teacher's efforts to inform them. Parents get the feeling that the teacher is quite capable as well as proud of what is going on and he or she wants to share it. The classroom newsletter also provides a chance for teachers to relay helpful advice to parents of children of a specific age, as well as to tell parents what they can do to facilitate and reinforce the child's specific learning at this level. For instance, a third grade teacher might include in a newsletter the fact that children are learning their multiplication tables and that parents can increase their child's memory by practicing at home with flash cards. Such newsletters don't have to be sent regularly—but it is best if they are. Classroom newsletters that are unexpected, however, can also come as a nice surprise.

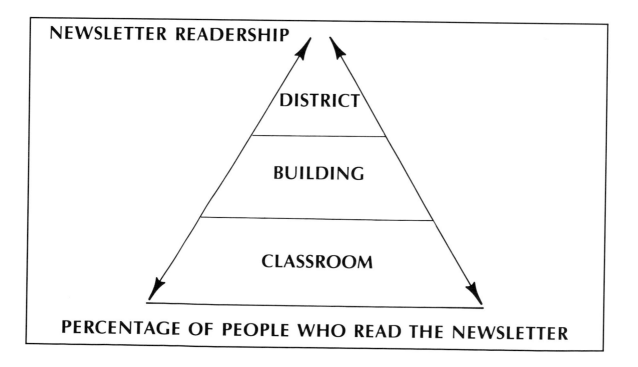

NEWSLETTER READERSHIP

DISTRICT

BUILDING

CLASSROOM

PERCENTAGE OF PEOPLE WHO READ THE NEWSLETTER

District Newsletters

Though district newsletters have appeal to the community at large, the information tends to be general in nature and, thus, readership is not as great as for newsletters originating at the building level. District-wide newsletters have great value for relaying financial figures, board decisions, policies, and information that affects every citizen. Beware that sometimes we tend to use district newsletters to fulfill the function of a "house organ" by publishing tidbits about specific school employees which have little interest to anyone but the employee and the employee's friends. Teachers who are anxious to receive publicity will turn in such stories regularly and may even exert pressure to be featured. As a result, these teachers are usually featured time and time again. Remember, the function of a district newsletter is to inform the public about the overall work and mission of the schools, and not to publicize specific people. Unless the frequency of the district newsletter is especially high—once a month or more— stories on specific school employees may have a negative effect on the morale of all the district employees who are *not* featured in the newsletter. The employees who are

Figure 6-7

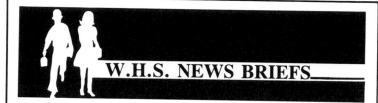

W.H.S. NEWS BRIEFS

OFFICE PRACTICE CLASS OPERATES CLERICAL BUSINESS

High-school business instructor, Mrs. Mary Dawson, reports that the students in the office practice class have organized a clerical business. Under the direction of "office manager," Joyce Prockish, the students have completed typing, proofreading, and duplicating for school organizations, teachers, the high-school office, and churches of the community. The work is done during the class period, and the students receive points for doing clerical projects. Through this first-hand experience, students have developed responsibility for scheduling their work as well as producing accurate and acceptable clerical work. In addition to this unit of study in the course, the students are also developing skill in using the transcribing machines and calculators plus taking simulated Civil Service examinations.

ALAN HARSHBARGER NOMINATED AS CANDIDATE FOR LEADERSHIP SEMINAR

Wamego High School sophomore Alan Harshbarger was nominated by the W.H.S. faculty to be the school's candidate in the competition for the Hugh O'Brien Youth Foundation Leadership Seminar on Government. The state winner will be announced in February and will attend the seminar to be held in Washington, D.C., in March. Alan is the son of Mr. and Mrs. John Harshbarger.

LAUNDRY UNIT COMPLETED IN HOMEMAKING I

Homemaking I students completed a laundry unit of study early this month. During the unit, the students tested water for its degree of hardness and softness and then calculated the amount of detergent or soap needed in different instances. Too, the students studied the effect of chlorine and oxygen bleaches on different fabrics. During one laboratory period the different techniques and methods for removing various stains were demonstrated.

As a result of this unit of study, the students will be better able to select garments that launder well, as well as understand the different types of laundry products available and the purposes of each. In addition, the students will better understand that by following the basic steps in laundering clothes, the garments will look better and last longer.

KSU FRESHMAN CONFERENCE TO BE HELD FEBRUARY 20

On February 20, W.H.S. Principal W. G. Trimmell and Counselor James Ethington will meet with Wamego High School graduates who are now enrolled as freshmen at Kansas State. The visitation allows school personnel an opportunity not only to visit with W.H.S. graduates but also to gain valuable feedback which can aid in the development of suitable curricula which will better meet the needs of W.H.S. college-bound students.

ART CLASSES CROWDED FOR SECOND SEMESTER

All classes in the high school art department operate on a semester basis. Those courses in art which will be offered second semester include: Introduction to Art, Survey of Art; Drawing, Painting, and Graphics I and II; Sculpture and Ceramics I and II; and General Crafts I and II.

Due to a small classroom and the tools available for only a limited number of students, several courses have a waiting list for enrollment. These classes are closed to new students until some of those previously enrolled drop the class or leave school. Interested students should check with the counselor, Mr. James Ethington, or art instructor, Mr. Dick Simpson, about enrollment in art for second semester.

W.H.S. STUDENT HELPS PLAN FOREIGN AND DOMESTIC AFFAIRS CONFERENCE

Joyce Prockish, W.H.S. senior, met in Emporia on Monday, January 7, to help plan discussion topics for the upcoming Foreign and Domestic Affairs Conference. The conference will be held in Emporia on February 23 on the KSTC campus. Joyce is one of four officers for the conference which will be attended by over 500 students from thirty schools.

The conference gives students an opportunity to exchange ideas and attitudes as well as allows them to experience first-hand the political process during the business session when the students campaign for offices.

Figure 6-8

featured become the targets of jealousy and resentment. All in all, this becomes a very unhealthy practice. However, newsletters at the building level can accomplish publicity for the school staff with much greater tact. The staff at the building level is small and much more tightly knit. Thus, staff members can be apprised of how you select the articles for inclusion and what your plans are for the entire year. It might be possible to cover every employee some way in the course of the year.

Effective Use of Word Tools

Figure 6-7 illustrates two key elements. First, the logo which encircles two students immediately establishes a child-centered focus for the information which follows. Second, the major headline states a decided benefit. There's no question that people who are interested in psychological services will read further. In addition, note that you read the major headline before you read the smaller headline to the right of it.

Figure 6-8 illustrates the effective use of smaller headlines. The typical reader will read all the smaller headlines, beginning with those headlines on the left and moving to those on the right, before he or she reads any body copy. Only if something in one of the smaller headlines attracts his or her attention will the reader read any of the body copy.

Figure 6-9 shows how a chart can increase readership *and* understanding of complicated material. A typical reader will go straight to the chart, bypassing any other information on the page, only to stop at the small headline which indicates what the chart is trying to illustrate. If the chart explains everything adequately, the reader may not even need to read the body copy. The body copy should therefore supply *additional* information. It should not just repeat what has already been stated by the chart. If readers discover that the body copy only repeats the information in the chart, they will become conditioned *not* to read your body copy. In this case, body copy should be used to interpret the data.

Figure 6-9

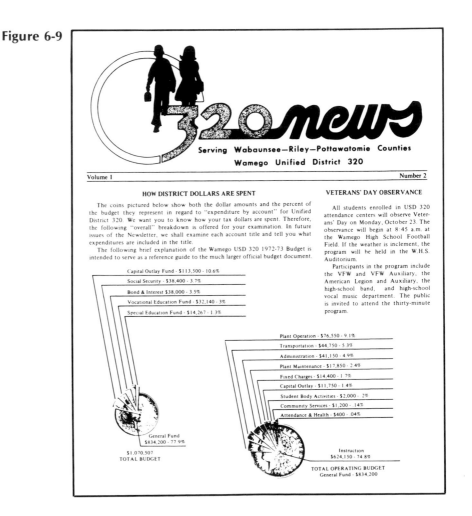

Ideas For Creating Interesting And Functional Newsletters

In the first newsletter of the year, include a list of what was done over the summer to maintain the school building(s). People like to read about how you are maintaining their investment in their schools. This is also a terrific feature for a summer newsletter, as illustrated in the following example.

Summer Maintenance Work Continues

The summer is a busy time for maintenance and custodial personnel of the XYZ District schools. Custodians are charged with getting their buildings in shape for the opening of school while other maintenance crews are formed to perform various other necessary tasks. A primary goal of the program is to reach a point where maintenance can be performed on a preventative basis rather than from crisis to crisis.

Countless minor jobs have been completed this summer in addition to some major accomplishments which are as follows:

1. Remodeling of the cafeteria at the junior high.
2. Complete retubing of two heating plants at the high school.
3. Repair or addition to asphalt surfaces at Central, Washington, Northview, the high school, the junior high, and Head Start.
4. Converted a porch at the elementary school into a room to be used as a library.
5. Remodeled two restrooms in the buildings at the high school.
6. Converted the kitchen at the high school into a classroom and temporary serving area.
7. Installed a new heating coil in the air handling unit of the gym at the junior high.
8. Executed a contract with the Urban Renewal Agency for demolition of the old red brick building at the middle school.
9. Resurfaced the tennis courts at the high school.
10. Sold and replaced 24 teachers' desks.
11. Purchased 180 desks for anticipated new students.

A crew of five painters has been working since June 1. They have applied over 200 gallons of paint to 45 classrooms and various other facilities in practically every school in the district. A highly washable epoxy base paint has been applied in heavily used areas such as hallways and restrooms.

Another crew of workers has been working practically all summer performing odd jobs such as: outside washing of windows, repairing doors and windows, clearing brush, trimming trees, repairing fixtures, repairing plaster, repairing tackboards, moving furniture and equipment, repairing roof leaks, and doing countless odd jobs.

The maintenance staff has made a concentrated effort to see to it that our facilities are as trouble-free, functional, and comfortable as possible with the available resources. It is a realized fact that a good maintenance program is a team effort with school personnel and students cooperating to preserve school facilities. It is also a realized fact that a good maintenance program costs a great deal less than a program where the cooperative effort is meager.

Make a list of new teachers. Include when and from where they graduated, academic descriptions, honors won, and what their teaching assignments will be in your school (system).

Include a clip-out coupon that parents can sign and return after reading the newsletter. Classrooms can compete for 100 percent return of these coupons and prizes can be awarded.

List the names of students, teachers, and parents you wish to congratulate or thank. People will comb the newsletter to read these names. Remember to explain each award. We sometimes assume that people know what we mean by "Golden Badge" students, or "O.K. Club" students when they don't.

13 PUBLIC RELATIONS IDEA

Give instructions in the newsletter. The newsletter is the perfect place to instruct parents on what to do with children's report cards, what to do on snow days, or how to register a child for a special activity. Such instructions should be highlighted with a border for maximum readership.

PUBLIC RELATIONS IDEA 14

Include the cafeteria menu for the month on the back cover of the newsletter for easy clip out.

PUBLIC RELATIONS IDEA 15

List what is being purchased with PTA and PTO funds.

PUBLIC RELATIONS IDEA 16

Summarize school board policies or decisions that are of special interest and concern to parents, such as student dress. However, be sure to state them as positives.

PUBLIC RELATIONS IDEA 17

Supply good news about student progress, achievement, and test scores.

PUBLIC RELATIONS IDEA 18

Reproduce surveys and survey results.

Supply information to educate parents on such matters as how to prepare students for tests or how to determine if a child has symptoms of a disease that is spreading in school.

Never put in a weekly bulletin or newspaper, "Have a question? Call your school," or "Have a complaint? Call your school," and give a number. Rather, always make it a three-fold statement. Say, for instance, "Have a question? Have a complaint? Have a compliment? Call (913) 539-0555." The results of this are obvious. You are always pointing out the fact that the school is doing many things right which deserve recognition as well as the fact that the school wants to help with problems.

Good news about the graduates of your school always makes interesting reading and is testimonial to your staff's efforts on these students' behalf.

Publish questions and answers about certain subjects that affect students and parents. Invite parents to write in with their questions. Then, publish their questions and your replies in the newsletter.

"Answers To Your Questions...
About The School Bond Election" (See Figure 6-10.)
The question and answer format always receives high readership. That's why it's especially effective for explanations of complicated issues, programs, or school

Answers To Your Questions...

About The School Bond Election

One of the primary responsibilities of the Board of Education and the Superintendent of Schools is to bring to the attention of citizens the facts which affect the education of children within the district. The schools belong to the people, and it is the Board of Education's responsibility to assure the school community that all facts are known to them, so that the best possible education—as dictated by the community—is available for each and every child. This is the reason for this question-and-answer brochure.

The following has been compiled in an effort to answer some of the questions you may have pertaining to the upcoming Bond Election on June 5, 1973, for construction of a new high school. If there are any questions that are left unanswered, the Board would welcome an opportunity to answer them either in person or through the many people who will be helping in this community effort. Only through complete understanding and community participation can this endeavor become a reality and the best interests of the children in our schools be served.

Q. *Is the Board of Education, Administration, and Staff certain we need a new high school?*

A. Yes. Several years ago it was realized that student population growth caused by area growth would ultimately demand more school facilities. This belief was confirmed by studies made by the State Department of Education, Kansas State University, and consultants from the University of Tennessee working in conjunction with the architect firm. Local studies made by the Board, administration, and staff supported these findings. Two years ago the Board began to intensify efforts to provide additional facilities for the district. It was becoming quite obvious that a state of emergency would soon exist. Industry interest in this area and a predicted population shift intensified this urgent need.

Q. *If the high school is built, what grades will attend the three school centers?*

A. A new high school would be constructed to house grades nine through twelve, the existing high school would be used to house grades five through eight, and the existing elementary school would house grades kindergarten through four.

The school system is now operating under a K8-4 plan, in two types of attendance centers, elementary (Kindergarten through grade 8) and secondary (grades 9 through 12). The Board of Education, by unanimous decision, after studying several alternatives and much deliberation, conclusively decided that adopting the master K4-4-4 plan would be the most economical and feasible solution to the problem. By choosing this alternative, long-range plans would be flexible and practical and could be altered later if necessary. With the long-range planning, the school district would then best be served in the most economical way, and quality education could best be served.

Q. *What area of the school is the most crowded?*

A. The greatest emergency exists in the elementary school. Over 400 children, which is approximately one half of the elementary enrollment, will be housed outside the elementary building next year. However, high-school enrollment will increase by 70 students within the next two years, not including population growth increases.

Q. *Are all classrooms overcrowded in the elementary schools?*

A. No. Kindergarten, first, and second grade rooms are not overcrowded at the present time. Recommended classroom space is thirty square feet per child, and rooms in the permanent building contain approximately this footage. However, rooms in the moveable buildings and annex are crowded with twenty-five children because the rooms are small.

Figure 6-10

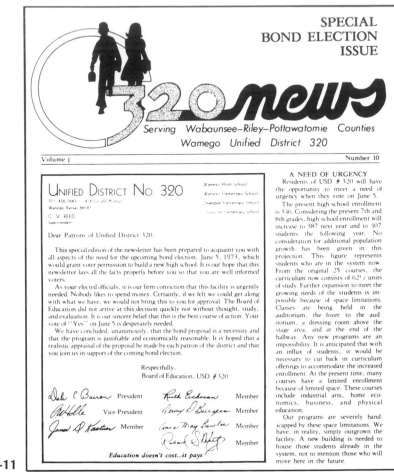

Figure 6-11

activities. The reader immediately identifies with the article when he or she finds the question that he or she would have asked you given the opportunity.

The question and answer format also helps neutralize negative attitudes. The way this is done most effectively is by stating a known negative concerning the issue in the form of a question and then answering it positively. For example:

> Question: "I have heard that this bond election is only the tip of the iceberg and that there are plans to hold one every year for the next five years."

> Answer: "The answer to this question is decidedly false. The school bond now being considered incorporates our plans for expansion over the next five years . . . (continue your explanation)."

Signature Letters (See Figure 6-11.)

People are interested in what other people think, believe, and endorse. Never overlook this fact. That's why signature advertisements for political campaigns are so effective. People comb them to see who has signed and who has signed next to whom. Using signatures on letters or articles that you publish in your newsletter can markedly increase readership for this reason.

A suggestion that is quite useful for getting staff members to contribute to the newsletter is to have them sign or by-line their entries. And allowing bus drivers to contribute material and sign their articles is one way to ensure that the newsletters won't be left on the bus.

23 | PUBLIC RELATIONS IDEA

Include a paragraph of news from each classroom at each grade level. Have teachers sign or by-line their entries. People are attracted by writings that are signed.

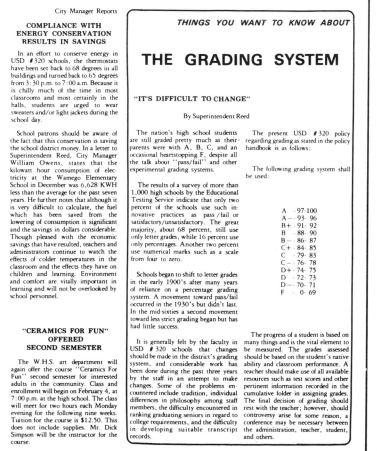

Figure 6-12

"The Grading System"

This example (see Figure 6-12) illustrates two important graphic elements of any well-laid-out newsletter: borders and white space. An important rule to remember is that anything inside a border will be read before anything outside a border. Therefore, your most important messages should be placed inside borders. Second, note how the white space around the headline and around the grading scale helps compel the reader to read the material. People won't read copy that has no "breathing room." It's simply too much and looks too complicated. Therefore, don't be afraid of using white space. And never believe this is wasted space. It is not, because it helps ensure that the rest of the newsletter will be read. Too, remember that any information that won't fit or that must be crowded in can be used in another issue.

"Board Of Education Report..."

This is an example of artwork that is used to highlight a regular column in a newsletter. (See Figure 6-13.) The benefit of highlighting regular articles is that the

Figure 6-13

Figure 6-14

CALENDAR OF EVENTS
WAMEGO UNIFIED DISTRICT 320

OCT

mon	tue	wed	thu	fri	sat
16 *"B" Team Football Holton-Here 6:30	**17** *Grade School Football Ft. Riley-Here 4:00 *Fall Y-Teen Conference	**18** *Kansas Highway Patrol Safety Program H.S. *Faculty Inservice Meeting 3:45	**19** *Freshman Football Logan Junior High-There 7:00	**20** *Varsity Football Effingham-There 7:30	**21**
23 *"B" Team Football Manhattan Soph.-Here 6:30 *Veterans' Day Observance 8:45 a.m. **AMERICAN**	**24** *NMSQ Test (Juniors) *Freshman Football Marysville-Here 6:30 **EDUCATION**	**25** *Faculty Inservice 3:45 **WEEK**	**26** *Grade School Football Abilene-Here 6:30	**27** *Varsity Football Marysville There Pep Bus leaves 5:30 p.m. returns 11:00 p.m.	**28** *Debate-Manhattan *State Cross-Country Meet-Manhattan *Spanish Contest Wichita University *Girls' Regional Volleyball

NOVEMBER

mon	tue	wed	thu	fri	sat
30 *Jr. High Basketball Practice Begins	**31** *Halloween	**1** *Report Cards Due *Basketball Rules Meeting - Manhattan *Freshman Football Northern Hills-Here 3:00	**2** *Report Cards Mailed *Varsity Football Santa Fe Trail-Here 7:30 HOMECOMING *Homecoming Parade 3:00 p.m. *Parents Conference	**3** *K-NEA CONVENTION NO SCHOOL *Jr. High Ensemble-Topeka	**4**
6 *NCKL Fall Meeting-Concordia	**7** VOTE	**8** *Faculty Inservice 3:45	**9**	**10** *District Football Playoffs *Mobile Art Gallery	**11**
13 *Teachers Assn. Meeting 8:00 p.m. *Mobile Art Gallery	**14** *Mobile Art Gallery	**15** *Faculty Inservice 3:45	**16**	**17** *Senior Play *Regional Football Playoffs	**18**

320

reader becomes conditioned to look to a particular place for this information. It is a convenience measure that helps readers see your newsletter as a useful and comprehensive publication.

Calendar Of Events

This is a very important feature that should be included in every newsletter. The primary reason parents read a newsletter is to make sure they don't miss something that is coming up. Therefore, include a calendar of events which covers the time frame of each newsletter, but also highlights special upcoming dates of which parents should be aware. In addition, record faculty and department meetings on the calendar. That way, the calendar will not only highlight important dates, but will also show that the school building is used both day and night and that the staff has night as well as day activities. Place the calendar on the back page of the newsletter so it can easily be clipped out for posting on a refrigerator or bulletin board. (See Figure 6-14.)

Layout Tips For Newsletters

1. Use thumbnail sketches to lay out the newsletter. (See Figure 6-15.)

A thumbnail sketch is a device used by commercial artists and professional layout people to give themselves an overall organizational scheme for a publication before copy is actually typed or typeset. Figure 6-15 gives you an idea of how thumbnail sketches look. They usually don't take more than a few minutes to do and are easily changed since items can simply be rearranged. A thumbnail sketch will save you or your secretary hours of time in laying out articles.

2. Newsletter formats. (See Figure 6-16.)

There are many ways to lay out a newsletter. We have illustrated some possibilities in Figure 6-16. Once you decide upon a format, stick to it. Newsletters that are laid out one way one month and another way the next month will not be perceived as consistent professional publications. And people won't like them any more than they would their local newspaper if it changed formats every day.

3. Variations in folds. (See Figure 6-17.)

There are several ways to fold an 8½-inch-by-11-inch, 8½-inch-by-14-inch, or 11-inch-by-17-inch sheet of paper to provide interesting reading for your newsletter. Folds lend themselves to showcasing particularly important items or stories by setting them apart from other items. However, a word of caution about too many folds: They can be confusing. Therefore, choose a format that makes good readership sense—and not one that is simply clever.

Figure 6-15   **Thumbnail sketches help give an overall organizational scheme to your newsletter.**

132

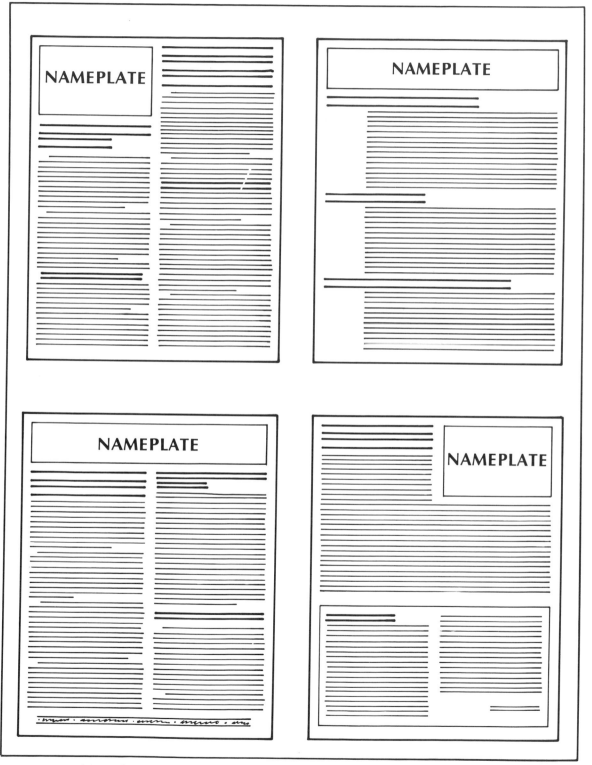

Figure 6-16   Newsletter formats

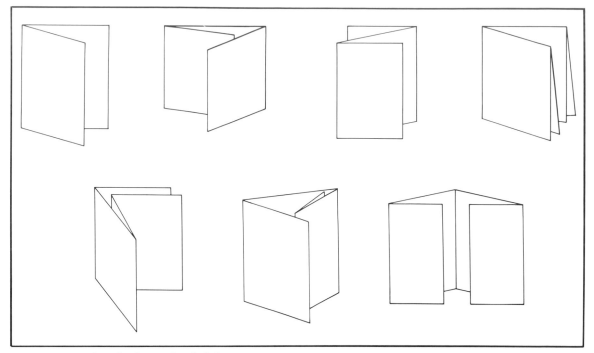

Figure 6-17 Variations in folds.

Use Of Photographs In Layouts

As we have said, photographs have a great deal of interest and emotional appeal. Therefore, we recommend their use as much as possible. However, for photographs to be reproduced effectively a printer needs to make what is called a half-tone, and print the newsletter on an offset press. If you duplicate your newsletter on a copier *do not use photographs.* They will not reproduce well and will give your newsletter a muddy appearance.

Likewise, never distort a photograph with posterization, mezzotints, or other graphic techniques if you want it to be clear. Though these techniques are great for book and magazine covers and posters, they are confusing to most readers who look to photographs to clarify and enhance the information you are presenting.

PUBLIC RELATIONS IDEA

Getting news home and then getting it read once it is home is a perennial problem. Some schools have solved it by establishing a communication day one day each week. Each student is given a colored folder with pockets that has his or her name on it. These folders are kept by the classroom teacher or the assigned homeroom teacher of each student. In each folder the teacher compiles the important information that parents should read. Parents know, in advance, when communication day is and they look for their children to bring home the brightly colored folders on that day each week. A typical communication folder might include a weekly newsletter from the principal, a classroom newsletter from the teacher, and a flyer about an upcoming school event. Such folders may also contain report cards, tests, and other examples of student work. In some schools the parents are required to sign the folder before the student brings the folder back to school the next day. The folders' pockets are ideal for ensuring that money for lunch, pictures, or tickets is returned to school safely.

MEMOS

The memo is used every day in school business as a communication tool. It can be a powerful device when written clearly, to the point, and for the right reasons. It can be a very negative tool if used in the wrong way or for the wrong reasons. If you want to know the effectiveness of your memos, simply check the wastebaskets after school the day your memo was sent out.

**Let
The Memo
Work For You**

Always clarify your memos by answering the "who," "what," "why," "when," "where," and "how" questions about your subject matter. In the process, be aware that the memo **may** be used in the following ways:

1. To fix responsibility. Such a memo should leave no doubt as to who is responsible for a task. Example: A memo identifying all teachers who have special after-school duties, and what their duties are can be invaluable.

2. To clarify policy. A well-written memo can eliminate misunderstanding about policies and rules. Example: A memo aimed at informing teachers and support staff where they should direct children during fire drills would be helpful.

3. To reaffirm a spoken directive. A memo can confirm and prevent misinterpretation of the many spoken directives you give each day. Example: A memo summing up what happened at a particular staff meeting is always appropriate.

4. To bring a person or persons up-to-date. The memo can be used to keep people current on various situations that exist in the school. Example: Your school is undergoing remodeling. A memo which brings teachers up-to-date on the remodeling timetable and which projects a completion date would be appropriate.

5. To communicate with a person who is hard to approach or busy. A memo can prompt action from hard-to-reach people by making them aware of your needs.

6. To communicate with many people at once. The memo is a way to reach a lot of people with a concise message. Therefore, the memo facilitates the possibility of what is referred to in media circles as "total penetration simultaneously" with the entire staff.

The memo should **not** be used:

1. When another form of communication could be used, such as the weekly bulletin. Because memos do not and should not come out regularly or become a habitual practice, they have an attention-getting quality that is both a blessing and a curse. The blessing is that they are usually read, but they can also be alarming or cause negative emotions. You don't want to cause unnecessary alarm or depreciate a memo's value—which will surely happen if you use memos improperly or become known as a "memo freak" by issuing them to handle every conceivable situation.

2. To "come down on" or reprimand individuals or a group of people. First, you never want a reprimand to be written. Its tone can be blown too far out of proportion. Second, memos that are written to reprimand tend to blame all for the mistakes of a few and offer no practical way for a person to respond. When this is the case, there will always be repercussions. Make no mistake, written reprimands are very negative and widely resented. And if they have been typed by a secretary, the breach of confidence may permanently destroy your relations with the staff.

Therefore, ask yourself if there is any better way to communicate your message than the memo. Many necessary reminders can be given in person, on the intercom, or in the weekly bulletin.

STAFF BULLETINS

The weekly staff bulletin is a very important form of school communication. That's because the staff bulletin communicates with some of our best public relations people: teachers. Weekly staff bulletins are the primary way administrators keep all of their staff members informed of current happenings for the week. Staff bulletins don't need to be fancy, but they should be frequent and available to all staff members who work in a school. (See Figure 6-18.)

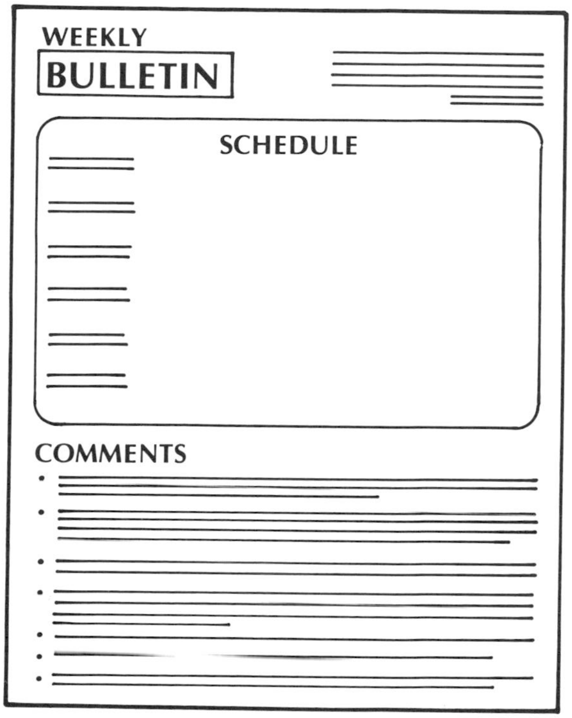

Figure 6-18   Staff Bulletins

Do's and Don'ts For Staff Bulletins

1. Do...publish your staff bulletin weekly. This is the ideal frequency—and the overwhelming majority of schools publish bulletins weekly. Don't try to save a little money by publishing your bulletin biweekly or monthly. It will be outdated in three days.

2. Do...include upcoming events day by day.

3. Never reprimand the whole staff in your bulletin. Negative comments should be made verbally so that your point can be made, but your temperament forgotten.

4. Do...keep your weekly bulletin positive.

5. Do...use the bulletin to set the tone for the week. In other words, give the writing some personal flavor and spirit. Using a "thought for the week" is a good beginning.

6. Do...keep the format consistent so that if people need to refer to the bulletin for something they can do it easily.

7. Do...expand your distribution list to include others who work with your school. PTA president, chairperson of an advisory group, football boosters, club members, and local newspaper editors might be included.

8. Do...distribute the bulletin on Friday to facilitate planning. If this is not possible, have the bulletin waiting in mailboxes Monday morning.

9. Do...make extra copies to replace those lost by teachers.

PURCHASE ORDERS

Whether we think so or not, even our purchase orders leave an impression with our public—especially our business public. The amount of excess paperwork required by many schools just to purchase the smallest of items is seen as wasteful and inefficient by the business community. The businesses in your own community as well as your suppliers outside of your community are very much aware of the mounds of paperwork it takes for you to buy something. The collective impression that is often created is of a system which reeks of bureaucracy, waste, and inefficiency. Needless to say, this image does not serve you, your school, or the district well. Therefore, when assessing your current paperwork procedures for purchase orders, use these guidelines:

- *Purchase orders should be no larger than 8½ inches by 11 inches and should, at the most, contain only as many duplicate copies as is absolutely necessary.*

- *Purchase orders should fit in a number 10 envelope.* A number 10 envelope is the most economical size to buy in large quantities. Oversized envelopes send the message that you are wasteful and not concerned about how much supplies cost.

- *Purchase orders should never be stapled through the envelope.* This is a discourtesy to the person who must open it, and the staple can cut the hand of the person who opens your letter. It is also unnecessary.

- *Unless required by law, refrain from asking the supplier to read through pages of state regulations before he or she can qualify as a vendor.* This makes it difficult for the supplier to serve you. Most of the time, this information can be confined to a few lines and made a part of your purchase order.

PROGRESS REPORTS

The most universal communications used by schools are reports regarding student progress. These reports may be in the form of report cards, achievement test scores, or vocational interest or aptitude test results—as well as parent conferences and home visitations. Public communications may involve reports of student attendance and behavior. Regardless of the kind of report, it's exceedingly important that the reporting be as accurate and uniform as possible. Unfortunately, some schools are very careless in their reporting. Over a period of time, this carelessness can result in a loss of confidence in the schools and public skepticism about the quality of the schools—including those who work in them.

To gain uniformity, consistency, and accuracy, administrators and teachers must make sure that the form of the reporting isn't left to chance. For example, schools must have a student grading system that parents and teachers both understand and accept. It must also be as objective as possible. Whenever the subjective judgment of teachers is involved—as is almost always the case—there ought to be firm guidelines regarding how grades are determined. When test results are revealed, they should be reported in a specific format in the same way to every parent. While the way in which the results are reported may vary from community to community, it should not vary from school to school within a community. Where the reporting is done in conferences or home visits, each teacher should understand the kind of information that is required to be reported to parents.

Schools will always have difficulty achieving uniformity and accuracy when many different employees are reporting to many different parents. That's why specific guidelines are needed. Although guidelines may not ensure absolute accuracy and consistency, they will go far toward reaching this desired goal.

While the following aren't all of the questions that an administrator may want to ask, they provide a good starting point.

● Is the information easily understood by those who do not have a special knowledge of educational language?

● Is the information accurate, precise, and uniform?

● Is the information in a form which can be accurately reported by employees and used by the news media as well?

● Do the employees of the schools understand the necessity for observing the administration's guidelines for reporting to others?

PUBLIC RELATIONS IDEA

One of the underlying themes that run through current criticism of education is the failure of the school to be specific about a student's performance. In spite of the difficulty that exists in reducing the achievement of a student to some simple statement and communicating it to a parent or guardian, many schools have adopted the position that one of their goals will be to work toward more exact reporting to parents. In some states, this has become mandatory.

Regardless, there are several ways this can be done. Some school systems are mailing the results of standardized achievement tests to the parents. In the process, they also include information as to whether a student exhibited certain competency levels in the basic skills.

However, there are often objections to these procedures. Some teachers and administrators believe that parents will not understand the test results or will misinterpret what they actually mean. Some educators feel that such test results are damaging to the student's self-image if they do not indicate a high achievement level. Yet, sending the test results home can be very beneficial. Other communications should be included, of course. Needed is a brief cover letter explaining the test procedure and what the results mean. Likewise, an invitation to discuss the results with a teacher, counselor, or administrator should be included.

Schools that have used this procedure report that it's possibly the most satisfactory step they have taken in a number of years to gain parental support and interest in the schools. Comments from parents have been favorable, regardless of the test results that their children received. If the results are known, a discussion—whether formal or informal—can begin on a note of forthrightness and honesty. Certainly, this stance can do much to build confidence in the schools.

THE
GRADE
CARD

The process of communicating with students about their grades is covered in Chapter VII. But the subject of the actual grade card document is an important one, so we will discuss it here.

The grade card may just be the school document that has the highest degree of importance and readership to students and parents. We often miss this point and it is reflected in our use of standardized forms or computer-generated forms. Without doubt, there is much to be said for the ease and convenience of such methods. However, we must also be aware how cold and noncommunicative such methods can be. Therefore, the following are some basic points to consider regarding grade cards.

1. *A grade card that contains your school slogan such as, "Where we consider every young mind important" (see good and bad slogans, p. 103) will help to reinforce the school's stand and mission in the minds of parents—whether the news on the grade card is good or bad.*

2. *Grade cards that don't contain at least a line of narrative from the student's teacher(s) leave much to be desired.* In fact, such a void may be demotivating. If we consider how teachers would feel receiving an evaluation from their principal that only contained a number or letter evaluation, we will be able to see how put off students and parents can be with a computerized form. It has no note. It has no privacy envelope. It has no human contact, but it is heavily laden with machine computed, typed, and delivered messages.

**Possible
Notes For
Grade Cards**

Here are some sample notes teachers can use on report cards and letters home which are designed to offer parents two distinct messages. The first part of the note offers a word of praise. The second part of the note is a statement that recommends specific goals their child should attempt to achieve. As we all know well, teachers often need to deliver both messages.

Note 1: Jim does a fine job in math. He studies hard and completes his work consistently. However, he should be encouraged to keep his work better organized. He has to spend too much time searching for materials, homework, and completed assignments.

Note 2: May is showing a steady rate of growth in all aspects of class work. However, she needs to be reminded not to let up following the completion of one assignment and before the beginning of another. The lost time is not working to her advantage.

Note 3: Keith is an excellent student with a fine attitude toward responsibility. He should strive to find more enjoyment in his accomplishments, however. He needs to be encouraged to view mistakes as valuable learning experiences rather than negative or destructive events.

Note 4: Sharon grasps new ideas easily. She is both quick and accurate in oral interpretation and responses in class. However, she should be encouraged to set time aside each day to work on her writing skills so as to perfect her total communication efficiency. Writing letters to friends or relatives could be a big help.

NEWSPAPERS

Newspaper reading tends to be a ritual. Usually a person will read the newspaper at about the same time of day in the same manner. For example, he or she may read the headlines and news on the front page, and then turn to a favorite section such as the sports page, financial page, society page, comics, or others. People who are newspaper readers rarely skip a day. Their natural curiosity compels them to get their daily "fix" of news.

Newspapers remain the primary source of daily local news for many people. Unlike newsletters, newspapers cover the news of the day rather than a large segment of time. A newspaper also has the ability to provide in-depth coverage of the news, while air time on radio and television is more limited. Newspapers, unlike radio or television, offer the schools an ideal medium because newspapers can afford to devote space to local news, including school events. A newspaper is like a newsletter in one respect. Both can be used at the reader's convenience, and may be saved until the reader has the time to read them. In contrast, if the viewer misses the broadcast of the 6:00 p.m. TV news, he or she has to stay awake long enough to catch it on the 10:00 p.m. TV news. If the viewer misses both broadcasts, he or she may miss that day's news altogether.

**Typical
Newspaper
Markets**

Figure 6-19

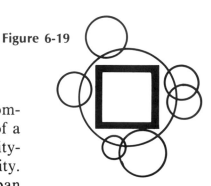

In Figure 6-19, the bold square represents the community. Each circle indicates the circulation range of a particular newspaper in the community. There's the city-center paper which reaches people throughout the city. There may be a number of daily and weekly suburban papers, each dividing the total newspaper audience. And of course, not everyone gets a paper and few get *all* the papers in a community.

**Typical
Radio
Markets**

Figure 6-20

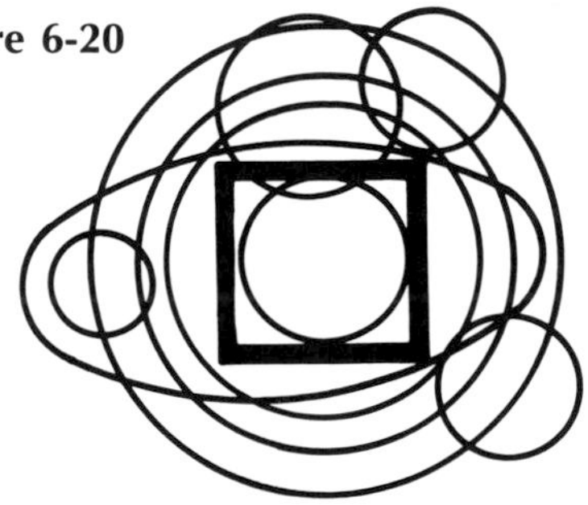

Radio covers a vast area. (See Figure 6-20.) It is usually larger in range than a newspaper. But there are many radio stations on the air that people can listen to. Each station is trying to win its share of the total radio audience. Therefore, several stations might have to be used with a public relations effort to reach everyone. In addition, each station may play predominantly one kind of music and, therefore, some are regarded as country and others as rock, etc. Too, some stations reach an audience which may not be interested in our messages. Therefore, we have to pick the stations that reach our audience or the most dominant station in the area.

Figure 6-21

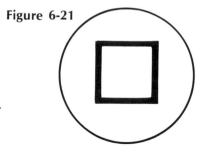

A
Typical
Television Market

A limited number of stations is a big benefit of television—even with the advent of cable systems and satellites. (See Figure 6-21.) Therefore, coverage of city-center, suburbs, and rural areas all at the same time with the same message is possible. Yet, we may not have access to any television station and it may be costly to utilize it if we do. However, we need to be aware that television is an extremely powerful medium. It cannot be overlooked as an influence.

Tips For Working With Media Representatives Or Reporters

1. Designate someone in your building to deal with the media. This may be the superintendent at the district level or principal at the building level. It might also be a journalism teacher or—at the elementary level—a secretary. This person should be responsible for collecting releases from teachers and students. However, if you are new at the business of dealing with the media, make sure you give yourself the experience firsthand before you decide you can delegate the responsibility to someone else.

2. Have this person sit down with representatives from the newspaper, radio, and television. Depending on the size of the community and the media with which you are dealing, there may be someone designated as the education reporter or editor. Don't wait until there's a crisis that the newspaper, radio, or television wants to report to get to know your reporter. If you do, it is unlikely that you will have any leverage at all concerning how the news story is presented—or when it is released. In addition, make a point to have lunch with reporters every six weeks or so—to discuss the work and mission of your school, answer questions, receive and offer suggestions, and even squelch rumors before they are started.

3. Make sure reporters know whom to call. And when they call, make certain that factual information is at hand. Reporters live with deadlines. Be sensitive to this fact. If you give a story to the newspaper at 4:00 p.m., it won't be in the paper until the next day. However, it will be on the radio at 5:00 p.m. This can cause bad feelings because the radio "scoops" the newspaper which makes it seem that the newspaper is publishing old stories. If a story is delivered to both media at 10:00 a.m., however, it will be on the noon radio news and in the evening paper. Then everyone will be happy. Regardless, don't guess—ask your local media people what time is fair for all.

4. Read the by-lines in your local newspaper and keep track of which reporter or reporters you prefer—and request meetings with those people.

5. If a reporter is assigned to your school or district, invite him or her to spend a morning in your building or central office to get a taste of what goes on there.

6. From time to time, write a letter to the newspaper or station when you feel the media has done an especially good job of covering an event. It's a fact that newspeople get a lot of criticism and little praise. Therefore, they are especially appreciative of any sincere praise but will resent being manipulated. (See *PUBLIC RELATIONS IDEA #27.*)

7. Remember, reporters are people. The press really does want to do more than report bad news. Your job is to give reporters enough information to allow them to feel generally favorable toward your school(s). Though it is a reporter's job to report objectively, you can help a reporter be "objectively positive" by explaining to him or her the school's goals and how they are being achieved. You can also help by delivering good news on a regular basis and even communicating some of the problems that you encounter. Let reporters feel that you are a person rather than an institution. Institutions are cold. People are warm.

8. Tell the media how you intend to operate. The only way to operate successfully is to be totally open and truthful. Therefore, tell reporters that you understand that they feel they are entitled to the bad news along with the good. In addition, add, "Feel free to talk to any school employee, on any subject, at any time other than during class time." Though reporters usually won't take you up on this offer because it is inconvenient for them to do so, this gesture makes your "open door" policy believable.

There will be times when a reporter will call, of course, and you will be truly unable to take the call at that time. When you first meet with reporters, explain, "I will return all phone calls as soon as possible." Then do so. This statement will allow the media to trust that you will return calls and that you aren't being evasive or stalling.

9. Superintendents should send members of the media every piece of information they send to board members, including agendas and recommendations. Only confidential information regarding personnel should be excluded, of course.

10. Building administrators should send copies of their media releases to the central office as a courtesy, as well as for informative purposes.

11. Make arrangements to have the press take photographs whenever possible—or purchase a camera and supply the media with black and white photos as per their specifications.

12. Give the press plenty of lead-time—at least a week—if you want them to cover a story.

13. Ask if you can write a monthly guest column on subjects such as:*
- Importance of education.
- Your school's successes.
- How parents can help their children at school.

14. Make plans to develop at least one news release each month about some positive aspect of the school. The release might be about student success, curriculum changes, test results, or a successful graduate.

15. Always make sure your stories are current and accurate.

 PUBLIC RELATIONS IDEA

Many school boards and administrators complain about the amount and quality of coverage that the news media provide their schools. Unfortunately, complaining is about the extent of the action that these boards and administrators usually take to remedy the situation. That is to be regretted, for there is an action that a board can take which often results in improvement of media coverage of school news.

Invite representatives from the newspaper, radio, and television stations to appear before the board or the faculty, and review their needs for education news with you. The meeting can be an informal one. In fact, it should be. Ask the representatives to detail the kind of information they would like to have about the schools, and then ask them how much of the job they expect to do for themselves and the extent they expect you to gather the information for them.

Will such a meeting guarantee improved relationships with the news media and result in better coverage for the schools? Those results are not guaranteed, but such a meeting will leave both the board and the news media representatives with a better understanding for each other's position. That is a good start for improved relations in any situation. After all, taking some positive steps is better than complaining that the news media representatives do not want to serve the public interest. Asking them how you can help will likely pay dividends in better and more positive news coverage for the district. It will also help the school board to see the overall needs of the news media personnel and the responsibility that they have for providing adequate coverage of education.

About Our Schools is a 4-in-1 public relations program for schools published by The Master Teacher. Each month, the ordering administrator receives a newspaper column, an article for a newsletter to parents, ten brochures to display in the office, and the text for a short speech when an administrator is asked to say a few words in public. Call or write, The Master Teacher, Leadership Lane, P.O. Box 1207, Manhattan, Kansas, 66502; (913) 539-0555.

PUBLIC RELATIONS IDEA

Perhaps one characteristic that is commonly shared by almost all of us—from boards of education to teachers—is that we expect everyone with whom we deal to do quality work. Although boards almost universally hold this expectation and may criticize or even condemn those whose work does not meet their expectations, they are often very slow to praise or acknowledge those whose work does meet their standards.

The failure to commend employees when praise is due is a big mistake. Likewise, the failure to praise the news media when it's due is also a blunder. If a board of education expects to build a relationship of respect and cooperation with the news media, it's a mistake that we must seek to avoid.

A close look will reveal that the news media are often in the same position as the board of education and the schools. They receive little acclaim and plenty of criticism from the public daily. As a result, they may become nearly immune to negative responses from their listeners or readers. On the other hand, praise is so seldom offered by readers or listeners that the use of it has considerable impact.

There is nothing that motivates an individual to do better the next time like a comment regarding a job well done. An appropriate note sent to the editor, station manager, or reporter when a story is well done is also in order. And don't wait to give praise until you read or hear a story which is highly favorable to the schools. Instead, write your note when a news report is accurate or interesting. And remember, a little praise at the appropriate times to reward the news media for a job well done is a small action. However, it's a positive start for any public relations effort by a board of education or school.

**Format
For A
Press Release**

A press release, just like any news article, should include the "who," "what," "why," "when," "where," and "how" aspects of the story. The key to writing a good press release is to include three or more of these elements—particularly the "who," "what," "when," and "where"—in the first paragraph of the release. Subsequent paragraphs can be used to give these four elements more depth and to explain the "why" and "how." Figure 6-22 is a form which may be used for compiling this information before writing a press release. (This form may be photocopied.)

Newspapers are used to receiving press releases in a standard format. A press release should be typed *double-spaced* on 8½-inch-by-11-inch sheets. There should be one-inch margins on all sides. The writer's name, address, and telephone number should appear in the upper right-hand corner, or the writer should use letterhead paper. The writer should identify the release date at the top of the page. Example: FOR IMMEDIATE RELEASE, JULY 15,

PRESS RELEASE INFORMATION FORM

Submitted by _____

Grade or Dept. _____

Date _____

School _____

PUBLIC RELATIONS   For the School _____   For an Event _____   For an Activity/ Service _____   For a Person _____

TARGET PROSPECT(S)   Senior Citizens _____   Adult Women _____   Adult Men _____   Middle School/ Junior High _____   High School _____

WHO:

WHAT:

WHY:

WHEN:

WHERE:

HOW:

I WANT TO CONVEY THIS BELIEF OR EVOKE THIS REACTION: (CONVEY THIS BELIEF) _____

_____

_____

TO MAXIMIZE ITS OPPORTUNITY FOR SUCCESS, THIS MESSAGE SHOULD INVITE SUCH CONCLUSIONS AS: _____

_____

_____

_____

NOTES:

1. Specifically: What objective is *this particular message* to be designed to serve? (What message do you want it to convey?)

2. Thought Guide: "How do I want the public to react, i.e. How do I want them to *feel;* what do I want them to *believe* regarding the school, event, service, etc., after reading this particular message?"

Figure 6-22

<u>PRESS RELEASE</u>

Name _____

School _____

Telephone _____

FOR IMMEDIATE RELEASE, JULY 15, 19__

TEACHERS TO ATTEND NUTRITION WORKSHOP

Teachers of kindergarten through grade six classes at _____(school)_____ will be learning to help children make wise food choices on _(day and date)__. They will be participating in a workshop introducing <u>FOOD...Your Choice</u>, a sequential nutrition learning system.

The workshop will be conducted by Dairy, Food and Nutrition Council, Inc., and is part of the school's continuing inservice training program for teachers. According to <u>(name and title of person in charge)</u>, <u>FOOD...Your Choice</u> adapts nutrition learning experiences to the developmental stages of children at various grade levels. Developed by The National Dairy Council, the program has been field tested nationwide and validated by experts in the educational field. Over <u>(number)</u> teachers in New York and New Jersey participated in <u>FOOD...Your Choice</u> workshops last year.

(Mr., Mrs., Miss) ____(name)_____ explained, "<u>FOOD...Your Choice</u> teaches the basic principles of nutrition and suggests learning activities appropriate for use in the classroom."

Divided into three levels, the system provides a wide variety of educational goals for both teachers and students at each level. Level I, for grades K-2, introduces basic concepts. The attitudes and concepts

MORE

Figure 6-23

148

developed here will assist students in forming lifelong attitudes and interest in nutrition. Level 2, for grades 3 and 4, provides an opportunity to relate nutrition information to the student's own decision making. At level 3, grades 5 and 6, students focus on understanding and evaluating factors that influence eating patterns. All learning activities encourage wise food choice.

As they participate in the workshop, teachers will receive the educational materials geared to the level of their students.

The workshop is being conducted by the staff of Dairy, Food and Nutrition Council, Inc., a nonprofit educational organization serving communities in New York and New Jersey. Milk producers and milk processors in this area provide the funds for Dairy Council to conduct its educational program promoting good health through good nutrition, including the beneficial use of milk and milk products.

or 30

19____. The title should be centered and put in all capital letters. If the story should run over to succeeding sheets, the writer should type "MORE" at the bottom of the page. Then at the top of the next page the writer should type a few words to indicate the nature of the story along with the page number. At the end of the story, the writer should type "30" or ### to indicate the end. It's important to use short paragraphs and to write in third person. All people in the story should be identified by using their full names and positions. (See Figure 6-23.)

RADIO
AND
TELEVISION

People use radio often as an accompaniment to other activities. Radio itself becomes a companion and tends to be regarded as a part of the background climate in which a person works or lives. The important emotional benefits which people receive from radio are the following: aesthetic pleasure which for the most part comes from music; human contact, in terms of personalities with which listeners become familiar; friendship, particularly when people listen to the radio alone; and information or knowledge as it pertains to the news, weather, sports, and advertising. Radio also seems to *involve* people through the use of such information, humor, and music and thus comes across as a friendly, unobtrusive medium. However, the radio stations which have the most listeners are those which feature regular programs rather than simply news, weather, and sports, followed by music the rest of the hour.

Television is a medium not available to most schools. However, more and more local cable systems are televising board meetings as well as school events. Many schools do use television internally for staff, student, and parent meetings. Television is a powerful mass medium because it utilizes sight, sound, motion, and emotion. It is able to involve people emotionally because it communicates in terms of human situations with which the viewer can identify. From the reasons people give regarding precisely *why* they turn on television, a pattern emerges. This pattern shows that people are more apt to accept television as a replica of a direct experience. It is television's realism, its ability to bring things to life, that enables this medium to involve people in so many different ways and with great depth.

In the case of television, the individual *expects* to be involved emotionally when he or she turns the set on. A person anticipates being absorbed. Equally important, he or she is often likely to set aside relatively long periods of time to experience this activity. People either find that they become relaxed after turning on the television, or they turn on the television for the sole purpose of relaxing. Studies and polls reveal that watching television puts a person in a highly receptive mood.

In reaching your community, you'll find that television offers many significant and exclusive advantages. First, television offers the priceless combination of pictures, words, demonstration, music, and sound effects. These are all the ingredients that an ideal medium should provide. And television provides all the advantages that are inherent in a personal contact. Neither radio, newspapers, newsletters, outdoor signs, or magazines offer all of these benefits.

Second, television reaches people in the quiet of their own homes when and where important decisions are usually made. Third, when television is being watched, the viewer is absorbed and involved in the telecast rather than easily distracted as is the case with other media. Fourth, television offers group viewing. You can, for instance, talk to both the man and the woman or the whole family at one time with your message on television. This is, of course, possible with radio, but not as easily achieved with any of the print media.

Fifth, television gives in-person communication. You project your schools and student services—you don't talk about them actively—and at the same time build a warm, caring human image of your organization. Sixth, on television every word is a headline. Viewers receive the full message. They don't just read the big type or see the dominant picture. Seventh, television covers broad areas in your community intensively. Television reaches out to the fast-growing suburbs while maintaining great popularity within the important central city. It reaches urban and rural areas with the same effectiveness. Eighth, television promotes viewer involvement. Television involves people emotionally in both the program content and the public relations message. Viewing is active, not passive. This gives your message quite an impact.

Tips For Using Radio And Television

1. Contact media representatives and discuss their preferred mode of reporting. Many radio and television stations run what are called public service announcements, or PSA's. These might be used to announce upcoming school events such as those events open to the general public; deadlines for scholarship exams; important meetings at school; or adult educational opportunities.

2. Try to be featured on "local news briefs" whenever possible. Radio stations feature short hourly, or even semi-hourly, news segments that include local news. Ask the news director at the station about possible coverage for your school(s).

3. Ask the media representatives what possibilities they see for joint projects that benefit both the schools and the radio stations. For example, you might have a regular segment such as "The School Lunch Menu" that could be sold to an advertiser in your community for sponsorship. This kind of programming benefits the schools, the radio station, and the sponsor.

4. Remember, television is more selective than the other media. But anything that has visual interest has many possibilities. People do love to see the activities of children. Therefore, if students are going to be involved in an activity that is fun to watch, it might be of real interest to a television station. All you need to do is call the station and tell them what you are going to do—and when you will do it. A telephone call is better than a letter. Too, be sure that you give the station at least a week's lead-time.

PUBLIC RELATIONS IDEA 28

Almost every community has one or more service clubs. Invariably, one of their primary purposes is to help children and youth. Traditionally, this has taken the form of sponsorship of ball teams, food baskets for the poor, aid to crippled children, the purchase of eye glasses, and other worthy efforts needed in the community.

No fault can be found with any of these activities. Yet, in recent years, clubs in some communities have been making commendable efforts in another direction. They've been funding announcements on radio, on television, and in newspapers commending individual students and groups of students for success in the classroom and in extracurricular activities.

As an example, a recent spot announcement on a radio station by a service club noted the success of a mathematics team in a regional contest. The announcement named and highlighted each student involved. A day later, that same club commended a group of students for a dramatic production. A week later, they featured the merit scholars in the school district. Another club in the same community focuses on success in athletics and student activities. They call people's attention to the activities and the successes of youth and the value of extracurricular activities.

There's really no substitute for good examples and models for young people. Service clubs can do an excellent job in bringing these models to the attention of the public. If the clubs in your community are looking for a project, you may find a similar activity worth suggesting to them. The media will be glad to help. Students are doing good things in schools. Getting a third party to report those things will benefit students, parents, the community, the service club, and the schools as well.

VIDEOTAPE

One of the most exciting new technologies of our time is the videotape. This medium holds untold opportunities for both presenter and viewer. It is already being used by most schools as an instructional tool as well as a vehicle for staff development.* Yet, its power as a device to enhance public relations is still very much untapped. The following is a list of ideas which you may not have thought of.

---

*The Master Teacher offers a variety of instructional videotapes including a series of video field trips as well as tapes on leadership, motivation, parent-teacher conferences, and mathematics. For more information, contact The Master Teacher, Leadership Lane, P.O. Box 1207, Manhattan, Kansas 66502; (913) 539-0555.

29 | PUBLIC RELATIONS IDEA

Videotape certain speeches that you as the administrator make to your entire staff. These can be played back by teachers who are absent or by others who want to clarify in their own minds something that you said. This procedure cuts down on unnecessary rumor and innuendo. This concept is especially useful for superintendents who are in charge of many buildings and a very large professional staff.

30 | PUBLIC RELATIONS IDEA

Use videotape to film school plays, musical performances, variety shows, and the like. This procedure is very beneficial to parents who are unable to get away from work to see such performances in person. Such tapes are also very useful in stimulating student participation in these events in the following years.

31 | PUBLIC RELATIONS IDEA

Have teachers at the same grade level videotape certain segments of their classes throughout the year and put these together in 10- to 15-minute segments that describe the course work at that grade level. Use these tapes at the end of each year to create an anticipation in students for moving on to the next grade level. Use the same tapes at registration time to give parents an idea of what their children will be learning. Put segments of all the grade levels and subject matter tapes into a 30-minute video. Then, show the video at PTA and board meetings as well as to parents who are just sending their children to your school for the first time, including new families just entering the district. The chamber of commerce, the local library, and the local television station, along with local businesses such as banks and real estate companies would probably be interested in showing such a tape at specific times during the year.

It is an unusual school or district that does not have several new employees each year. Almost every school or district makes some attempt to orient these new employees to the "housekeeping" portions of their assigned duties. Usually, however, we overlook the necessity of orienting new employees to the basic philosophy and goals of the district. As a result, new employees may have little or no knowledge regarding an administrator's or the board's expectations for students, the philosophy of classroom management and discipline, or how the school fits into the district and the community.

Don't assume that anyone who starts to work for a school or system is already knowledgeable about these matters and that, therefore, it's only necessary to orient new staff members to the day-to-day requirements of the school system. You'll find it helpful to develop a 30- to 45-minute slide or videotape program that gives new employees a "feel" for their employers as well as an understanding of the board's—and the administration's—expectations for students and employees. Such a program can show how decisions are made about education in the community as well as the way in which each employee fits into the total educational system.

Putting together even a short orientation program requires considerable effort. But it is well worth it. School systems that have developed a program have found that it's useful in creating good relations as well as reminding the existing staff and even board members themselves about some important aspects of the work of the schools that they may have forgotten. Best of all, it can give the entire staff a real lift and make them feel good about their work and about the school with which they are associated. Some have even found it to be a good public relations program to use in the community.

SCHOOL SIGNS

Many schools, particularly high schools, have large outdoor signs built near the school entrance or parking lot on which messages can be posted concerning the happenings at the school. Such signs are extremely beneficial in educating the public—including children and teachers—about what's happening at school. Schools that do not have such a sign might do well to consider one. The uses are limitless and the advertising is free—once the sign is paid for. However, the sign should conform with the identity package of the district and not be unique or different. Only the school name should be different. The following is a list of ways such a sign can be used.

1. *To post the outcome of national tests:*
   Examples:
   "Fifty percent of Jackson School students tested in the upper twenty-five percent on national tests this year."
   "Ninety-six percent of Washington Elementary School students are reading at grade level and above."
2. *To post the names of national merit scholars.*
3. *To post the names of students who win prizes at math, science, or media fairs.*
4. *To post the outcome of important course tests:*
   Example:
   "Congratulations sixth-graders, on passing your Constitution tests."
5. *To post a message to parents concerning an upcoming academic event that will affect all students.*
   Example:
   "Students will be taking Iowa Basic Skills tests October 6-11. Parents can help by making sure that students are well rested and that they eat breakfast on those days."
6. *To generate good feelings about your school's extracurricular programs: post dates and times for school plays, music events, sports competitions, fairs, etc.*
7. *To post congratulations to the winners of sporting events.*
8. *To post congratulations to any teachers who win awards or who attain advanced degrees.*
9. *To post the name of "Teacher of the Week" or "Teacher of the Month."*
10. *To post the names of teachers who have more than 10 years of experience teaching. (15 years, 25 years, etc.)*

DEVELOPING A REPORT CARD FOR YOUR SCHOOL

Many state legislatures across the nation are mandating that each and every public school in the state deliver, on a yearly basis, a written report card to the community to show how each school is doing. Though the states vary on the kind of information they require schools to report, the basis for the information is similar. The following are some of the items that schools are asked to report.

- Student attendance rate
- Percent of students *not* promoted to the next grade level
- Graduation rate for high schools
- Student mobility/turnover
- Composite and subtest means for college bound students
- Average class size

- Percent of enrollments in high school mathematics, science, English, and social science
- Amount of time devoted to mathematics, science, English, and social science at the primary, middle, and junior high school levels
- Percent enrollments in college preparatory, general education, and vocational education programs
- Percent of students placed in the top and bottom quartiles of nationally normed achievement tests

Though there is much fear felt by school personnel about the reaction from the public to the figures that will be reported, educators must adopt a visionary stance toward such a report. The truth is that the public can't and won't make the necessary commitments to resources for education in the future without knowing the *results* of the educational system that is already in place. For growth and change to occur in the schools, the public must have adequate knowledge of what type of student the schools are producing, whether the schools can retain students, and if the instruction is adequate, before it can request that schools do more. The public deserves this information. And in many states it is no longer a question of *whether* we give such information to the public—only *how*.

The states that require such reporting have left it up to the individual schools to determine how much additional explanation each school will give the public concerning its reported statistics and in what format they will give it. Therefore, there are wide variations between schools and districts as to the thought, expense, and design that will be incorporated to expound upon the excellence of their school(s). Some will go to great effort and expense to produce a professional and colorful document that serves as a promotional piece for the schools and the community. Others will give such a piece little thought—either to content or to presentation. The latter is, very definitely, a public relations mistake.

In the years to come, the school report card may just become the single most important document that is published by the schools. As the public demands that schools become more results oriented, it will demand more of this kind of information from school personnel. Private schools will be wise if they too issue such a report, even though it is not required of them. After all, people will be comparing schools on the basis of the quality of students the school is reputed to produce.

The following are key questions that Illinois administrators are now asked to report on. You may wish to use the questions that follow as a guide to help you formulate answers to questions that your public would like to have. These questions might also help you to begin explaining the particular issues and problems that face the schools in your community.

STUDENT ATTENDANCE RATE

A. _____ SUM OF THE NUMBER OF STUDENTS IN
   (put in number)   ATTENDANCE EACH SCHOOL DAY (average)

B. _____ SUM OF THE NUMBER OF STUDENTS ABSENT
   (put in number)   EACH SCHOOL DAY (average)

In regard to this data, ask yourself:

What does this statistic measure?

- The socioeconomic class of your students?
- The dedication or apathy of parents?
- Student interest in school?
- Correlation between achievement and grades?

Then be prepared to report to your public:

1. What you think is an outstanding attendance record.
2. What you are going to do in your school or district to try to maintain this record, or achieve a better one.

PERCENT OF STUDENTS NOT PROMOTED TO THE NEXT GRADE

A. _____ NUMBER OF STUDENTS NOT PROMOTED
   (put in number)   TO THE NEXT GRADE OR LEVEL

B. _____ SCHOOL ENROLLMENT ON THE LAST DAY
   (put in number)   OF SCHOOL

In regard to this data, ask yourself:

What does this statistic measure?

- The philosophical stance of the school on student promotion?
- Mastery of skills before students move on to the next grade?

Then be prepared to inform your public:

1. Your policy on student promotion.
2. What happens to those students who are promoted but who haven't mastered all the skills of the previous grade including:
    - Tutoring
    - Special programs
    - Individualized instruction

GRADUATION RATE FOR HIGH SCHOOLS ONLY

A. _____   NUMBER OF 1986 HIGH SCHOOL GRADUATES
   (put in number)

B. _____   NINTH GRADE 1982 FALL ENROLLMENT
   (put in number)

In regard to this data, ask yourself:

What does this statistic measure?
- Our ability to keep students interested in school?
- The socioeconomic level of the students?
- Demands of the job force?
- With increase in standards does it show the ability of schools to adjust so students don't flunk out?
- Maturity of student population?
- Support of parents?

Then be prepared to inform the public:
1. What you think is a very good graduation percentage. Why?
2. What you are going to do to try to achieve the same or better percentage.

STUDENT MOBILITY/TURNOVER

A. _____   SUM OF TRANSFERS IN
   (put in number)

B. _____   SUM OF TRANSFERS OUT
   (put in number)

In regard to this data, ask yourself:

What does this statistic measure?
- Satisfaction? Dissatisfaction with the education experience?
- Mobility of population?
- Economic conditions in the work force?
- Difficulty of teachers to teach students who come in and out?

Then be prepared to inform your public concerning:
1. What you consider a good transfer percentage.
2. Data that your community ought to be aware of that would affect this percentage.
3. What you are going to do in your school to deal with student mobility.

COMPOSITE AND SUBTEST MEAN SCORES FOR COLLEGE-BOUND STUDENTS

In regard to this data, ask yourself:

What does this data measure?

- The standing of students in your district with students nationally who have taken an ACT or SAT test?
- Mastery of knowledge rated on a national scale?
- Quality of teaching rated on a national scale?
- Intelligence level of students as rated on a national scale?

Then be prepared to inform your public:

1. What you consider to be a good composite and subtest means.
2. What you are going to promise your community to maintain this statistic or improve it.

AVERAGE CLASS SIZE (On The First Regular Day of Classes in May)

High Schools:

A. _____ (put in number)   NUMBER OF SECTIONS TAUGHT DURING THE SECOND CLASS PERIOD

B. _____ (put in number)   TOTAL ENROLLMENT IN THESE SECTIONS IN THAT CLASS PERIOD

Schools having grades below grade 9:

	Grade 3	Grade 6	Grade 8
Number of sections/classes (on the first regular day of classes in May)			
Total enrollment in all sections/classes (on the first regular day of classes in May)			

In regard to this data, ask yourself:

What does this data measure?
- The amount of time each student is likely to receive individualized instruction?
- The quality of the general instruction?
- Need for aides to assist teachers?
- Ability of some students to do well?
- Interpersonal interactions between teacher and student, student and student?

Then be prepared to inform your public concerning:
1. What effect class size has in determining the quality of instruction.
2. What you are going to do to maintain the class size you've got, or to improve it.

159

PERCENT OF ENROLLMENT IN HIGH SCHOOL MATHEMATICS, SCIENCE, ENGLISH, AND SOCIAL SCIENCE

	Mathematics	Science	English	Social Science
Total Course Enrollment (High Schools Only)				

In regard to this data, ask yourself:

What does this data measure?

- The emphasis of the core curriculum?
- Career preferences of students and board of education?

  Then be prepared to inform your public concerning:

  1. What a very good enrollment is in each of these subjects.

  2. What you are going to do to maintain or increase this percentage.

AMOUNT OF TIME DEVOTED TO MATHEMATICS, SCIENCE, ENGLISH, AND SOCIAL SCIENCE AT THE PRIMARY, MIDDLE, AND JUNIOR HIGH SCHOOL LEVELS

Schools having grades below Grade 9 only

Average number of minutes per week of instruction

	Mathematics	Science	English	Social Science
Grade 3	(put in minutes)			
Grade 6				
Grade 8				

In regard to this data, ask yourself:

What does this data measure?

- Emphasis of the core curriculum?
- Career preferences of the community?

  Then be prepared to inform your public concerning:

  1. What you consider to be optimal for each program area.

  2. What you are going to do to maintain, increase, or decrease this time standard.

PERCENT OF ENROLLMENTS IN COLLEGE PREPARATORY, GENERAL EDUCATION, AND VOCATIONAL EDUCATION PROGRAMS (HIGH SCHOOL ONLY)

	College Preparatory	Vocational Education	General Education
Number of Students Ending the Year as 12th Graders	(enter number)		

In regard to this data, ask yourself:

What does this data measure?

- Our curriculum emphasis?
- Preferences of students and community?
- Are there factors in your community that impact on these percentages?

Then be prepared to inform your public concerning:

1. What you consider to be a good percentage in each area.
2. What specifically you are going to do to maintain or increase this percentage.
3. What ideas you have to fulfill your promise.

PERCENT OF STUDENTS PLACED IN THE TOP AND BOTTOM QUARTILES OF NATIONALLY NORMED ACHIEVEMENT TESTS

In regard to this data, ask yourself:

What does this statistic measure?

- How students in your school rank with students on a national basis?
- Mastery of subject matter?
- Quality of teaching?
- Intelligence level of student population?
- Climate of the school to facilitate learning?
- What factors outside of the school impact on this data?

Then be prepared to inform your public concerning:

1. What you consider to be a good percentage.
2. What you are going to do to maintain or increase this percentage.

161

DEVELOPING A BROCHURE ABOUT YOUR SCHOOL OR DISTRICT

In many communities, the practice of "shopping" for schools is becoming more and more popular with the public. In larger cities, people don't necessarily live in the same area in which they work. Therefore, those with children often pick a living area on the basis of the reputation of its schools. Likewise, people within a school district often pick an area to live based on the specific school their child would be able to attend. As a result, the public is inquiring more and more about the differences between schools and school districts, so that it can make informed decisions.

While private schools have known for a long time the value of informational brochures which stress the benefits of their individual institutions, public schools have not. Private schools know they must sell themselves or they may not have an enrollment from year to year. Private schools also use such brochures for the purposes of raising money for the everyday operation as well as to establish endowments and scholarship funds. The best of these brochures or catalogs utilize similar components, highlighting the *benefits* of each component. Remember, the key to a good brochure or catalog lies in information and benefits—not just raw data, descriptions, or listings.

**The Components
For A Brochure Or Catalog
On Your School Or District**

1. Mission statement for your schools.
2. Pictures of students and teachers in classrooms. This is far more important than pictures of your school buildings.
3. A brief history of the school:
   A. When it was built.
   B. Why it was named as such.
   C. How many teachers, aides, cooks, custodians, and bus drivers are employed by the school.
4. Special features of the school or curriculum.
5. Outstanding test scores and achievements of graduates.
6. Per pupil expenditure.
7. Personal statement from the principal or superintendent about the school(s).

FACE-TO-FACE COMMUNICATION

"Communication is something so simple and difficult that we can never put it in simple words."
—*T.S. Matthews*

Internal Communications:
An Atmosphere of Achievement and Cheer

Before we can even attempt to have an excellent external public relations program, we have to have an excellent internal program. In other words, people inside the school need to be able to communicate with one another—freely and without fear. In this regard, there are at least nine primary relationships we need to consider.

They are as follows:

Administrator	←-----------------------------→	**Administrator**
Administrator	←-----------------------------→	**Teacher**
Administrator	←-----------------------------→	**Student**
Administrator	←-----------------------------→	**Support Staff**
Teacher	←-----------------------------→	**Teacher**
Teacher	←-----------------------------→	**Student**
Teacher	←-----------------------------→	**Support Staff**
Student	←-----------------------------→	**Student**
Student	←-----------------------------→	**Support Staff**

As the arrows indicate, these relationships must be two-way relationships. It's not enough, for instance, for administrators to be able to talk to students. Students must be able to communicate their ideas and feelings back to administrators. Nor is it enough for one teacher to be able to speak his or her mind to colleagues. The teacher's colleagues must feel free enough to say what's on their minds without fear of repercussions.

The building administrator sets the tone for all other relationships between people within the building. A positive tone is established when an administrator attempts to maximize the goals of climate—productivity and satisfaction. That's why we say that in the internal public relations program the administrator needs to position himself to promote two vital elements—*achievement* and *cheer*.

Achievement, though an obvious goal for any school, is sometimes misinterpreted as meaning achievement for one group of people who work in a school—*students*. However, the truth is that everybody wants to achieve. Therefore, it's the administrator's responsibility to see to it that the school's stated and nonstated values support the achievement of everyone, at the expense of no one.

The second thing an administrator must do is help create a friendly, cheerful, and enthusiastic climate for working and learning. The only way this is possible is to put a halt to behaviors which are political, backbiting, and vengeful—and replace them with an atmosphere that promotes growth-producing challenges and dialogue. Since principals are the schools' leaders, they must take their responsibility in this regard very seriously. Although specific individuals in schools may try to create a growth-producing atmosphere in their classrooms, whether such an atmosphere pervades the whole school is up to principals.

Therefore, let's explore some of these relationships in depth, and we will discover that there are some guidelines we should follow and some practices we should encourage—because any time any one of these relationships breaks down, the atmosphere in the school suffers.

ADMINISTRATOR◄------►ADMINISTRATOR

Partners In the Work
Of The Schools

There are a number of factors necessary to maintain good administrator-administrator relationships. Effective administrators know, for example, that they must view the goals and directions of a school system as a shared development that involves the needs of students, the requirements of the state, the interests of the board, the desires of the community, and the professional knowledge of teachers, fellow administrators, and other employees in the district. If any of these elements is left out, efficiency, competency, and goodwill will suffer.

Effective administrators are also aware that building principals along with assistants and the superintendent must agree that there will be no surprises for one another. That's why none of them should make announcements or pronouncements that have not been thoroughly discussed or shared beforehand. The building principals have a responsibility of keeping the chief administrator informed of situations that could cause undesirable and irreparable effects. The superintendent owes the building principals the same courtesy.

Above all, effective administrators strive to maintain working relationships with one another that are open, friendly, assistance oriented, supportive, and professional. And yet, the administrator-administrator relationship is one that should not be strictly a social relationship. If the primary emphasis is on a personal rather than a professional basis, administrator recommendations may rest upon friendships and the "good-old-boy syndrome" rather than educational soundness.

Even in the best situations, friction between administrators will develop from time to time. For that reason, there should be a well-understood process for working out differences prior to that eventuality. The goal of this process *must be* results rather than a forum for airing concerns or grievances. Without reservation, administrators should work out their differences together—always. And these differences should not be aired to friends, school personnel, or the press. Administrators who air criticism of colleagues publicly are not solving problems, they are fueling them. When such is the case, both internal and external success are unlikely, and a positive public relations effort is impossible.

Administrators can never forget that anger, bickering, hostility, and fighting make any situation worse. Tensions are best reduced in a calm and rational environment. When principals and the superintendent can always count on one another to act in a rational manner, our schools are the beneficiaries.

Regular meetings between principals in the same district are always beneficial. These meetings can be held in the central office or rotated among schools. Such meetings help administrators more fully understand their individual roles, as well as how each fits into the whole. In addition, building principals will find annual visits to colleagues' schools very advantageous. Likewise, interdistrict memos and copies of weekly newsletters can help keep the team together. Above all, no community member should ever see administrators from different schools competing against one another. When this is the case, public relations is destroyed internally and externally.

ADMINISTRATOR←------→TEACHER

Verbal And Nonverbal Communication

There are two methods of communication—verbal and nonverbal. Verbal communication is the use of words, and nonverbal communication is often referred to as "body language." We all use both methods when we communicate with one another.

165

And both methods complement, reinforce, and help each other. But they can also contradict each other. An administrator needs to know and understand these realities in order to communicate effectively with teachers.

When verbal and nonverbal communication are in direct conflict, they put people in a bind. And it's important to note that people will usually accept the nonverbal message over the verbal one—when the two conflict. This fact is vital to administrator awareness and gives us important clues concerning our efforts to communicate totally our messages to teachers and vice versa.

Understanding Nonverbal Communication

Tests conducted on nonverbal communication indicate that administrators who are evaluated as good leaders perceive nonverbal communications from teachers better than other people in the lives of teachers. Tests also show that these administrators send better nonverbal clues to the staff. That's why it's important to understand how we send nonverbal communications and how they are sent to us.

Teachers are among the best nonverbal communicators. For example, teachers who turn their attention away from us during a meeting may be telling us they're bored. Likewise, when we ask a question and a teacher avoids eye contact with us, the nonverbal clues may indicate to us that the teacher may not be prepared to answer or that he or she disagrees with us.

Administrators also send nonverbal clues to teachers. Silence or a lasting stare may be used in a meeting to indicate to teachers that we are irritated.

By closely observing ourselves, we can learn to recognize nonverbal communication. That's why we should watch for physical mannerisms—sweating, blushing, head scratching, and smiling—which give us clues to messages being sent. When we send these communications, teachers will respond. When they send them to us, we should respond as well.

People are constantly communicating through both words and movement. As administrators, there are many things we can do to set the tone of communication we want with teachers. We can greet them warmly whenever we see them and we can always make eye contact when listening to them. We can understand that how we communicate nonverbally with teachers can make a big difference in how they function and relate to us.

Factors
Which
Distort Communication

There are several additional factors which can distort listening—and an administrator should always be aware of them. The first is listening for facts only and missing people's feelings. Second, a lack of interest in communication can distort listening. And the third is seeing people as stereotypes. Often, teachers say, "That's an administrator talking." Likewise, we say, "That's a teacher for you." Each phrase locks understanding into a static state and locks out the possibility for growth of one person toward the other.

In addition, having advance information about the sender or receiver, making premature decisions about the message, or failing to seek feedback to determine what is being received, are all factors which distort communication. Many of these "misjudgments" can be averted if we realize that people send and respond to communications differently. They tend to *send* their communication messages the way *they receive* them. This is called style. And there are three basic styles of which we should be aware.

THE
THREE MAJOR STYLES
OF COMMUNICATION

There are three main styles of communication—*action, senses,* and *scholarly.* All three are present in any professional staff, every student body, and every community in the world. The chances are that we, as well as our teachers, use one more dominantly than we do others, when we should use all three. Which style we use determines, to a great degree, how we are perceived and accepted by those we lead. Too, our dominant style of communication also reveals to others our professional ways, means, and preferred method of operation. In many ways, the style of communication we use always shows our dislikes as well as our areas of tolerance and intolerance.

If others are like us, chances are they can relate to our style of communication—and all is well. However, if others aren't like us, then we will have trouble communicating with and relating to them—and they will have similar difficulty with us. That's why we need to utilize all three communication styles when speaking to groups. And this is true whether we are talking to a group of students, teachers, administrators, board members, parents, or community members. Remember, our understanding of the communication styles helps us realize how we are communicating. Equally important, our communication style helps or hinders others' understanding and acceptance of us and what we are saying. Likewise, watching how *others* communicate can help us understand the communication we receive from others.

Let's discuss the action, senses, and scholarly styles. Each style tells us something about human behavior and helps us decide how best to utilize that behavior in accomplishing the work of the school.

The Action Style:
Short And To The Point

The action style of communication emphasizes action and getting things done. People who are dominant in this style don't like red tape, treading water, structure, and attending required meetings to get action. Neither do they like worrying about the past or trying to foresee the future. They want to do something, and they want to do it now. And any communication which does not suggest or result in action turns them off.

They are usually uncomfortable and annoyed with anyone who is not an action type person. They are also usually direct, abrupt, and to the point. Observation will reveal that they often wear clothing that is simple, informal, and functional. They may also make it a point to have people think they are too busy and preoccupied with important things to be neat. They usually write and communicate in brief terms and with a sense of urgency. As administrators, if we don't relate to them in action terms, they may not identify with our management or communication style at all.

The Senses Style:
Communicates Through The Emotions

The senses style of communication is warm, friendly, and sympathetic. These people work best with human emotion appeals. In fact, they may be suspicious of or turn off to any urging or plan that does not have caring, love, and the welfare of children or people as a foundation. Such individuals listen well, show empathy, and sort out complex emotional problems more easily than other staff members.

Senses style people are easy to identify. Usually, they speak and write in friendly, humorous, and exuberant ways. Their communications are highly personalized. They sign notes "Your friend," "Enjoy," "Have a happy day," or with the mark of a circle with a smiling face. They usually dress in colorful and informal clothing. And their desks and offices contain every personal memento they have ever been given by students and adults alike.

As administrators, for instance, if we communicate with them using only the action style, but without a degree of humanism, they will classify us as hard, cold, and void of caring for students, teachers, and people in general. In reality, they may think our only concern is for ourselves and the achievement of *our* goals. This is important, because many teachers, especially those who are good with students, are senses style communicators.

168

The Scholarly Style:
Organized and Objective

Scholars are cool and objective, and they view everything constructively—and from all dimensions. Their evaluations include the past, present, and future as they relate to the topics under discussion or consideration. And they love systematic investigation and inquiries when it comes to decision making.

The scholarly style communicators are the ones who like new ideas—but may not like how they are approached or considered. They are business-like and highly professional. Their communication is specific, and they write in an organized and commonly understood way. Because they love logic and facts, administrative communication which does not contain background coverage, research, or study in any aspect of decision making will be regarded as shallow, irresponsible, without foundation and, therefore, a waste of time. In truth, these teachers will call administrators "shallow," "dumb," and even "stupid" if the scholarly dimension is not covered in their communication plans. And they believe senses style people operate on emotions and are void of substance.

Understanding these three communication styles can help every administrator be a better communicator. When we understand these communication styles, we can communicate in ways that encourage people to listen, to understand, and to do what we know needs to be done. That's why we need to use all three styles in our communication rather than ever hang our hats on just one.

Availability:
An Administrative Necessity

Though there are many concerns teachers have about us, a constant concern of teachers is what they refer to as "the availability" of the administrator. When teachers wish to see administrators, they feel that they *must* and that this need for contact should receive first priority. No matter how much we would like it to be otherwise, we must recognize and accept that when a teacher wants or needs us, it's now—not tomorrow or next week. And there is no need to fight this belief. Such efforts will be useless. This sense of urgency is accented and exaggerated, however, if the administrator is not highly visible throughout the school. That's why we need to make an honest effort to make sure that sometime during each day, we walk through halls and stop by classrooms as well as set aside time when we are available for appointments with teachers. And one thing is certain: We should be available in our offices before and after school.

In addition to being available for meeting teachers' immediate needs, you will find it very worthwhile to take time to be visible in the lounge, the cafeteria, the library, and other gathering areas. This is especially important during passing periods and at other times of high traffic. Whenever possible, you should not be out of the building at these times because they are peak times for promoting your image of availability. The fact that you are highly visible to teachers is important. It reminds the staff that you are administrating as well as available to help them in any way possible. This practice also gives you the opportunity to be constantly aware of what is happening in the school and to get to know your teachers. Likewise, it offers your teachers the opportunity to become better acquainted with you. These daily informal invitations develop feelings of presence and security which lead to better administrator-teacher relationships as well as a more productive staff.

Making yourself visibly available and taking time daily to make your presence known to teachers lends a new professional dimension to your relationship with the staff. Your presence also gives you the opportunity to acknowledge exceptionally well-done work, and to offer constructive suggestions. With every interaction, you are demonstrating evidence of your concern for your teachers and, most important, your concern for the work of the school.

FACULTY MEETINGS

If handled wisely, the faculty meeting can be one of the most successful means of disseminating information and helping administrators perform the teaching function inherent in good management as well as successful internal public relations efforts. It is, without a doubt, an activity during which internal relations are either made or destroyed. In most schools, faculty meetings are scheduled regularly throughout the year. In some schools, however, faculty meetings are only scheduled when the administration feels a need to call a meeting.

On A Regular Basis... Or As Needs Arise?

It is most effective, for both the administration and staff, if faculty meetings are scheduled on a regular basis. This practice allows the staff and the administrator to plan for meetings. It lets teachers record the dates of faculty meetings on their calendars. Regularly scheduled meetings also make it possible to set a definite time period for holding each meeting and conducting school business. Remember, knowledge is vital to gaining support and, therefore, disseminating information is vital to your internal public relations program.

Regularly scheduled faculty meetings provide other benefits as well. They present an opportunity for the staff to get together on a regular basis. This is vitally important to teachers as individuals as well as to the whole of the school. After all, independent parts that are not joined together periodically cannot be expected to run very well. Too often, teachers come to feel that they are acting alone without support, direction, or adequate information in their task of teaching students. Bringing the staff together on a regular basis helps eliminate this problem. Remember, when teachers feel alone, they may automatically start acting as isolates rather than as part of the team. Therefore, regularly scheduled meetings should be the administrative rule.

Finally, regular faculty meetings allow an administrator to develop a plan to teach the staff. This teaching ought to include the practices which are successful as well as special insights at specific times of the year. This includes the beginning of the year, before and after grade cards, holiday times, and the end of the year. If nothing else, our experience at specific times can help take some of the trial and error out of a teacher's life.

Your Opportunity To Enhance Morale And Cooperation

Faculty meetings are vital to school year success. As leaders of our schools, we can use faculty meetings to improve morale, cooperation, and communication among staff members. Too often, unfortunately, administrators suffer setbacks in various areas of staff relationships because they approach faculty meetings in a haphazard, scattered, humorous, self-righteous, or unprofessional manner. An administrator may see faculty meetings as "me-against-them" situations, and may become insecure, defensive, or dominant as a result. Sometimes, an administrator simply feels uncomfortable about getting up in front of the entire staff, and he or she may lose control of the faculty meeting out of fear. Teachers quickly pick up these signals. Then, they come to dread faculty meetings as much as the administrator does.

As a leader, be aware of the problems involved in speaking to a group. In many ways, faculty meetings are no different from any other public speaking experience. If public speaking scares you, you're not alone. According to *The Book of Lists,* 41 percent of Americans list "speaking in public" as their number one fear—above fear of flying, financial difficulties, snakes, and heights. However, your position as leader demands that you minimize the effects of fear and nervousness as much as possible.

You must devote as much effort to preparation for a faculty meeting as you would to a speaking engagement outside school. If you are prepared, you are more likely to feel confident and at ease in front of the staff. There isn't an administrator alive who wouldn't be wise to start working on public speaking skills to improve presentations. *Here are six essential guidelines for conducting successful meetings:*
- Get organized.
- Show empathy for staff members.
- Improve your delivery style.

- Choose the right type of meeting to facilitate effectiveness.
- Choose a suitable location and prepare the room in advance.
- Establish an agenda prior to the meeting.

1. Organization: Doing Homework, Stating Purpose, Following Agenda, Closing On A Positive Note

One of the secrets of every tension-free speaker is organization and preparation. Organization starts with doing your homework. The administrator must know all the facts relating to his or her ideas, proposals, or topics for discussion. Equally important, the administrator must know the staff, both individually and collectively, and must keep them in mind when deciding how to approach the business at hand. Any format and plan you present must be one that the staff could accept. Ask yourself what you want the staff to think, feel, or do as a result of the faculty meeting, and present your message accordingly.

Once you have developed the content of the presentation, your main task is to prepare an opening statement which will explain the direction and purpose of the meeting. It should capture the audience's attention, make them want to hear what you have to say, and set an appropriate tone. No matter how many times you have a faculty meeting, an opening statement is always mandatory.

The statement should include telling the staff that the meeting will be structured, but that there is planned flexibility within the structure. This allows the staff to know they can make additions, ask questions, and bring up their own ideas, but only at planned times or when relevant to the guidelines of the meeting. With this kind of careful organization, the focus of the meeting will remain where it should be at all times. The faculty will see you as efficient, open, thorough, thoughtful, well informed, receptive, and positioned to lead.

Regardless of the nature of the material to be covered in a staff meeting, time will be used most efficiently if you state, in advance, the beginning and the ending times of the meeting. Then, begin on time and end on time, regardless of the circumstances. If you follow your time schedule, the staff will understand that you mean what you say. Thereafter, they are more likely to be at meetings on time, because they know you will start and end the meeting on time. And you can deal individually and privately with those who are repeatedly late. Too often, we begin meetings ten minutes late—and go past our scheduled quitting time. This kind of mismanagement causes annoyed teachers and gives us an image of incompetency. Remember, at the end of a meeting people forget about *their* late arrival—they only see *your* late adjournment.

Finally, you must take the time to formulate a conclusion. The words you choose to close a meeting are very important. No matter what has happened during the meeting, always end on a positive note. If the leader sounds pessimistic, he or she will not motivate or inspire anyone. The long-lasting effects of a negative conclusion cannot be measured. Remember, the final impression you leave with staff members may be the one that they take back to their classrooms.

2. Empathy: Focusing On Staff Members' Needs And Worries, Not Your Own

Empathy is one of the vital strengths behind all great communications. To show empathy when speaking to a group in a staff meeting, a leader must make people feel that he or she is more concerned with their needs than with his or her own. If an administrator is worried about whether or not he or she comes off as the boss, teachers will sense this preoccupation and resent it. If an administrator uses the meeting to dump his or her problems on a captive audience, the audience will conclude that the administrator is insensitive. Instead, the administrator must show concern and compassion for teachers and the work they do. Teachers must know that the administrator is aware of the difficulties they face in the classroom, day in and day out.

The leader who is empathetic is organized and concise—because he or she is sensitive to both the objectives and the time demands of teachers. We all know what it's like to have to sit through a seemingly interminable monologue by a long-winded, rambling speaker. The caring administrator makes sure he or she does not subject the staff to such an experience in any meeting. The first step to ensure that this does not happen is to plan every meeting.

Another way to express empathy is to establish eye contact. There is nothing worse than a speaker who reads from notes, looks at the ceiling, focuses on the back wall, or stares out the window the entire meeting. Looking people directly in the eye sends them the message that you are sincere and you care. Eye contact can help your presentation in other ways. For instance, by observing facial expressions and body language, you receive instant feedback from each person. Use these reactions as cues in determining your pace. If members of the audience seem confused or lost, slow down. If they seem bored, speed up. Looking for these specific messages will also help you concentrate.

Maintaining eye contact with your staff increases the chances that they will ask questions. Don't be afraid of questions. Welcome them. Keeping in mind the following tips can help you handle questions better:

- ***Repeat and rephrase the questions you are asked, especially if you are addressing a large group.*** This way you can be sure that everyone has heard the questions. By paraphrasing, you can also put the question in clearer, friendlier, and more specific terms, making it easier to answer.
- ***Listen for the intended meaning as well as any hidden meaning in each question.*** Some people may try to ask loaded questions, trap you, or test you in order to undermine your credibility.
- ***Use evidence to support your answers whenever possible.*** Remember, facts are more convincing than opinions.
- ***Don't get involved in a long dialogue with one person.*** The rest of the staff will lose interest, and small groups will begin to hold their own "meetings."
- ***Be brief so others can ask questions and the meeting can end on time.***
- ***If you don't know the answer to a question never hesitate to say, "I don't know."*** Always add, however, that you will find out and get back to the group directly.

3. Delivery: Speaking To Inform And Inspire, Not To "Get Through" The Meeting

Your delivery style directly affects how people react to your presentation. It's not just what you say but how you say it that counts. The style you use can even determine the outcome of your ideas, suggestions, requests, recommendations, and proposals.

Before the meeting, take time to rehearse your speaking voice. If you have insecurities about getting in front of the staff with an unsure feeling or even a shaky voice, practice a few breathing exercises: Take a few long, slow, deep breaths, inhaling from your diaphragm and drawing the air up into your lungs. To exhale, let the air slowly out of your lungs, then tighten your stomach muscles to push out all the air from your diaphragm. These exercises will help you relax, and clear your mind before the meeting. While you are speaking, remember to take good deep breaths. This will prevent your voice from cracking or rising to a higher pitch.

When speaking, try to sound interesting, but natural. Use inflections in your voice so it doesn't become monotonous. Learn to avoid a lot of "uh's," "and's," and "er's." Change tone and volume to give special emphasis to your most important points. Concentrate on giving your words real meaning, instead of delivering them mechanically. After the meeting, seek feedback from the staff. You might also try tape recording the meeting and listening for areas that need improvement. Practice these techniques and you will develop a speaking style which presents you at your best.

4. Type: Vary The Meeting Style To Facilitate Effectiveness

When planning faculty or staff meetings, keep in mind the choices you have in organizational styles and time schedules. Select a type of meeting that fits the needs of the particular situation: your needs as an administrator, the needs of the staff, the need for discussion among participants, or the need to provide information. Whatever type of meeting you select, keep in mind that meetings of any kind must be meaningful for everyone in attendance or participation will not occur.

Morning
And Afternoon
Meetings

Morning meetings must stay within a strict time schedule so that staff members have enough time to get to their classrooms. You might want to suggest starting some meetings fifteen minutes before the time teachers are normally required to be at school. This allows enough time to conduct an ordinary meeting. On the days that morning meetings are held, teachers could be allowed to leave the school fifteen minutes earlier in the afternoon.

The same kind of arrangement could be used for an afternoon meeting. Set the meeting ending time for fifteen minutes after the normal staff dismissal time. Then allow the staff to leave fifteen minutes early the following day.

Dual
Meetings

Using both the morning and afternoon for one staff meeting has certain advantages. The morning session may be used to present information. The afternoon session may provide the opportunity for open discussion of the information presented in the morning meeting.

This type of meeting might cause a slight delay in reaching decisions if you allow lengthy discussions in the afternoon session. Nevertheless, the dual meeting is an excellent way to conduct business in a crisp and efficient manner in the morning with everyone present. Those who desire further discussion have the opportunity in the afternoon. An example might be the announcement of a new policy. Perhaps there is a need to gain input from the staff about how to implement the policy. It may be necessary occasionally to require everyone to return in the afternoon in order to finalize certain issues that day. Whether attended by everyone or just some of the staff, the dual meeting helps keep you within the confines of the teachers' workday.

Evening
Potluck
Meetings

Another type of faculty or staff meeting that many administrators have found effective is the potluck dinner meeting. Once or twice a year you may need to conduct a meeting that deals with one specific major issue, such as an end of the year evaluation of goals and objectives. Or you may need to have a planning session to set goals or define problems and concerns for the coming year.

Both teachers and administrators have stated that a meeting this important should not be conducted immediately after school when no one has enough time or energy to give the matter the attention it deserves. Therefore, allowing everyone to go home immediately after the students have cleared the building and to return about 6:30 p.m. for a potluck dinner and meeting has definite advantages. The staff is able to take care of family responsibilities and maybe get a little rest before tackling a major issue.

An evening meeting also allows time for studying specific issues in depth. Likewise, staff members have the opportunity to get to know one another personally and explore issues together. Too, people are fresher and more likely to be eager to face a major task—rather than want to go home from the minute the meeting begins. This type of meeting is best introduced early in the school year. It may help to obtain staff consensus when scheduling this style of meeting.

Conference
Period
Meetings

The planning or conference period meeting is best used when you desire a lot of input from small groups of staff members or from individuals. The meeting should be scheduled so that teachers come to the administrator's office during their planning periods. Other staff members, such as the librarian, should schedule themselves with the secretary for the time slot they prefer.

The purpose of the planning or conference period meeting is to meet with staff members in small groups or individually throughout the entire day to discuss certain issues. It's important that the staff receive agendas ahead of time so that they are prepared to begin discussion immediately when they get to your office.

This type of meeting can be fatiguing for the administrator, who must conduct five to six meetings in one day. But the rewards of such meetings make the effort very worthwhile. Lines of in-depth communication can be established with individual staff members—and these are lines which would have little chance to develop in larger group situations.

After-School
"Rap" Sessions

Another way to improve communications is to schedule a time after school during which the administrator can meet and talk with anyone who has concerns he or she would like to discuss. This type of meeting can neutralize staff members' negative attitudes. It is difficult for people to be negative with one another if their administrator makes himself or herself available to the staff on a regular basis. This willingness to discuss issues, explore problems, and just listen to staff has a very positive effect on people.

Department
Meetings

The department meeting, another important type of meeting, is well suited to deal with the specific needs of individual academic or interest groups. Department meetings should not be limited to just curriculum departments (social studies, music, English), but should include separate meetings for custodians, cooks, secretaries, and aides. It is important that regularly scheduled department meetings are held separately with the custodians, bus drivers, cooks, aides, and secretaries. It assures them that they are a recognized professional group and that their opinions and needs are important. Many of their suggestions can be helpful in determining policy and in working with certain students. With some students, they prove to be the best counselors and teachers in school.

Department meetings should be scheduled well in advance, and department chairpersons should submit agenda items to the administrator in advance of the meeting. This enables the administrator to determine which meetings he or she should attend or if someone else should be present at a specific meeting.

The administrator can also coordinate department meetings by getting together with the chairpersons a few days before the scheduled department meetings. An appealing format for the chairpersons' meeting is the breakfast meeting. The administrator may even want to prepare breakfast for the chairpersons, allowing adequate time for the meeting and cleanup before teachers have to be in their classrooms. Breakfast meetings can be fun and provide an opportunity for the leaders in the school to get to know one another personally as well as professionally.

**Fit
The Style
To The Purpose**

When choosing the style of staff meeting to use, you will want to consider the circumstances and the nature of the material to be covered. Each type of staff meeting—morning, afternoon, dual, evening potluck, conference period, afternoon rap session, or department—meets a specific objective. Variety adds interest, so don't limit yourself to one style.

In addition, don't decide to continue or discontinue a certain type of meeting after just one try, because you will not yet have enough valid input. Remember, after you introduce anything new to the staff, you may not get any immediate feedback, or you may hear only negative responses at first. Evaluate and make adjustments after each type of staff meeting. Then, after using one particular type of meeting several times, decide whether or not to continue that style. By striving for the most effective communication possible during each type of staff meeting you will reduce your crisis situations and enhance the team attitude of your staff.

5. *The Room: Comfortable, Nondistracting, Prepared In Advance*
The room you use for the faculty meeting also has a great effect on your presentation and the receptiveness of teachers. Here are some tips for choosing and preparing a room:

● *The room should be large enough to hold the group comfortably, but not so large as to allow the staff to spread out.* You cannot remain in control of the meeting if people are too far away from you, or from one another.

It is sometimes necessary to meet in areas that are much too large for the number of people at the meeting. But a leader should never allow meeting participants to scatter throughout a large room as they seat themselves. Under such circumstances, control of the meeting can be totally lost for several reasons. First, people can't see or hear well. Second, participation in the meeting is difficult. Third, the group will feel disjointed. Fourth, such a seating arrangement allows and encourages cliques to sit together. This is not conducive to listening because some small groups will end up holding their own private meetings, preventing adequate involvement, unity, and discussion among all participants.

● *If possible, use a windowless room.* Windows provide too many distractions. However, make sure the room is well ventilated in order to prevent drowsiness.

● *Provide refreshments if you can.* Most faculty meetings are scheduled at the end of the day and teachers are tired and ready for a break. If you can't supply food, then at least tea and coffee should be served.

Time should be allotted prior to the beginning of the meeting for staff to obtain their refreshments. Allow staff members to return to get additional refreshments during the meeting if you are comfortable with the disturbance involved. State clearly at the beginning of the meeting that they may return to get more refreshments. You will find that most staff members who do return for refreshments will do so quickly and quietly. If this is not the case, then address the issue privately with the violators.

● *Make sure all the materials and equipment you will need are in the room prior to the meeting.* There is nothing as disturbing as delaying a meeting in order to get the necessary accessories. It makes you look disorganized. Therefore, make sure *everything* you need—including a glass of water—is in the room *before* the staff begin to arrive.

● *A lectern can be useful to hold notes, but it can also create a psychological barrier between the leader and the staff.* Therefore, move away from it as much as possible. When you need your notes, stand far enough from the lectern so that your hands rest comfortably on top. Don't squeeze the sides of the lectern, which is a common practice when speakers are annoyed, nervous, intolerant, or angry. Remember, the staff will pick up on your body language—and white knuckles caused by squeezing the lectern can be revealing.

● *If you need to use a microphone, test it before the meeting to make sure all sections of the audience will hear your voice.* Don't lean into the microphone and say "Testing, one, two, three, four." Rather, simply begin by talking to the audience, not to the microphone.

● *Before people arrive for the meeting, make a final check of the room.* Make sure there is a chair for every staff member, and that tables are provided—if the staff is expected to take notes. Recheck the lighting, temperature, and cleanliness of the room.

Remember, it's the little things you do to prepare for a faculty meeting that count in both the short and long run. If you show attention to detail and consideration for the staff's physical and mental comfort, they will be more willing to attend your meetings. They may even enjoy them.

6. *The Agenda And Minutes: Important Aspects Of Faculty Meetings*

Whenever possible, an agenda of the upcoming faculty or staff meeting should be placed in staff mailboxes the afternoon prior to the meeting. The agenda allows the staff to think about the topics to be covered in the meeting. It's helpful to have extra copies of the agenda at the meeting for those who forget to bring their copies. The agenda sheet can also be used for taking notes during the meetings.

A secretary, or some other designated person, should record all action taken at the meeting and should prepare minutes of each meeting to be distributed to the staff on the following day. (See Figure 7-1.)

Too many times administrators do not prepare agendas or minutes of meetings. Preparing and distributing thorough agendas and accurate meeting minutes is a good management and internal public relations practice. In truth, it is the only effective way to operate any organization. Such practices create good meetings, clear communication, and permanent documentation. They also help keep the focus and discussions on the subject at hand. Therefore, they promote high productivity at meetings. Likewise, giving written copies of policy and procedural changes to staff members following a meeting provides for quick and easy application. Unfortunately, some administrators issue directives to staff members in faculty meetings for which there are no written records. Minutes can be a reliable source of confirmation when a staff member questions a directive or policy. Reference can be made to minutes of previous meetings to clarify decisions that were made at that time. Certainly, minutes take the pressure off everyone when it comes to remembering discussions, decisions, or policy changes.

Reviewing staff meeting minutes at the end of the school year will be a great assistance in making necessary revisions in staff handbooks for the coming year. If teacher handbooks are three-hole punched and placed in a notebook, minutes may also be placed in the same notebook. Then, all policy changes and decisions can be kept together. This practice greatly assists the staff in their record keeping.

33 PUBLIC RELATIONS IDEA

How we refer to colleagues in a meeting is important. All people should be addressed in a consistent manner. We can't call one person Mary and another Mr. Walker—and generate the relationships or feelings we want with the entire group—for obvious reasons. It's these kinds of careless communication moves which alter our effectiveness in groups. Therefore, decide before you begin a meeting, or respond in a meeting, to use a consistent approach when you address colleagues. If you do, you'll be a more successful communicator.

179

```
                        MEETING MINUTES

Date:     August 29, 1987
To:       Lancer Middle School Staff
From:     John Smith
Subject:  Staff Minutes of August 28, 1987


1.  Present:  All staff except Mr. Walker, Mrs. Smith, and Mr. Jones.

2.  Lunch Room Procedures:  A discussion was held to determine how to cut
    down on the long lines in the cafeteria.  It was determined not to change
    the procedures, but to attempt to stay on assigned room schedule for
    bringing students to lunch.

3.  Classroom Inventory:  A proposal was made to take classroom equipment
    inventories in February instead of during the last week of school.
    Everyone is so busy at the close of the school year that it's difficult
    to take an adequate inventory at that time.

    It was moved (Julie Winters) and seconded (Martha Koch) that we take
    classroom equipment inventories the first week of February.  Carried.

4.  Attendance Task Force Report:  A proposal for a change of the attendance
    policy was passed out to each member of the staff.  No action was taken,
    as the new policy is to be discussed at the next meeting.

5.  Announcements:

    5.1  All reports of weekly attendance should be turned in each Friday
         at check-out time.

    5.2  Please check your handbooks to make sure you are familiar with
         the car, motorcycle, and bicycle policies.

    5.3  The next staff meeting will be held September 14, 1987, at 3:15 p.m.

    5.4  Department chairpersons meeting in principal's office on Tuesday,
         September 10, 1987, at 3:30 p.m.

Action Taken at Staff Meeting

1.  The annual classroom equipment inventory will be taken the first week
    of February.
```

Figure 7-1

PUBLIC
RELATIONS
IDEA

To improve communication effectiveness, tell people immediately why you are talking to them. Be careful about using small talk or a beginning approach which allows "lead time." In truth, such tactics lure people away from your message. Likewise, rather than an open-ended question such as, "Are you having any problems with Jerry Smith?" Use this more direct technique: Say, "I'm having a problem with Jerry Smith; he won't stay in his seat. Are you having any problems?" You'll find that you'll create trust and get a better response if you connect the key people with the key issues and reveal both immediately.

PUBLIC
RELATIONS
IDEA

Three communication skills can improve your effectiveness. First, reinforce your spoken words by making them visually appealing on the chalkboard or an overhead projector, or with charts whenever possible. Second, remember that color adds a positive factor, while harsh lines and check marks are usually regarded as negative and turn attention away. Third, focus your appeals on the concerns of your audience. Too often, we focus attention on our needs or the requirements of the task. Both can be communication mistakes.

PUBLIC
RELATIONS
IDEA

One method of communication is to schedule opportunities throughout the year for staff members to visit with you about any concerns they may have. In addition, you can announce that you will be in a certain classroom on a particular day immediately after school to talk to anyone with a desire to visit. You may also set up individual conferences for the entire teaching and support staff at fifteen-minute intervals over a period of two weeks. Any staff member who would like to discuss anything with you may come at his or her designated time.

PUBLIC RELATIONS IDEA

The weekly bulletin is a standard means of communicating frequently with the staff. However, a bimonthly or monthly letter to the staff can be an excellent way to deliver good news as well as react to concerns expressed by the staff. The letter should deal with one particular topic or concern. For example, one issue may deal with curriculum and another with student achievement.

PUBLIC RELATIONS IDEA

Have an "open door" hour once a week during the noon hour. Let teachers and students know that this is the time they can come in and see you casually and without an appointment on a first-come, first-served basis.

School System Staff Development...
A Vital Communication And Learning Component
For Teachers And Administrators

To be successful, every organization must have a plan for encouraging and assisting employees at all levels to become more skilled and capable in the performance of their duties. School systems are not an exception to this need for a plan.

Yet in many ways, school systems are unique in their requirements for a staff development plan. Each district, and each school within each district, has needs different from other districts and other schools in some way. Schools and districts vary in the socioeconomic status of community members, in the ethnic culture of the majority of students, and in the pay scale for teachers and administrators. They face different problems depending on whether a school is in a rural, suburban, or urban area. There are different legal requirements for certification. There may be different legislative mandates for specific curriculum or testing. And because education deals with so many different populations, there are fads and trends that influence and direct staff development. In addition, many employees and administrators also have a high level of education and may believe that they are beyond the need for further enhancement of their skills.

Regardless, as any principal, superintendent, board of education, or staff development committee considers the creation of a staff development plan, there are some realities that must be acknowledged.

First, many professional employees are not convinced of the need for staff development activities. Certainly, every school system has some teachers and administrators who eagerly participate in nearly every staff development activity that is available. If none are readily available, these teachers and administrators will seek out opportunities to enhance their skills and increase their knowledge—on their own time and even at their own expense. Unfortunately, these eager learners do not constitute a majority of professional employees.

Second, it is difficult to schedule in-depth staff development activities in a school or district. Negotiations concerning salaries and work conditions in many school systems often mean that there is little time available for staff development activities—unless teachers and administrators are released from their classroom or office obligations to participate. This is not an easy arrangement.

Third, many school boards and superintendents do not have a real commitment to staff development. They are not convinced of the need for it and, as a consequence, little time and few funds are made available each year for staff development. This lack of commitment exists—despite the common knowledge that good teachers may cost more, but poor teachers cost the most.

Without question, there is only one way to ensure that children receive a quality education and that is to provide them with quality teachers. Every study that has ever been made on teachers has proved conclusively that there is nothing more significant to students' learning than the classroom teacher. Likewise, all studies prove that you can have good teachers in a school without a good principal, but you can't have a good school without a good principal. Therefore, both improvement and excellence are almost impossible without an administrative staff development priority in a school or district.

Fourth, little time is given to planning staff development activities, and many of the offerings are arbitrarily chosen—mostly on the basis of their ability to entertain, inspire, or provide a program which will fill either an identified need or a time slot on the program. Little effort is made to plan staff development activities that will help teachers and administrators to meet the needs of students, staff, parents, or the work and mission of the school system.

Even though these blocks to effective staff development exist, they can and must be overcome. Without doubt, our employees need meaningful and appropriate programs to upgrade their skills and knowledge—and to keep abreast of the latest developments in education. Our students need teachers and administrators who are continually improving their skills and knowledge. This is necessary—if we are to fulfill the mission of the schools and achieve our goals and objectives.

We *can* overcome these impediments to effective staff development programs. Although there are many ways to do so, we have outlined a step-by-step process for creating and organizing a program that will meet student, teacher, administrator, and school system needs.

A Quality
Staff Development Program
Has Three Major Components

These are the following:
1. A process to identify the skill needs of employees.
2. A process for involving employees in the creation and planning of a staff development program.
3. A procedure for making available the specific help and training programs to meet the needs of employees after those needs have been identified.

Let's examine these three components.

There are several ways you can attempt to determine the needs of employees. You can simply ask employees to list needs. Or, you can provide a list of possible training programs and then ask them to check those that appeal to them. Both of these methods are frequently used and both leave much to be desired. The major problem with the results of these types of surveys is that they do not consider the needs of the school system regarding how to improve the education of boys and girls along with the needs of the employees.

Regardless, before you schedule a single staff development activity, it is recommended that you involve employees. Any program that you expect to be successful must include employees in planning and implementation. There are many ways this may be done. Indeed, in some instances the state has established guidelines for implementing a program. Always, however, the professional employee must have a voice in selecting a program by being represented on a special staff development committee.

On the following pages is a Needs Assessment Document that is based upon the criteria of effective teaching and administrating.* It can be modified to fit the unique requirements of each school system. Or, you can use the document to make copies for each educator in your school system.

How To Use The Self-Assessment Of Teacher Or Administrator Needs (See Figure 7-2.)

In using the Self-Assessment Of Teacher Or Administrator Needs instrument, you will find that it is of most value if you follow these specific steps.

Step I: Modify the Needs Assessment Document to meet the needs of your school or district.

Although the document may be used as is to assess the needs of your professional staff since it is based upon some essential criteria for effective teaching, you may well

_____

*Information derived from the research which substantiates the curriculum for *The Master Teacher Academy.* For more information write: The Master Teacher, Leadership Lane, P.O. Box 1207, Manhattan, KS 66502.

SELF-ASSESSMENT OF (TEACHER) (ADMINISTRATOR) NEEDS

(Specifically list areas in which you would like more training.)

EFFECTIVE TEACHING
1.
2.
3.
4.

LEADERSHIP & MANAGEMENT
1.
2.
3.
4.

MOTIVATION
1.
2.
3.
4.

PUBLIC RELATIONS
1.
2.
3.
4.

CLIMATE
1.
2.
3.
4.

DISCIPLINE
1.
2.
3.
4.

Figure 7-2

SELF-ASSESSMENT OF (TEACHER) (ADMINISTRATOR) NEEDS, (cont.)

(Specifically list areas in which you would like more training.)

PROFESSIONALISM AND ETHICS
1.
2.
3.
4.

COMMUNICATION
1.
2.
3.
4.

CONFLICT MANAGEMENT
1.
2.
3.
4.

PARENT RELATIONSHIPS
1.
2.
3.
4.

GRADING AND TESTING
1.
2.
3.
4.

OTHER
1.
2.
3.
4.

Figure 7-2 (cont.)

find it advisable to make modifications in order to provide employees with an opportunity to have some input into the assessment. If you decide to modify the document there are several procedures for doing so. You may choose to do this by board and administrative directive—although this is not recommended. It is better to have the revision considered by the staff development committee or a special committee of employees convened for this specific purpose.

Step II: Orient employees to the Needs Assessment Document.

In a faculty meeting or a meeting especially called for the purpose, review briefly the Needs Assessment Document. Request that staff members study it carefully and give serious thought to their own needs as well as those of students before completing the form.

The needs assessment should be made at least once each year. The best time is in the spring, so that the implementation can begin the following school year.

Step III: Tabulate the responses.

Step IV: Decide upon the training.

After the responses have been tabulated, you will need to decide upon the training to be offered. It will not be possible to fulfill everyone's training requests immediately. You will need to decide upon a specific number of programs depending upon the number of staff members and resources of the school system. However, you should consider offering any training or educational activity which two or more staff members have requested as long as it is likely to benefit the school system.

Step V: Decide how the training will be delivered.

You need to be imaginative and flexible in ways in which you deliver the training to staff members.

Step VI: Conduct the training.

Establish times and dates for the various training programs scheduled over a two-year period.

Step VII: Evaluate the program.

Ask each participant to complete an evaluation sheet at the conclusion of the training program.

PUBLIC RELATIONS IDEA 39

All administrators should participate with the staff in all inservice sessions. Administrators should not simply introduce the speaker and then go to their offices to work. Nothing disturbs teachers more than or damages relationships as much as this common administrative error. There are very few days which we can spend working and learning with our teachers. This is one of them. And if you say, "I would like to stay, but I have (an appointment) (work I must do)," you have compounded the problem. Teachers could say the same thing—and you have automatically stated that the work you have to do is more urgent or more important than what teachers will be learning in the inservice session. Therefore, clear your calendar. Get in there on the *front row*—and let your teachers see you working to be a better educator. You gain more by this one act than you can imagine.

PUBLIC RELATIONS IDEA

Typically, when inservice and staff development activities are scheduled for teachers and administrative personnel, school board members do not attend and participate. Worse, they may not be invited. Their absence, however, makes a statement about their attitude toward teachers' needs, concerns, and improvement efforts, whether they mean to or not. On the other hand, board members' presence at inservice functions indicate that they consider the activity important and valuable enough to take time from their schedules in order to attend.

Indeed, board members' and administrators' attendance at inservice activities will help to create positive attention and involvement. It also allows a board to make several observations. First, a board can determine whether the inservice is of genuine value in meeting district goals and the needs of teachers and administrators. Second, it can provide the board member with insight into educational problems that confront teachers as they work with students. Finally, it enables the board and administration to monitor the quality of inservice programs and make necessary changes or suggestions for future programs.

It's no secret that individuals who direct inservice activities are quite vocal in their belief that the value of inservice increases in direct proportion to participation by school board members and administrators. And it cannot be denied that the full development of the staff is one of the primary functions of management. It's for these reasons that the board of education should attend inservice day activities whenever possible. Certainly, they'll enhance educational understanding and relationships with the staff if they do.

**Study
Groups**

A highly effective form of inservice meeting is the study group, in which a few staff members gather for professional study. One means of organizing study groups is to select five or six books which deal with a certain topic and to let people choose which book they would like to study. Each group should be formed on the basis of which book participants selected. Then determine when the group can meet: before school, evenings, Saturday mornings, during planning periods, during lunch periods, or after school. There should not be a set length of time the groups should meet. Rather, the group itself and the amount of material to be covered should determine the length of the study.

The study group is an opportunity for an administrator and staff to get to know one another and to increase insights and skill simultaneously. Of course, the administrator cannot be involved in all study groups. However, it is recommended that he or she participate whenever possible. The administrator who participates with the staff is demonstrating the importance of learning and communication, in terms of both professional staff growth and closer working relationships among the people of the staff. A word of caution is needed, however. Do not be concerned with the size of the groups. If only a few choose to meet, it is reason enough to get a group going. A few participants today may mean many more six months from now, when the word gets out that you are doing something significant. Be aware that you should always encourage others to participate if they have the inclination. Otherwise, your study groups may appear cliquish.

In addition, participation in study groups should not be required of the staff—and we should never indicate by attitude or action that it is. If the administrator participates and encourages others to participate in study groups, this program will grow with time. When other staff members see the enjoyment and the fellowship among members of a study group, they will be willing to venture into the next study group. Some may organize their own groups and select their own materials. Even when less than 100 percent of the staff is willing to participate, the communication skills and professional competence which emerge from study groups—as well as from the mere knowledge that they exist—will have a positive effect on everyone.

41 | PUBLIC RELATIONS IDEA

School board members and school administrators often overlook the possibility of using the leadership skills of others to motivate and encourage superior performance on the part of employees. However, they can make regular use of this idea by inviting well-known public figures to address employees just before the start of school or at midterm. The experience of one school system this past year illustrates one good and practical possibility.

The board invited the governor of the state to address employees just prior to the start of school. They specifically asked him to speak on the importance of education and the vital part that each school employee plays in the education of young people.

The governor accepted the invitation and spoke directly on the requested topic. The employees were impressed that he would take time to address them and, regardless of their political persuasion, they responded in a positive and professional way. After all, a fifteen or twenty minute talk by a governor, especially for many people who do not have an opportunity to hear, see, or meet one, can be a powerful motivator. Perhaps of equal importance is the fact that it directly involved the governor in education in a local school system. One cannot ignore the present or future possibilities of this involvement and action.

Obviously, a governor is unlikely to make very many such appearances in any given year. Yet, a school system can use the same idea to invite leaders outside the field of education to address the staff. Many of these leaders would be honored to make such appearances. And their speaking in your schools can increase employees' motivation and goodwill. Keep one important point in mind, however. Ask that they speak on a specific topic of your need or desire.

Point Out
The Benefits
Of Staff Development

Do not apologize or minimize staff development efforts or expectations. Rather, boldly and forcefully stress these points to teachers, students, staff, and the public. Here are four strong, logical, and beneficial stances to include in your public relations efforts.

1. Talk about your inservice days to your public. At the same time, however, assure the public that inservice days are not "free" days for teachers. Point out that inservice days—held only one or two days each year—are important and necessary for educators' professional growth. And tell the public that the number of inservice days is inadequate—and takes up little time in relation to the weekly efforts put forth by teachers. When we point out that teachers work to educate community members' children every week of the school year, inservice days will not produce negative public feelings or receive public criticism. Remember, there are few professionals who are not engaged in continuous learning in similar ways.

2. Remind teachers to tell students that they are studying and learning continuously too. Modeling is very important to young people. One of the worst things we, as adults, could do is to let children believe that learning ends with a formal education. Learning is a lifelong process. Educators are teachers, but they are also lifelong learners.

3. Say to parents, "We urge you to show your children that mothers and fathers have to continue learning in homes and on jobs—in order to run more efficient households." Children need to know that mothers and fathers who work are learning continually. Our children need to know that parents have to read, go back to school,

190

attend conferences and meetings, and engage in other activities to keep up-to-date professionally. Teachers are doing the same at school.

4. *Reinforce this point to all your publics: Professional growth is a necessity in work and life—including education.* To our publics we should be able to say, "The answer to increasing teacher competency clearly lies in a program of constant challenge, intense stimulation, and training that continues for a lifetime. That's why every faculty member of our school is participating in a carefully planned and precisely controlled program of staff development."

SOCIAL ACTIVITIES:
A PART OF ADMINISTRATOR-STAFF
COMMUNICATION AND INTERACTION

Think about it a minute. Have you ever had a significant relationship with anyone with whom you haven't broken bread—or whom you haven't "touched"? It's almost impossible to have a significant relationship with someone without any kind of social interaction. Herein lies the value of socializing on a personal level with your staff. However, this is one of the most difficult roles for some leaders. Functioning as the principal or central office administrator by day and then socializing after work or in the evening is something some administrators feel can't be done. It is certainly a practice that must be considered, however, if good communication and rapport are expected to develop between administrators and staff members. Many administrators fear such contact, are uncomfortable with it, and think it is a mistake. Yet, socializing can and does offer many benefits. First, socializing with the staff allows them to see you in a different role—as a human being. As a result, they will come to understand you as a person—as well as to understand your personal likes and dislikes. In turn, you will come to understand them as people as well as to understand their preferences. Unless you attend social events, staff members may only see you in the authoritative or professional role.

The staff will also have the opportunity to grow to appreciate your ability to be the administrator and colleague during the day and a friend at other times. It seems that some staff members are more willing to talk openly to administrators outside the building or outside the formal school day schedule. If you don't want to talk business in social situations, don't refuse to socialize. Rather, make it clear that you believe it is inappropriate. Simply say, "After hours, I'm Joe—not the principal," or "At social functions, Joe has no influence on the principal." If people try to "buttonhole" you at a social event, tell them to call and schedule an appointment or that you will call them.

Second, the administrator has a chance to see the staff outside of the professional setting and to meet their spouses and children. This way the administrator can gain insights into what is important to the staff, other than teaching. After all, staff members are people with personal as well as professional lives.

Without doubt, social events allow sharing of our humanness as individuals. And people who have personal regard for one another work better together. Like it or not, it's very hard to convince people that you care about them if you refuse to have anything to do with them socially. It should be noted that the teacher who sees children only in the classroom may never get to know them. If teachers want to know and understand children so as to better relate to them, they must see students in the halls, on playgrounds, in the cafeteria, at school events, and even in restrooms. Beneficial insights can be gained in all these places. As school leaders, we would be wise to see the parallel between teachers learning about children through activities outside the classroom and our learning about teachers via social events.

Suggestions For Organizing Staff Social Events...

There are several ways social events may be organized. For instance, events may be scheduled to celebrate the holiday seasons. Both dinners and breakfasts are excellent ways to get the staff together on such occasions. As a suggestion, you may celebrate by having the male staff members prepare breakfast the last day of school before Thanksgiving, and having the women prepare breakfast the last day of school before spring break.

Likewise, the principal may on occasion sponsor a "Thank Goodness It's Friday" gathering with light refreshments in the lounge. Or administrators might accompany a group of staff members to a local coffee shop on Friday evening after school for an hour.

Picnics, fishing parties, steak fries, sports events, or other activities are all ways to become better acquainted and aware of one another. Following school athletic, music, drama, or other extracurricular events, the staff and administrators can get together. Social participation by an administrator can contribute to the productivity and satisfaction of staff members, which in turn provides the opportunity for students to be the real winners in our schools.

Do not insist on setting dates so everyone can attend—it's impossible. Instead, schedule many different kinds of activities, and thus provide several opportunities for people to participate. Above all, do not pressure people to attend. Remember, you are simply having different activities for different people. You are trying to reach all your people with different activities. It's impossible to satisfy everyone with one event or get everyone to attend social functions. However, with different activities and varied communications, you can reach and be in touch with every staff member during the year.

ADMINISTRATOR←------→STUDENT

ASSEMBLIES

In schools we often have only one vehicle for bringing all the members of the student body and faculty together. This vehicle is the school assembly. Even here, however, the size of our auditorium may necessitate split assemblies. Therefore, many times our only whole-school assemblies are pep assemblies which focus on athletic events. Other times we have assemblies to focus everyone's attention on a specific subject such as alcohol and drug abuse. In either case, we know that we are bringing people together to focus on "exceptions" of school life. As beneficial as these experiences are, wouldn't it be terrific if we could incorporate the body and soul of what school life is all about into an assembly? Two principals have accomplished this feat as described below.

Monday Morning Assemblies

Every Monday morning for the past sixteen years, Todd Roberson, principal of Inverness Elementary School in Cheboygan, Michigan, has conducted an assembly with the faculty and students of his 300+ enrollment public elementary school. Why has he done it? The reasons are numerous, but his teachers say the following:

"It helps to draw the school (staff and students) together; also coordinates events and happenings of the week."

"I feel it's a great feeling of togetherness. After a weekend, we need this. Also it is reminiscent of taking time out to smell the roses."

"All students and staff are together at the same time."

"We have a feeling of 'family unit.' "

"We review the good points of school—staff and students."

"We have the chance to remind the students of the 'trouble areas.' "

"The whole school population receives positive feelings and messages from the choice of songs—and the singing itself."

"It makes the principal highly visible and is continuing evidence of his leadership."

"It's a rallying together to ready everyone as a unified body to begin the week."

"We have a positive approach to school problems or areas of concern."

"We become a family—sharing and caring about each other."

"It provides an opportunity to honor/recognize students for special feats in school and outside."

"Parents think it's a fine idea."

"Special groups can 'perform.'"

"It seems to begin the week just right."

"The students have a chance to see the principal (some children never have a chance or reason to see a principal)."

"A weekly assembly seems to get the week off to a good start and sets the tone for the week when held on Monday morning."

"This is also a good way of getting the whole school body together at once where rules, awards, announcements, etc. can be given and explained via the group. It is very definitely missed when it is not held."

"A great way to begin the week. All of us joining together as a school family. Sharing those first minutes of the week seems to set a pleasant atmosphere in our school. We miss it when we can't have the assembly."

"It sets the tone for the week. It gives the students and teachers an opportunity to feel a part of the total school environment. It reinforces values."

A sample format for a Monday morning assembly for students and staff might include:

A. Monday Morning Assembly
1. Game Scores—Girls Basketball—Weekend
2. School Song
3. "It's a Small World"—song
4. A discussion of citizenship. For instance, one topic could be cafeteria manners—such as courtesy at the service window.
5. "Learning Song"
6. "I've Been Working On My Costume"—song
7. Student Demonstration
8. Permission slips—discussion—access to art field trip
9. Thought for the week: "To win is not just having a higher score.
                            To lose is not just having a lower score."
10. One moment of meditation
11. "God Bless America"
12. Pledge

B. Other Ideas
1. A student's creative writing (read by the student)
2. Student talent (singing, rope jumping to music, gymnastics)
3. Awards (community and school)
4. Teacher-of-the-year (special assembly presentation)
5. Skits by large or small groups
6. Visiting musicians
7. Campbell Soup project (Motivation)

The format for the Monday morning assembly is put together by Mr. Roberson the prior week. Both teachers and students bring him ideas for inclusion, but he remains the final judge of the content.

Academic
Pep
Assemblies

A former Kansas high school principal successfully implemented several programs in her school, including an "Academic Pep Assembly."

At the completion of each grading period, a pep assembly is held with cheerleaders doing cheers about scholars and studies and the band playing the fight song. Speeches are made by administrators, counselors, and teachers about what's good about the school academically. Honor roll students are called onto the gym floor for recognition, cheers, and applause.

MEETINGS
WITH
STUDENTS

It's always a good idea for administrators to meet with students in both large and small groups. Too often, administrators see only those children who are discipline problems. They don't see and work with the whole student body. However, it can be extremely beneficial to break the student body into groups of 50 or 100 and visit with them at least semi-annually. Here is a format that has proved successful.

First, have all second-hour or second-grade students, for example, meet in the auditorium.

Second, relate to students those areas in which all is going well. Tell them all the things you are happy about.

Third, ask them if they have anything they might like to tell you that they like very much—and hope will be maintained.

Fourth, relate your areas of concern—and make specific recommendations to them.

Fifth, ask them to relate their concerns and questions. Give answers whenever possible. If you can, tell them when they can expect an answer—and how that answer will be delivered. Begin your next meeting with "What resulted from the previous meeting?"

Do's And Don'ts For Meeting With Students

1. *Don't*...schedule long meetings with students. If you need a lengthy period of time to discuss a subject, schedule several short meetings rather than one long one.

2. *Do*...always say something positive before you say anything negative—regardless of what you want to say to students. And never start the meeting on a sour note by introducing a negative stance without introducing a positive first.

3. *Do*...end every meeting on a positive.

4. *Don't*...be repetitious. Be very careful about repeating yourself when you're talking to students. It doesn't take young people long before they say, "I've heard this before," and turn off. When they do, they won't hear another word you say.

5. *Don't*...repeat a point that is readily accepted—or you may talk past the point of being influential.

6. *Don't*...have a meeting with young people without getting their viewpoints. If you're just going to state your side you'll miss out on getting vital information, and you'll have some students who are turned off immediately.

7. *Do*...all you can to make one and all feel welcome at a meeting. This is best done by greeting each student as he or she comes in the room. If you don't take such action, some may feel that they don't belong.

8. *Don't*...let the group feel that you have "pets" or "favorites" within the group.

9. *Do*...tell students the objective of your meeting. Some will enter the room knowing why you are meeting with them and some won't. And there may be fifty rumors regarding why you are meeting with students. Therefore, simply state your objectives before the meeting—and again in your opening statement.

10. *Don't*...lecture. Share rather than tell, request rather than demand, and try to persuade rather than order. Then you have the best chance for results.

11. *Do*...join the key students with the key issues in problem situations—and don't have students in the meeting who are not affected by what you say. In other words, never call a meeting with all students when the issue only involves or affects a selected few.

12. *Do*...appeal to what motivates students rather than appealing to your needs, to what motivates you, or to your position of authority.

13. *Don't*...be afraid to "bounce what you intend to say and how you intend to say it" off a few select students or faculty members before you begin the meeting.

14. *Don't*...use slang when talking to students.

15. *Don't*...try to be a buddy.

16. *Do*...be friendly and approachable rather than unfriendly and distant regardless of the situation. Remember, you may even get mad at what students have done—but you can't get mad at students.

17. ***Don't***...say anything to students that you wouldn't say in front of their parents.

18. ***Do***...be concerned for students' welfare rather than concerned only for your wants.

19. ***Do***...talk about opportunity rather than limitations, restrictions, and punishments.

20. ***Do***...tell students what *you* expect. Remember, people need to know what is expected of them in order to perform to standards.

21. ***Do***...let students tell you what *they* expect of you.

22. ***Do***...select a square-shaped room over a room of any other shape. Students can be seated more closely together and can see one another more easily in a square room.

23. ***Don't***...use a long room. Consciously or subconsciously, some may feel too far away from you to participate. The spread-out effect in a rectangular room makes individual participation and paying attention more difficult. A rectangular room allows students to disengage themselves from the meeting. That's when they can escape listening as well as participating.

24. ***Do***...choose a large room over one that is cramped. Physical closeness does not make a good meeting. Most important, people don't feel good or always behave well when crowded. In fact, they may act more like a mob than individuals who are responsible for their behavior. If you forget this fact, you may automatically set up a situation in which the "mob" takes on the speaker.

25. ***Don't***...seat students in a classroom or theater arrangement. It is the poorest seating arrangement you can use to conduct a meeting.

26. ***Do***...use a horseshoe arrangement for twenty-five or fewer students.

27. ***Don't***...always stand behind a lectern.

28. ***Do***...always use a circular table for small groups. This makes it easy for people to see and talk to one another.

29. ***Don't***...have more than twenty-five feet separating you from the farthest student in the group. If you do, linkage is made more difficult. Worse, you will find students doing other things during the meeting. They will only listen when they choose to listen—or they will try to make you think that they are listening.

30. ***Do***...openly and freely admit when you are wrong.

31. ***Do***...walk among the group if you can, especially while listening to questions, responses, or discussions. It can make the entire group more alert and encourage those who have stopped participating.

32. ***Do***...get back to the group to cover unanswered questions.

33. ***Don't***...stand much higher than the audience. In addition, don't use a raised platform or a lectern. Both increase the psychological distance between you and the audience and inhibit discussion as well as identification with you. If possible, don't put any physical object between you and the group.

34. ***Don't***...feel you must always make a decision on the spot. But you do have to reveal a date or time when your decision can be expected.

35. ***Do***...place a small table at the top of the "U" for the person talking. However, use a table, not a lectern.

36. ***Don't***...ever say that some input is not admissible.

37. ***Do***...make sure students do not have to strain to see anything, including you. If students have to strain, they will sit back, relax, and detach themselves from the meeting in a short period of time.

38. ***Do***...make good questions out of poor ones—and never "put down" a question.

39. ***Do***...thank students for attending the meeting.

40. ***Do***...thank students for giving their time and interest to the meeting.

41. ***Do***...commend individuals in specific ways whenever you can.

ADMINISTRATOR◄-------►SUPPORT STAFF

**Effecting
Performance**

School objectives are difficult to establish, much less accomplish, unless a staff is united in philosophy and action. That's why staff unity must be all-inclusive—from custodian to teacher. And unity can't be achieved by putting administrators in another classification either. The staff includes everybody. Remember, when people are excluded, they act and react differently toward objectives and work—and toward one another. Mostly, they are placed in a position where they are almost forced to think and act alone. They seldom feel good no matter where they are or whom they are with. Trust is nonexistent and suspicion is likely to become everyone's companion. For these reasons and more, it is almost impossible for the excluded persons to operate to the highest level of their ability. This is true whether the person excluded is a secretary, a cook, an aide, a nurse, a teacher, or an administrator.

When staff unity is void, we must all assume responsibility for any deficiency revealed by one of our partners in work. Young people probably suffer the most when staff unity is lacking, but administrators run a close second behind them. Putting out brush fires and mending fences between personalities consume the majority of administrators' time. Worse, administrators are likely to be blamed for every woe and looked upon as the obstacle which prevents the success of any undertaking.

We can begin effecting staff unity by accepting and appreciating those with whom we work and the roles they play in the work and mission of the school, and by showing that appreciation. In addition, we can show professional respect by encouraging and allowing each school worker to fulfill his or her need to belong as well as his or her need for self-actualization. This cannot be done unless we know and value each person and the work he or she does. We can continue promoting unity by never talking "out of school" about people and the work they do. Such behavior is disunity revealed via total disrespect. We should always remember that when we criticize the things people do, we criticize those people. Therefore, we should refrain from second-guessing people— whether it's the way the floors are cleaned, the way a meal is prepared, or the resources a teacher chooses for teaching a unit. These are private matters which demand private counsel with the parties involved—not discussion with a third party or with any ear that will listen. Remember, when we criticize one person publicly, we may be seen as condemning all publicly. And it will certainly be recognized quickly that if we will criticize one publicly, we will criticize *any* publicly.

The wise administrator knows that how the members of a family disagree privately is one thing. How they disagree publicly is quite another. What family members can do together is limitless—because they have one another. The only thing they can do alone is go in different directions, sometimes destroying the whole in the process. That's something we can't do if we are members or the leader of a school team. When we do, we do so at the expense of students—and maybe even the entire organization.

Helping
The Support Staff
Feel Appreciated

One of the most important ingredients in establishing good internal public relations and getting productivity from support personnel is to let them know that they have administrative respect and that they provide a valuable service to meeting the needs of students—and helping educators get the work of the school accomplished. The best way to let support staff know this is by extending to them our cooperation and help in doing their jobs. This is one way we, as administrators, actually prove that we consider support personnel important as people, and that we consider the jobs they perform important, also.

Certainly, it should not get to the point that "the tail is wagging the dog." The support staff do not and cannot run the school. They can't, for instance, be allowed to clean rooms when they want to. Rooms must be cleaned when they aren't being used by teachers or students. Neither can secretaries dominate to the point that the office becomes secretary-centered rather than student-centered. They should perform a service that takes care of all school needs first, not their own needs. Then, the education of children can take place. Therefore, you have to be careful as the administrator to do the leading—and make sure that *you* decide when things are done and how they are to be done so that they agree with the work objectives and mission of the school.

One of the ways we can bring support staff into the mission is by treating them as full-fledged members of the total professional team. This doesn't mean that support staff should take over in the faculty lounge. But neither does it mean that they should be excluded from the lounge. We can't provide a lounge for teachers while restricting custodians to the boiler room and expect to generate good internal relations. Rather, the lounge should be a place where all people who work in a school gather to relax, rejuvenate, and recharge. It's a sanctuary. Therefore, we must determine whether or not we really consider the support staff in the terms we should. If teachers don't want them included, we need to ask why. It might be that they don't want support staff to hear certain conversations—conversations that should not occur in the lounge, regardless of who is present.

You can't exclude people purposely at certain times and include them at other times, however. Juggling acts simply don't work. For best results, therefore, we need to include every person on our staff at all our functions. This means begining-of- and end-of-school celebrations, inservice days, social functions, retirement parties, and recognition events should include the support staff. They work in a school daily. We work with them and rely upon them each day. If we want them to share in the objectives, work goals, and mission of our school, they need to be included. This means invitations are in order. Therefore, we may need to discuss this issue with our faculty and make some definite decisions about how we should collectively include the support staff.

The Administrator
Should Meet
With The Support Staff Regularly

It's very important for an administrator to meet with the support staff both formally and informally. It's vital that we don't restrict our meetings to a formal style or a one-on-one format. If we have a superintendent of buildings and grounds, it is vitally important that we develop a close and compatible relationship with him or her. Regardless, the principal might sit down and have a cup of coffee with the custodian during the custodian's breaktime. This can be a time to praise, get input, and make some suggestions. We can ask, "How are things going?" as well as ask questions regarding areas about which we are concerned. This should be done in a positive way without criticizing. Likewise, the administrator can have similar conversations with cooks in the cafeteria and playground supervisors on the playground.

Administrators should perceive the support staff as extremely important parts of the total educational program. If you keep this perspective, you can get your support staff to keep a positive attitude and to work with high standards in mind instead of just trying to get through each day. When administrators make the support staff feel like a part of the team, the support staff will take pride in their school and their work will show it. The truth of the matter is that we can't function without them.

Faculty Meetings:
A Place
For Support Staff As Well

In many schools, there is disagreement about who should attend faculty meetings. Some feel such meetings should be only what the name implies, a meeting for members of the faculty. But if you wish to obtain greater cooperation from everyone in a building or district, the faculty meeting should become a meeting with the entire staff.

Meetings concerning the general operation of the school or district should be called *staff meetings* and include everyone who is part of that operation. This means that teachers and professional support staff such as the school psychologist, social workers, speech therapists, secretaries, aides, custodians, bus drivers, and cooks should attend staff meetings.

The reason for involving all staff members is to gain their cooperation to accomplish the work of the school. In fact, if you want nurses, custodians, secretaries, and cooks to support decisions made on building policy, scheduling, activities, procedures, building maintenance, discipline, or energy conservation, you must include them. If they don't attend such meetings, staff members will not know what the work of the school is. Those who aren't included are often among the greatest critics of teachers and administrators.

This management stance helps all personnel understand why certain decisions are made, and helps them feel included in the decision-making process. Remember, people who are involved in the decision-making process are more apt to carry out those decisions. People who can only say, "I do as I am told" don't make good workers or colleagues. Support staff are supposed to support, but we must put them in a position to do so.

Another reason a feeling of involvement as well as actual participation on the part of these staff members is important is that they often speak about the school and district to the rest of the community. Too often, we allow noncertified staff to represent the school in the community without giving them adequate information to present a situation correctly or represent the schools in which they work. And remember, the very fact that they are working in the schools means they have information about students, teachers, administrators, other personnel, or incidents. But, they may not know what to say and what not to say to the public when that public asks them questions. As a result, they often say too much or too little, or give the wrong information. Thus, in most cases, the administrator who chooses to ignore the noncertified staff when imparting information of all types makes a management and leadership error. Both the operation of the school and the positive public relations may be hindered as a result.

Secretaries work with staff, parents, and students daily. It's necessary that they understand policy changes, directives, and other decisions that affect people with whom they might work. Having secretaries attend staff meetings saves the administrator from having to conduct a second meeting with the office staff. Secretaries are usually asked to be the primary managers of reports and inventories, and to perform other necessary duties for the administrator. Their absence from staff meetings may lead to confusion or misunderstanding, and thereby directly affect teacher-administrator or teacher-secretary relationships.

Cooks also interact with staff and students daily. Many cooks, in fact, establish a fine rapport with students. During conversations, many students express their concerns to the cooks. When the cooks are informed about the operations of the school in a straightforward manner, they can give accurate answers to students' questions.

By keeping all staff members well informed, we can ensure that they will feel a part of the educational team. They will all support each other. That's why, when it comes to staff meetings, we would do well to remember that the best management stance to take is to make sure the "staff" includes everyone, and not just some of the people who work in the school.

"I Have A Problem...
What Can We Do About It?"

Too often we feel we have to provide all the answers when we deal with noncertified staff. Fortunately, such is not the case.

When approaching noncertified staff, instead of telling them what to do we should say, "I have a problem...what can we do about it?" Letting the support staff members decide how to handle problems will improve administrator/staff relationships by 1,000 percent. It's probably the most important technique for dealing successfully with people in any work.

Good internal public relations is not built by telling people what to do—or having all the answers yourself. Rather, it is created by bringing people into your orbit and getting them "tuned in" to what needs to be done. That's why the principal who will call a support staff member and say, "Hey, Al, I have a problem...what can we do to take care of it?" may get the best response. The support staff member may immediately think, "Hey, this guy needs help. I am going to get in there and help him." But if the principal calls and says "Al, *you* have a problem...when are you going to take care of it?" the response is predictable. The support staff member will become defensive. He may not want to, but he will.

The Role
Of Support Staff
In A Crisis

A close look will reveal that more often than not, support staff members are the ones closest when a crisis situation occurs in the building, especially when that crisis involves children. Support staff members see students everywhere in the building as well as on the campus. Often they get to know students in ways that teachers don't. Some custodians, cooks, and secretaries are even our best counselors and problem preventers. These same people also handle crisis situations unbelievably well. In fact, some can get results that no other adult could get. But a school needs to have policies stating that if a support staff member has to step in to prevent a person from being hurt, he or she should do it. As workers in the school, these personnel need specific teaching and policies in this regard. If they don't receive proper coaching, they may ignore problems or take inappropriate action.

Remember, support staff who really deal well with most people in life deal well with students. They can make valuable contributions to the functions of the school in addition to their daily work. We need to utilize them properly. The needs of the school are too many to overlook this valuable resource. And when we utilize these staff members to their fullest, we will make a better school—and a better public relations program.

PUBLIC RELATIONS IDEA

Staff Meeting #1

In a staff meeting, preferably at the beginning of the school year, hand out a 3-inch-by-5-inch card to each of your teachers and members of your support staff. Ask them to put their names on the cards and then answer three questions.

1. If I could predetermine what my professional image would be this year, *students* would think of me as _____ and _____.
   (adjective)   (adjective)

2. If I could predetermine what my professional image would be this year, *colleagues* would think of me as _____ and _____.
   (adjective)   (adjective)

3. If I could predetermine what my professional image would be this year, the *community* would think of me as _____ and _____.
   (adjective)   (adjective)

Then on a blackboard, list the results (noting the duplications). Example:

...Students	...Colleagues	...Community
Caring (25)	Professional (23)	Professional (16)
Supporting (12)	Knowledgeable (17)	Fair (13)
Knowledgeable (18)	Friendly (20)	Good Educator (10)
Disciplinarian (10)	Having Character (18)	Knowledgeable (10)
Fair (19)	Dutiful (6)	Important (12)
Accepting (4)	Honest (4)	Caring (15)
Principled (14)	Charismatic (4)	Trustworthy (14)
Dependable (13)	Loyal (14)	Competent (20)
Competent (20)	Competent (24)	

Teachers and support staff members will be very interested in how their colleagues wish to appear. For many, it will be the first time they have ever even thought about it. This is true even though they may be very satisfied with the image that they have with students, staff, and other community members. Asking people how they want to appear gets to the heart of the matter concerning what they want to achieve much faster than asking them what their goals are. This is due to the fact that stating goals causes people to concern themselves with objective things. Stating how they want to *appear* causes people to deal with subjective and emotional matters. Most often it's problems with how people appear that cause them not to achieve their objective goals.

The next step is to determine the top five or six adjectives in each category. (You will, however, want to save the entire listing. A poster with this information on it can be posted in the lounge and will serve as a great reminder to the staff of how *they* determined the way *they* wanted to appear.)

Once the top five or six traits have been established, the listing in each category would appear as follows:

...Students	...Teachers	...Community
1. Caring	1. Competent	1. Competent
2. Competent	2. Professional	2. Professional
3. Fair	3. Friendly	3. Caring
4. Knowledgeable	4. Having Character	4. Trustworthy
5. Principled	5. Knowledgeable	5. Fair
6. Dependable	6. Loyal	6. Important

Then, split the staff up into groups of no more than five staff members. Their task is to brainstorm ideas about how they can achieve their desired image through their:

Attitudes; Actions; Behaviors; and Accomplishments. Depending on the number of participating staff members each group could brainstorm one, two, or all four categories.

List all the results. This is not the time to make judgments about which ideas are good and which aren't.

Staff Meeting #2

At the next staff meeting, you and staff collectively are going to determine which ideas you will tackle for this school year. To do this, list on the blackboard under the appropriate category (students, teachers, community) all the ideas resulting from last meeting's brainstorming. Then, again hand out 3-inch-by-5-inch cards to your staff members and have them list their favorite two in each category. Then, tally these results. The voted favorites may represent the priority projects for the year.

Next, ask each teacher to sign up for a committee that will be responsible for executing one idea. With this action your teachers have a plan which includes steps of action. However, don't cast aside the entire list of ideas that your teachers brainstormed just because you have the time to execute only a few. This list is perfect to use as a starting point next year. Remember, each year you should attempt to build onto your current plan and strengthen your public relations image and effort.

The chain reaction of shared participation in education is enormous. When teachers and support staff accept one another and don't feel they have special territory to protect, team spirit can thrive. It's when educators share in positive ways that we can get the work of education done in total and healthy ways. The beneficiaries are students and staff alike.

We must realize that how we manage to come to such a point results out of mutual trust. When we fuse mutual trust with the intangibles of accepting, supporting, and giving, we come out with something called team spirit. As we all know well, with team spirit the whole school system is a functional unit and better learning is the result. We must constantly be aware that it's the team union that allows us to do together what we will never be able to do alone—and find greater fulfillment in the process. This is the inside and outside benefit of a strong public relations effort. Not only does the organization benefit, each individual does too.

**The School Secretary—
Your Best Public Relations Agent With Parents**

The following true story from a parent relates the role of the school secretary as one of your school's best public relations agents.

"I got a call from Mrs. Moser, the school secretary at my daughter, Sara's, school. Sara had forgotten her lunch money for the second day in a row. Could I come down and give them a check? Well, as it happened, I couldn't. I was scheduled tight with meetings that morning. So I asked if she could please see to it that Sara was fed and I would send a check the next day. Mrs. Moser was very agreeable. We had been in this bind several times before. But, of course, the next day in the bustle of leaving home in the morning, I forgot to write the check. When I arrived at work I was greeted with a message that said my frantic daughter had called. I didn't even need to ask why. I immediately called Mrs. Moser. Not having the courage to ask for another day's extension, I said I would deliver a check that morning—I asked that she communicate that message to my daughter. Mrs. Moser assured me that she would.

"Later that morning I came to the office to deliver the check. There were few words exchanged between us, but I was warmed by Mrs. Moser's welcoming, knowing smile. There was no message from her that even intimated that she was thinking, 'I hope this doesn't happen again,' or 'You're not doing much to build responsibility in your household, are you?' Rather, I got the feeling that Mrs. Moser knew that it probably *would* happen again and, what's more, that it was OK. I thought to myself, 'How nice for the children to have such an advocate on their behalf...a giant who is a noncritical helper...a person in their school life who isn't there to evaluate them or their parents—just as a facilitator for both.'

"I know we will have many occasions when we will need to communicate something to or through Mrs. Moser over the years. Sara will be sick. We will need to reschedule our parent-teacher conference, or Sara will get sick at school and we will need to pick her up; and, yes she will forget her lunch money again.

"It's reassuring to know that we will be talking to someone who will accurately communicate any message we leave for our child. And because of this we feel safe—and so does our daughter."

The truth of the matter is that school secretaries may see and hear from more parents than any other adult employed by the school system. As a result, they have the power to make or break the image that parents and other community members have of the school. Secretaries type the letters, answer the phone, make and screen appointments, file privileged information, collect money, notify parents for children, notify children for parents, and much more. The list is endless. Therefore, an administrator's relationship with his or her secretary is a critical one. The next few pages contain specific steps an administrator can take with a secretary to improve general communication with the public at large.

First, ask yourself some questions:
1. Does my secretary like children?
2. Is my secretary patient?
3. Does my secretary have a good telephone voice?
4. Does my secretary have the ability to deal with all types of parents?

An Overlooked Asset...
As Part Of The Team

Few members of the school team realize or appreciate the true value and importance of the school secretary. However, in an ordinary day, most secretaries will have direct contact with more children, will serve more teachers, and will talk to more parents than any other member of the staff. Their ability to handle the clerical needs—as well as human needs—of a school is of critical importance in determining the success of the institution. Their every action is a reflection of the school's proficiency. The professional attitude they project mirrors the attitudes of children, teachers, and administrators alike.

The good secretary knows that her role in the work of the school is to aid administrators and teachers to achieve their educational goals. Though she may work mostly with administrators, she does indeed work with and represent every member of the staff. During the school day the secretary is the agent for all school employees. She will receive all incoming telephone calls. Announcements, visitors, daily schedule changes, and teachers' messages are all routed through her desk. She may even type letters and tests for teachers. Those professional teachers who don't join hands and form a partnership with the school secretary are shortsighted. They are overlooking one of the school's most important assets.

A
Unique
Position...

The school secretary has a very difficult job and is in a unique position. Secretaries practice their profession as a minority within another profession. As professionals, they must adapt their skills to meet the needs of another profession completely. They are even expected to be as knowledgeable about the profession they serve as they are about their own.

Teachers must realize that secretaries are also "uniquely informed." Many times they know more about "what's going on" than most people in a school. They may even know the strengths and weaknesses of individual teachers as well as anyone. They have access to confidential information. They must. It is part of their work and their responsibility.

Secretaries, too, must be totally conscious that they represent every teacher on the staff in addition to fulfilling their regular secretarial duties. They must be completely loyal to each teacher individually and to the staff as a whole. This is a must! But it can also be very difficult, especially if the teaching staff does not treat the secretaries with equal loyalty and professional respect.

**Meeting
Our
Expectations**

Amid the hectic and exhausting routine of a normal day in school, teachers and administrators alike expect the secretaries to remain calm and efficient. We expect them to be totally involved with the work of the school and committed to the needs of the children. We expect them to be kind, courteous, and polite to everyone they encounter. They are expected to be as professional with the irate parents as they are with the teacher who attempts to "boss them around." We expect them to be as mannerly with the discipline problem waiting to see a principal or counselor as they are with the teacher who is mad because a telephone message was not delivered to him or her personally. We expect all these things and more—and rightly so. A professional secretary will be all these things—if she is good.

These competencies should also be valued, appreciated, and acknowledged by every member of the school team. If they are not, there isn't one secretary in a thousand who can do a competent job in meeting the needs of the schools and at the same time meet all of our expectations. The work load is simply too heavy to bear if an unfriendly teacher-secretary climate exists. Remember, with the tightness of money in schools today, clerical staffs have been "cut to the bone." The amount of paperwork and correspondence in schools today is staggering. Without extended appreciation, the rewards for the secretary are too small.

The effective administrator knows that many teachers fail to appreciate the contribution of secretaries to the school effort. In fact, many teachers think secretaries are "too influential" or "know too much," and teachers may resent their knowledge of privileged information. However, the good administrator knows it is not the privileged information secretaries know that is important, but rather *how* the secretary protects that information. A wise administrator understands that the knowledge of information is inherent in a secretary's duties in the same degree as the confidentiality to protect it is her responsibility.

The good administrator expects professional excellence from a secretary. He or she expects the secretary's efficiency, disposition, and maturity to strengthen the school team. But the good administrator also acknowledges the secretary's work as professional and extends to the secretary the same courtesies, loyalties, and respect that the administrator demands of her. That's why the effective administrator and the secretary are partners on the school team.*

---

*Positive help for your support staff is available through *The 5-in-1 Monthly Inservice Program for Support Staff*. For more information, contact The Master Teacher, Leadership Lane, P.O. Box 1207, Manhattan, Kansas 66502; (913) 539-0555.

WHEN THE PUBLIC CALLS—
A TELEPHONE POLICY FOR SCHOOLS

The telephone can be the friend or foe of the school. It depends upon the skill of the secretary who is seen, not through the eyes, but through the ears of each person who calls the school. Therefore, the secretary must be a master of telephone technique. Both the secretary's voice and manner should reflect an image of competency, efficiency, and a friendly willingness to serve. The following is a suggested telephone policy for a school or district. It is written for the professional secretary in the hope that it will assist the secretary in reaching a goal of excellence. We urge administrators to adopt the following telephone policy and give a copy to every secretary. Then, give a copy to teachers, because all the rules apply to them when they are talking on the telephone.

Telephone Policy
For XYZ Schools:
An Image Of Excellence

We say the telephone is either a friend or foe of the school because the personality and image projected on the telephone generate good feelings, bad feelings, or no feelings at all. If it's either of the latter, then you have not made this most used communication device work to your benefit.

The image you project on the telephone depends upon the skill of the secretary. People who call the school, regardless of the reason, make judgments about the entire school and the people who work in the school based on their experience with the secretary on the telephone.

Most People Come To School By Sound...Not By Sight

Professional secretaries need to understand the importance of each of the following guidelines. They need to recognize the reality that, individually and collectively, these guidelines project the image to each caller that the secretary either knows how important she is in conveying a friendly, caring, and competent image about the school, or she doesn't. And secretaries should be twice as aware of this fact because the vast majority of people who contact the school will never come through the school doors. They will form opinions by what they hear—not what they see. Their total school experience is by sound rather than sight. That's why the professional secretary must master the following techniques.

Answering Promptly Is A Necessity

No one likes to wait. By giving prompt attention to the caller, you get off to a good start. Answer at the end of the *first* ring. Be ready to talk to the caller as soon as you pick up the receiver. Speak directly into the telephone in a normal, conversational tone of voice.

Hold the mouthpiece about an inch from your lips. Be sure that you enunciate clearly. If you do not use this technique, you will not be heard. Therefore, stop what you are doing when answering the telephone. Give the caller your full attention and skill. Make no mistake: You can't do something else while you're talking on the telephone and expect to give the caller courteous service, even if he or she can't see what you are doing. You might be surprised how often a caller can "feel" your divided attention.

Identification Must Precede Conversation

A telephone conversation cannot really begin until the caller knows he or she has reached the right place. For the most favorable results, calls should be received in a school or district as follows:

"Good morning/afternoon, Roosevelt School, may I help you?" Do not say "Can I help you?" You *are* physically able; therefore, "can" is grammatically incorrect and reflects poorly upon your school.

Receiving Calls Graciously

If the person whom the caller asks for is in the office, transfer the call immediately. If your administrator wishes, you may ask, "May I tell Mr. Smith who's calling?" However, this must never be done if Mr. Smith is not in the office, unless Mr. Smith's absence has already been revealed to the caller. Never insist that a name be given if the caller doesn't want to give it.

When A Staff Member Is Unavailable

Many times an administrator or a staff member may be in the office, but unable to take a call at the moment. Since the caller cannot see what is happening in the office, give a sufficient explanation such as: "I am sorry, Mr. Smith is talking on another line," or "I'm sorry, Mr. Walker is talking to a student."

Then, offer the caller a choice, such as: "Do you wish to wait, or may I ask Mr. Smith to call you?" Never, under any circumstances, should a caller automatically be placed on hold or not given an explanation regarding why a person is not answering the call. Remember, people don't like to wait—and waiting on a dead line is likely to make them irritable or even angry.

When An Administrator Is Out Of The Office

A secretary should never tell callers that she doesn't know where an administrator is or that an administrator is out of the office "for coffee" or some similar reason. The image projected by such statements is never a favorable one. Therefore, give one of the following explanations. An administrator or staff member is either:

1. In conference.
2. Visiting classrooms.
3. Working with students.
4. Out of the office on school business and expected to return at (time).
5. Out of town on school business and expected to return at (time and day). Please note that whenever a staff member leaves the office, he or she should tell the destination and time of expected arrival back in the office. However, the wise secretary should ask an administrator, "May I tell your callers what time you will be back?"

In addition, when an administrator is not in the office, the secretary should attempt to:

1. Get the name of the caller.
2. Get the number where the caller may be reached.
3. Determine if anything can be done for the caller in the meantime.

The Use Of Titles Is Vitally Important

When speaking on the telephone, always address callers with their proper titles, such as: Mr., Ms., Miss, Mrs., Reverend, Sister, or Doctor. Be both formal and as polite as possible. Failure to use a proper title is a mistake, regardless of how well you know the caller. Remember, you are always safe using titles. Without them, you may be on thin ice.

Take Messages Accurately

Taking accurate messages reduces the number of times a caller must call back and promotes caller satisfaction. Keep a pad and pencil readily available for taking messages.

Request rather than demand information from a caller. For instance, you may say, "May I tell Mr. Smith you called?"

Get complete *details* and *repeat the information* to make sure it is correct. Remember, if you don't repeat information, you increase the probability that your information will not be completely correct. That's why you may have to spell names back to the caller rather than just pronounce them.

Handle Complaints Tactfully, Pleasantly,...And Professionally

Remember, you speak as the personal representative of your school. Never forget this fact. A good reputation is founded on a pleasant, competent, and helpful attitude. It is not founded on passing blame or on lack of knowledge.

Be a good listener. Remain calm and friendly regardless of what the caller says. Remember, only you can make yourself angry. And never, under any circumstances, should you act aloof or distant. In addition, don't take the matter personally. React professionally, and remember that people want one thing when they complain—action. If you don't have the authority to act, then make the caller a promise. Promise that you will cover the issue with someone who can resolve it and that you or the person in authority will get back to the caller within a specified time.

Never forget to apologize for mistakes. Simply say, "I am sorry that happened." Never be defensive; rather, be ready to offer assistance. If the complaint is of a serious nature, refer the call to your administrator. Always ask the caller, "Would you please talk to Mr. Smith because he will want to know about this immediately?"

Leaving The Telephone Momentarily

Avoid saying, "Just a minute," or "Hold on," because people simply don't like it. Some hate it. If you must leave the line, always explain why. You should say, "Will you hold the line, please, while I look that up?" Then wait for an answer and say, "Thank you."

If it will take some time to get the information, offer to call the caller back. If you discover, while looking up information, that it's going to take longer than you thought, return to the line and report to the caller. "I'm still checking on that. Will you wait further, or may I call you back?"

Always thank the caller for his or her patience before and after he or she must wait.

Plan Outgoing Calls

Be sure you have the correct telephone number. Keep handy an up-to-date list of the numbers you call frequently. Call information only if the telephone number is not on your personal list or in the telephone directory. Never, under any circumstances, should you have the receiver to your ear while you are looking up a telephone number. Do not pick up a receiver and tie up a line until you are ready to dial.

Intercom

Remember that on many school telephone intercom systems, if the telephone is not cut off or on hold, a caller may hear any conversation you are having within the office. Therefore, check the hold button before you say anything. Choose your words carefully, or your actions may be among your most unprofessional.

Reflect Personality

The picture you create over the telephone is formed entirely by what you say and how you say it. As harsh as it sounds, most people aren't good on the telephone because they aren't trying to be. In truth, if you're not getting a great number of compliments regarding how good you are on the telephone, then you're not very good. That's because when we experience people who are good on the telephone, it sticks with us. And we'll tell them how good we think they are at some point. You can acquire a good telephone personality by thoughtful consideration of the following items:

Express personal and empathetic overtones: You can reflect a good telephone personality by:

1. Extending courtesy.
2. Expressing a sincere interest in the caller and his or her needs.
3. Assuming the caller's point of view.
4. Revealing a desire to help—openly and freely.

Be heard clearly. A normal conversational tone of voice—neither too loud nor too soft—carries best over the telephone. If you have a soft voice, the majority of what you say is not being heard.

Speak distinctly. Distinct speech is essential, since the listener can neither read your lips nor see your expressions. Failure to move lips, tongue, and jaw flexibly may block the sounds being made. This will result in slurred speech instead of crisp, decisive speech. Remember, clear speech is interpreted as a sign of competence.

Talk at an appropriate pace. A moderate rate of speech is the most easily understood. However, the pace of speech should be related to the ideas being expressed. The following information should be given more deliberately:

- Technical information
- Lists
- Information that the listener is writing down
- Numbers
- Names
- Educational language

Choose the right word. Your ideas should always be expressed as simply as possible. Never try to impress a caller with your vocabulary. Use descriptive words where appropriate. Technical, cumbersome, and unnecessarily long words may confuse the other person and may require explanation or even cause misunderstanding. Avoid slang because it has no place in a school office.

Tune the voice. Variety and flexibility in the voice can help to convey the mood and attitude of your office. Variety and flexibility can be gained through pitch, inflection, and emphasis.

Pitch. A low-pitched voice carries best, especially over the telephone. It is much kinder to the listener's ear. High-pitched voices tend to become shrill and irritating.

Inflection. Inflection—or the rise and fall of your voice—not only helps convey your thoughts but also adds personality to your voice. A monotonous voice may show lack of interest because it is flat and lacks spirit. We are in a very exciting business, and your voice should show this spirit.

Emphasis. The stress or emphasis placed on words, or groups of words, may change the meaning of what is said. A thoughtful use of emphasis will also help to give flexibility.

End Calls Pleasantly

Leave a lasting, favorable impression. Always express appreciation for the call and add "Goodbye," plus the person's name, if known. Say, "Thank you for calling. Goodbye Mr. Smith." If the call was for information or in regard to a problem, thank the caller for taking the time to call, and express your willingness to handle calls any time there is a concern or problem. It's very important for a caller to realize that his or her call is welcome, no matter what the reason. Remember, many people do not feel welcome to call the school. Rather, they feel they are intruding.

Finally, Replace The Receiver Gently After The Caller Has Hung Up

If you can, listen for the caller to hang up first. You are trying to end the call without the caller hearing the "clang" of your hanging up first.

Self-Evaluation

The telephone is one of the school's most important vehicles of communication. Every time you receive a call, you have met someone, and he or she has met you and visited your office. And the person "sees" you and your school by the way you handle yourself on the telephone.

Your courtesy, friendliness, attitude, neatness—the efficiency of your entire school—will be measured each time a patron of the school calls. You will be judged every time that patron hangs up the telephone. That's why your professional *consistency* is a *must*.

As part of your self-evaluation, ask yourself the following questions on a regular basis:

1. What are my telephone strengths?
2. What are my telephone weaknesses?
3. What am I doing to correct those weaknesses?

Your answers determine not only how good you are on the telephone. They also determine how good you intend to be. Hopefully, you'll decide to be the best.

The team concept in the school means that everyone in the school—custodians, cooks, secretaries, teachers, students, counselors, aides, and administrators—works together to promote the mission of the school. If we are going to be effective in our public relations, everyone on the team should be inserviced about the use of the telephone and reception of visitors.

TEACHER←--------→STUDENT

The Four Relationships Of Students
"Student and Self"
"Student and Teacher"
"Student and Classroom Activities"
"Student and Peers"

The formulation of a student's mental health in school is, without doubt, the result of at least four relationships. That's why these four relationships should be prime considerations in your public relations effort. As a primary instrument for the development and fulfillment of these relationships, a teacher can never forget—even for a moment—that the student is the common element in all of them. Too, these relationships cannot be separated, for they are interrelated—and this must be the focus for teacher emphasis. The real question is, "How does a classroom teacher relate to students as they function within these four relationships?"

The
Student
And Self

First, a teacher can begin helping a child by not "writing a child off" because of behavior, achievement, or personality. Too often, we "size up kids" on the first day of school. How often have you heard someone say, "I've got his number"? Impossible! When we say this, we have stepped out of the arena of diagnostician and into that of prejudger. This is a mistake, for teacher and child alike.

Never forget that a student comes to the classroom with five to eighteen years to think about who he or she is, what he or she is, and what he or she wants to be. The role of teachers is not to view students through teachers' eyes. Rather, it is to view students as *they* see themselves. This is the key to understanding student behavior. It is the only thing that allows a teacher to detect truth.

When we size up students, and then proceed, we usually proceed in the wrong direction. Failure to view children as they see themselves causes teachers to put those children in positions—within each of their four relationships—with which they can't deal. The most drastic example of this mistake is the student who displays a change in behavior that shocks us. How many times have you heard someone say, "Joan was such a nice girl. She had everything going for her. What happened?" One thing happened for sure. Somebody did not see Joan as she saw herself. Had someone been alert enough to recognize how Joan felt about herself, maybe "what happened" wouldn't have happened.

There are students sitting in our classrooms whom we don't know. It's time to begin finding out how they view themselves. Then, and only then, can individualized instruction have any real meaning.

Student-Teacher
Relationships

Teachers must elevate their thinking regarding the student-teacher relationship. Many teachers' thoughts include, "How can I get along with students, and how can students get along with me?" Needless to say, the emphasis is generally on the latter.

Never overlook the fact that students do not come to class liking the teacher nor does every teacher automatically like every student. But all students do enter class, consciously or subconsciously, looking for help. A teacher's responsibility is to give it. Teachers' problems begin when, for one reason or another, they deny that help. And there are many ways to deny a child the student-teacher relationship which is necessary for sound mental health. Usually teachers deny students this relationship by what teachers are or are not doing, such as ignoring students' questions, failing to keep appointments, or classifying students' interests as trivial. Teachers need only to review

3. If I could have my wish, my *parents* would think of me as

_____ and _____ .
        (adjective)   (adjective)

Students should be told that their sheets will remain private, and that you will share with them the combined reactions, but not individual ones. Most children would not be able to share these feelings out loud to their peers.

Then tally their replies. Example:

...*Friends*	...*Teachers*	...*Parents*
Fun	Smart	Smart
Popular	Well-behaved	Well-behaved
Honest	Good Worker	Good Student
Smart	Neat	Loving
	Helpful	
	Happy	

Share the total responses with the entire class. Then brainstorm with the class constructive things students can do individually and as a group to start appearing the way they want to appear. The results of this brainstorming can be recorded on posters and displayed during the entire year. Example:

My friends think I'm fun when I:	**My friends don't think I'm fun when I:**
1. Maintain my sense of humor.	1. Make fun of others.
2. Can laugh at myself.	2. Call others names and embarrass them.
3. Am willing to try new things.	3. Always have to do things *my* way.
My teachers think I'm smart when I:	**My teachers don't think I'm smart when I:**
1. Do my work carefully and accurately.	1. Don't show up for class.
2. Participate in class discussions.	2. Don't do my homework.
3. Show a willing attitude to learn.	3. Can't participate in class discussions.
My parents think I'm smart when I:	**My parents don't think I'm smart when I:**
1. Get good grades.	1. Don't get good grades.
2. Study hard.	2. Skip school or class.
3. Use good judgment.	3. Don't use good judgment.

In addition, every teacher should keep the individual sheets of paper filled out by the students. Knowing how children would like to appear to others in their world, and then helping them to appear that way is one of the most important things teachers can do for students to heighten their self-esteem. The truth is that if a teacher can help a student win with his or her folks, the teacher is an advocate to that student. If a teacher can help students win with their friends he or she is a real discovery. If a teacher can help students to feel important themselves, he or she can become the most important person in their lives.

Fairness—
A Vital Aspect
Of Teaching

If there is one thing most teachers want and need in their relationships with students, it's to be regarded as fair. They must, for being regarded as fair by students is vitally important to how students perceive them as human beings and as teachers. It's difficult to believe that the unfair teacher is either accepted, respected, or effective.

The question is, "Can a teacher generate feelings of fairness with students?" How can teachers be reasonably sure that the way they act or what they do will be regarded by students as fair? Though there may be no absolute guarantees, there are some safeguards. Teachers should be reminded by administrators to use them.

A
Word
Of Caution

First, teachers should be reminded to heed an old adage: "Haste makes waste." Their triggered reaction to any situation can lock them into acting unfairly when they normally wouldn't. That's why they need not be afraid to proceed with caution. Time and time again we have heard that teachers need the ability to make decisions and act quickly, which is true. But, at the same time, they need to act wisely more than they need to act hastily.

Acting too quickly may confirm that teachers have not acted out of thoughtful and just decisions. Hopefully, they learn early in their careers that sometimes to do nothing is to do something. Just as commas and periods produce meaningful pauses between words and sentences, so do teachers' delayed responses sometimes produce more meaningful results for students than would hasty decisions. If teachers want to be fair, they may not be able to act quickly.

We can also counsel teachers to test their fairness by using one of the most valid criteria of all: putting themselves in their students' positions. This seems an obvious thing to say. Yet people often don't think to do it at the time they should. If we could teach teachers to ask, "How would I feel if...?" then we could make them see that their chances of responding fairly are much better than if they acted in a unilateral and untested way.

Student
Involvement

Likewise, there is another simple procedure we can use to help ourselves or teachers maintain fairness. We can check with students to see how they feel about what is being decided. Whether we believe it or not, this makes us neither weak nor indecisive. That is, it doesn't unless we regard consideration for others as a weakness.

It can't be stressed enough that making a decision is a tremendously important act. To include students in the decision-making process is to validate their abilities to contribute to the planning. Enough cannot be said about the positive aspects of this teacher and administrator action. Whether we happen to be the educator or the student, having others trust us may mean the difference between good resolution of a problem and a breakdown. If we think asking for students' input suggests leniency or permissiveness, we are mistaken. In the case of punishment, we will usually find students' suggestions far more severe than anything we might suggest. To be able to consider suggestions from students indicates teacher maturity. This in itself is positive, for it enables students to have a mature experience with an understanding teacher from whom they can learn. No matter how long it takes, a fair teacher will always set up a linkage with students by inviting both contribution and response.

Another way of testing fairness has to do with a particular set of students. Sometimes what might seem fair with one class will not with another, based on differences in ability or even in temperament. However, if students come away from a situation feeling that heavy pressure has been placed on them, this probably indicates an unfair burden. The teacher might not even intend to be unfair, but he or she certainly has to know students as people before placing requirements or making particular assignments. This is important to remember.

Wise teachers and administrators realize that none of us can guarantee fairness all the time. There will be those times that we may act unfairly even though we think we have exercised care and consideration. What should we do then? We should do what we teach students to do—we should apologize and mend fences. Perhaps we should keep in mind too that there are no more forgiving human beings than children. They can be wronged time after time and will still be willing to start again. It is a very touching thing about children that we adults don't notice often enough. Unfortunately, something seems to happen in this respect once children enter adulthood. But when they are children, they usually respond graciously to apology. Our role is really very small. We need only recognize a need to apologize and then do it.

A PUBLIC RELATIONS PROBLEM: SAYING YES OR NO TO STUDENT REQUESTS

When it comes to listening to requests for special consideration, whether it's permission to leave class early or to bring a pet snake to school, every teacher asks, "Should I say yes or no?" A decision has to be made. It's not as easy as one might think. Equally important, the tone of student attitude toward teachers may depend upon how teachers handle student requests. There are times to say yes, times to say no—and there is a *way* to say each.

A Question Of Fairness

Certainly, we all recognize three important facts about student requests. First, students usually want what they ask for. Second, they don't really always expect to get it. Third, some students are only "testing" us, and if our perception is wrong, we get manipulated in a way that's not good for us or the student.

Sometimes we feel that student requests put us "on the spot." Too, we often feel that a request is unnecessary. Regardless, we must handle it without damaging relationships. We want to be fair—so we hear each individual request. Even the most routine request, it seems, needs our decision. And we know establishing standard procedures for each request such as rules and regulations about going to the office, turning in late assignments, going to the restroom, or using the telephone can work against us more than for us—with students and staff alike.

But, make no mistake: Our handling of requests not only affects our relationships with students, it can even determine our reputation with colleagues and parents alike. For instance, if colleagues see students leaving classrooms continually, our judgment may be questioned. We may even realize that our colleagues sense our indecisiveness, insecurity, and lack of stability in our approach to handling requests. If this is the situation, there is a solution—and it begins with us.

Approach And Technique

If you have allowed requests to get out of control, stop. Discussing this fact with students is a "must" as a beginning effort to bring the situation back to normal. Point out to your classes that too many are taking advantage of your special consideration and that from now on, each request will be treated on an individual basis.

Never tell students that there will be no more requests. Perspective should tell you that requests are normal. You can't wall off requests or the students who make them. Some teachers, by nature, are "no" teachers. Every request elicits a "no" response. Such an extreme is not very healthy in a school. Some requests not only need a yes, they need a stamp of approval. That's why setting a tone of absolutes in either direction is not good. School rules must be obeyed, of course. But emergencies need to be met too.

PUBLIC
RELATIONS
IDEA

You must know students individually to handle requests. It would be untrue not to admit that some students can be allowed to do things others can't. The question we need to ask in each situation is this: Is it in the best interests of the requesting student to permit this request? If the answer is yes, so should ours be. Herein lie our foundation guidelines.

We tell students we want them to feel open and free with us as educators. The student who dares to make a request has believed what he or she was told. Most students have a certain sense of insecurity about making requests. They instinctively know when something that may seem like a good idea to them won't to their teacher. It takes a good deal of courage to ask. If requests are met with blunt negatives or automatic "no's," fear alone can prevent a student from pointing out why he or she thinks the idea is a good one. If the cut-off has been sharp enough, this may be his or her one and only try at making requests. If other students in the class see merit in the request, strong feelings may be built against the teacher for refusing it. An educator who lacks sensitivity may not pick up what is happening out of the refusal. A refusal without good reason only invites student alienation. Therefore, we must be aware that guidelines for requests rather than hard and fast rules are advantageous to teacher and student alike.

PUBLIC
RELATIONS
IDEA

Students must be taught one lesson about requests. They must be taught that the basis for a teacher's or an administrator's decision to grant or not to grant students' requests is consideration for the individual making the request as well as for those who will be affected by the decision. We must realize that students will usually accept a teacher's explanation if the rationale is explained in terms of benefits rather than limitations. Our explanation should always tell students that the individual and the group must be considered with every request, but that there are times when the needs of an individual must precede the needs of the group.

47 | PUBLIC RELATIONS IDEA

We should recognize that compliments have an important place in teaching. It's almost impossible to teach without them. Teacher compliments contain the basic ingredients in the teacher-student relationship that evoke positive participation from students. Compliments not only help us motivate students, but they allow students to realize that we are partners in their personal growth. Compliments also help us continually to accept those we teach rather than reject them.

Compliments help us keep our perspective too. When we recognize the need for compliments, we can see, for example, why a six-hour project may seem worthless to a student because we have overemphasized the misspelling of a word or failed to note his or her effort. Compliments help us realize that a student barely meeting minimum requirements may surge forward because we have attached importance to one of his or her ideas. But, above all else, we must know that compliments help students feel good about themselves and about us. That's the human connection we want and need to have for both today's and tomorrow's teaching and learning efforts as well as student and public relations.

GRADE CARDS:
THE PROCESS
REQUIRES A PLAN

Determining grades is not a responsibility teachers take lightly. A great deal of time and thought—as well as empathy and even sympathy—are part of the process. Even so, the end of a grading period can be an unpleasant time and experience for teachers, students, and parents. The difficulty often seems to lie not so much with a teacher's fair and accurate measurement of each student's achievement, as it does with the fact that students and parents are often not really prepared for the grade sent home.

**A
Natural
Response**

A low grade, fairly computed but unexpectedly received, often produces a natural response of defense or anger. The student often tries to rationalize away his or her classroom failure with a wide variety of excuses, ranging from not understanding the material covered to the teacher's computing the grade incorrectly. Many students explain their failure by giving their parents the impression that the teacher simply does not like them personally or that academic standards are unreasonable. Likewise, it is hardly uncommon for a student to infer that the real culprit is poor teaching rather than poor personal study habits.

That's why teachers need to recognize that it's natural for parents to listen sympathetically to their child, to conclude that a grade is unfair, and to voice their dissatisfaction to the teacher, principal, or anyone who will listen. After all, parents want to believe their child is doing well. They don't like facing the possibility that he or she may not be working hard or doing as well as his or her classmates. They may even feel that their child's low grade reflects on them as parents.

PUBLIC RELATIONS IDEA

A teacher can never assume that students know their grades or understand fully the basis upon which grades are computed. That's why teachers must communicate thoroughly and regularly with parents and students alike throughout the grading period. Above all, every communication must mirror the teacher as a helper and partner rather than merely as an evaluator or as an enemy.

This takes time. But we cannot fail to take the time periodically to explain grades to students and to send progress reports to parents whenever needed. Parents have a right to be kept informed. They should be the first—never the last—to know anything regarding their child. This is a teacher's obligation, and failure to fulfill it is a sure way to establish misunderstanding and bad feelings. A teacher only needs to recall his or her own experiences as a student to know this is true.

49 | PUBLIC RELATIONS IDEA

We should set aside the time to have a short conference with each student the week of grade card distribution. The conference may take place before or after school or during study periods.

One successful conference technique is to require the student to present a self-evaluation of his or her grade before you discuss the actual grade earned. Record this evaluation in your grade book. Then, review the actual grade for the period, explain it completely, and allow the student time to ask questions. You will find that most students will underestimate—and few will overestimate—their grades. But even if students overestimate a grade, explanations can be given and clarifications made before the grade goes home.

This procedure assures understanding and helps the student assume the responsibility for serious self-evaluation. It also allows the student time to prepare parents for the coming grade. During the conference, be sure your students understand that if they feel you have made an error or believe the grade is unjust, they should tell you *before* the grades are sent home. Tell them openly and freely that you wouldn't want to cause them any unnecessary embarrassment or difficulty at home. You'll find that when your students experience your consideration, attitudes about both you and their grades will be more positive. This procedure can reduce problems as well as tension and apprehension with both parents and students. It can also make it difficult for a student to complain to classmates or parents after receiving grade cards.

Make no mistake: Both student and parent communication must be continuous. One of the biggest mistakes we can make as professional teachers is to "surprise" either students or parents at grade card time. And, we must be fully aware of the fact that a teacher rarely hears the vast majority of feelings and responses from either students or parents following grade card distribution.

Grade card time is an opportunity to promote trust and understanding with students and their parents. Sound relationships with both can only be achieved if we are viewed by both as partners and helpers in the learning and grading process. Grade cards may be the vehicles which bring all together for serious planning, study, and learning. In addition, we need to recognize grade card time as a time to praise and a time to encourage. It's a perfect time to offer help and constructive suggestions which will be received and appreciated. That's why we must use grade cards as bridges rather than barriers.

PUBLIC RELATIONS IDEA 50

As educators, we should know that happy children are generally better potential learners. Therefore, helping children to be happy is part of the business of teaching and schools. Many times, when teachers sense that students are unhappy, they will make promises with the hope of making students happy. However, teachers must be careful not to make promises that cannot be kept. Whether you promise to let students "do something" or excuse them from some assignment or activity, remember that promise and keep it. Never think that students don't remember each and every promise or that they don't expect those promises to be kept. They do—even the little, seemingly insignificant promises. Any unkept promise can only result in a loss of student trust and confidence.

PUBLIC RELATIONS IDEA 51

A teacher should not and cannot be afraid to say "I don't know," at any time. In truth, pupils cannot be fooled by teachers who don't know what they are doing—but pretend to know. Never forget that teachers do not have to be the purveyors of all knowledge and truth. If you don't know an answer, simply tell the students that you will try to find an answer for them tomorrow. It's as simple as that—and any other course of action is a mistake which can and will destroy the student-teacher relationship.

PUBLIC RELATIONS IDEA 52

Somehow we have to get the idea out of people's minds that we only want to communicate when there is bad news. That's why it's a great idea to telephone students and parents at home after the first week of school. This provides you the opportunity to make sure things are going well, or to instill confidence or point out exceptional performance. What would you give to have a doctor who would call several days after an appointment with your sick child—to inquire how the child was doing? Would you ever switch doctors? How many people do you think you would tell? Principals and assistant principals can encourage teachers to contact new students by making such calls themselves.

53 | PUBLIC RELATIONS IDEA

Teach students how to greet visitors to the school. Adults learn a great deal by observing *if* and *how* children acknowledge them. Teach children that it is important to treat visitors as if they were guests in the children's homes.

It is equally important to teach students that their decorum while adult visitors are in the building has a tremendous impact on the public. Parents and other members of the taxpaying public are in our buildings many times for visitation, parent meetings, student performances, assemblies, and other special events. Schools are also used by the community as polling places and by continuing education programs. If parents see students running in the halls and treating each other badly, the effect on the parents will be negative.

54 | PUBLIC RELATIONS IDEA

Let students know when a teacher-parent relationship exists. It's a fundamental truth that when students find that a teacher-parent relationship exists, a beneficial condition is created. Children are more apt to be concerned about their performance and behavior in school if a flow of information to their homes is a common occurrence. It's when we don't communicate and don't develop relationships with parents that children stop worrying about their negative actions at school. Therefore, public relations efforts can be a motivating factor in the classroom as well.

Without question, teachers who open up new areas of communication with parents will see greater student effort. Too, as we share the work we do in a broader context, it's likely that we'll gain a new perspective on the importance of what we do.

55 | PUBLIC RELATIONS IDEA

Before you communicate, let a friend see what you're sending home for parents to read, and get some feedback. You'll be surprised at how often an objective third party will point out something in your message that you failed to see—something that could have been misinterpreted or damaging. And a friend may be able to make an addition to your message that would help it be received in a much more favorable light.

Go to parents and community members on *their* own turf occasionally. You may find parents more receptive when you're able to visit with them at their homes or clubs.

Avoid personal comments about specific children. Constantly ask yourself, "Is there anything in what I'm relating that is private—and not meant for public disclosure?" Never forget that you're trying to build credibility and support for the school—so be careful that you are not building one place and tearing down another.

COMMUNICATION TO THE PUBLIC AT LARGE

Key Communicators: Who Are They And How Are They Used?

Every community has a group of individuals who are asked questions about everything that is happening or going to happen in their community. Their opinions and beliefs are *sought* in both the private and public sectors. They are referred to as key communicators. A key communicator can be any person who talks with large numbers of people—and a key communicator is an individual whom people believe and trust. Key communicators do not need to be a part of the formal power structure of a community. They might be barbers, beauticians, bartenders, or bankers. But it's important that we identify key communicators who will talk with or be sought out by part or every segment of the community.

Key Communicators Can Be Used For Many Purposes— Including Four Important Ones

1. To stop rumors before they get out of hand. Some rumors have no truth to them whatsoever. Some are partially true. Some are entirely true, but are not totally believed because they were received as gossip. All rumors should be addressed and stopped or confirmed. This is where key communicators can be so beneficial. Key communicators can confirm or dispel rumors by communicating the facts.

2. *To get ideas and reactions from the public.* Many citizens are reluctant to give their opinions about school issues to school personnel directly. They are shy, or they fear that there might be some repercussion to them or their children who are in school. Therefore, school people are sometimes the "last to know" about a discontent in the community—or about the pro and con reactions that citizens have concerning some aspects of the school or school personnel. Key communicators can be used as designated listeners for public opinion. They can establish constructive liaisons between factions. They can ward off problems. And they can help school people stay in tune with community thought.

3. *To share the day-to-day story of the schools.* Remember, we have said that public relations consists of communicating the ongoing daily events of school life. No matter how much publicity schools receive in the media, community members need—and are often starving for—good information regarding what's happening in the classrooms and the schools. Key communicators in the community who are supplied with this information can serve as important human contacts in telling the story of your schools. Just remember, these people are going to be sought out. Therefore, they are going to spread the word in some way, regardless. And if people conclude that the key communicators don't know anything, they are apt to conclude that *nobody* knows anything about the schools. They are the leaders in business, industry, and the professions. They are the officers of service clubs. They are influential men and women in neighborhoods and in the community.

4. *Help to sell the community on an idea.* Before passing a bond issue, approving a major change in the curriculum, supporting a plan for restructuring the schools, or making any major shift or change, the community must be both informed and sold on the idea. People are persuaded most easily if other people whom they respect and trust can present them with facts that convince them of the benefits of the plan, idea, or change first. Key communicators in the community can be ideal sales people—if we establish a relationship with them and if they are supplied with enough positive information regarding any changes.

How To Set Up A Key Communicator System

1. Define all the various groups in your community that you want to reach. Don't leave out students and teachers in your school. They too are key to reaching very important parts of your public.

2. Identify one or two key communicators for each group that you might want or need to reach.

3. Send a letter to each of the people you choose, explaining the nature of the effort and why they have been chosen for consultation regarding an issue. Invite them to a

meeting in which you get prospective key communicators together. Remember to include an R.S.V.P. A follow-up phone call from the principal will usually ensure many "takers." Calls from a secretary are effective too, but only secondary to the principal's making calls personally. In truth, some people will not or cannot be handled by a secretary. Such people don't handle their own business in such a way and won't allow you to handle business in such a way either. Remember, their time is valuable. If they feel that you are attempting to save yourself some valuable time by having a secretary call, they aren't apt to give you their time by coming to a meeting.

4. At the meeting, explain to your key communicators why you need such a system and how you intend to communicate with them. And explain how each key communicator should communicate with the school. Each key communicator should have someone at the building level as well as at the district office whom he or she feels free to communicate with regarding any matter. Remember to place key communicators on all your mailing lists for school district publications. And send special invitations to these people for school plays, musicals, debates, and sporting events. Once a year you may even want to invite them to attend classes and have lunch with you and your students. This will allow them to feel more a part of the school and the school family.

OPINION POLLS

All parents have an opinion about what we are doing. However, not everyone is willing to voice his or her opinion directly or individually. Nor is it always easy to obtain parents' individual opinions face-to-face. After all, listening to another person's opinion can leave you feeling as if you're between a rock and a hard place. Likewise, giving an opinion can leave a person feeling very vulnerable.

According to Technical Assistance Research Programs (TARP)*, the following was determined about customers' attitudes toward most businesses they had to deal with:

> "One in four of your customers is unhappy enough with your organization right now to stop doing business with you. Worse yet, only 4% of those disgruntled customers are likely to complain—preferring to switch rather than fight.
> "Why is this worse? According to TARP, simply encouraging unhappy customers to complain changes the probability they will do business with you again from 30% to 50%. Listen to the unhappy customer and promise to look into the matter, and that probability goes to 72%. Respond

---

*Training Magazine, August, 1986, p. 43

immediately to the complaint, apologize for the problem and
guarantee to 'fix,' and the probability goes to 95% that the
customer will *remain* a customer."

The application of these data to schools can teach us a great deal. Let's just suppose
that schools do twice as good a job as business in serving their clientele. Instead of one
in four being unhappy with us, let's say we only have one in eight dissatisfied patrons.
Therefore, in a school of 240 families, there are 30 households that are very unhappy
with something we are doing—so unhappy, in fact, that they would like to withdraw
their children from our school or switch schools. If these are two-parent households,
that means 60 people are unhappy with us. And yet, only 4 percent, which is two or
three parents, will ever voice their complaint. However, using the TARP statistics, we
know that we can nearly eliminate our problem if we give parents a chance to voice
their concerns so that we can do something about them. This is why we must have
methods of polling the public—and why we must use these polls to determine part of
our public relations effort. Not only can such a practice reduce the number of
dissatisfied patrons, it can gain stronger support from other people in the district. And
this same procedure can be used with students to gain the same results. This is the
reason business and industry spend millions of dollars to find out what customers and
potential customers think about their products or services.

On the following pages is a questionnaire prepared by North Central Association*
which was used to poll parents on how they feel about the school in which their child is
enrolled. You may want to prepare a similar questionnaire to send to parents in your
community.

_____

*Used with permission from North Central Association.

PARENTS' QUESTIONNAIRE

Would you please take a few minutes to give us your opinion? It is very valuable to us.

The purpose of this survey is to help the school determine what the parents think about the school and the school program. The results of this survey will be used in the future efforts and planning of the school.

NOTE: If you have more than one child in this school, you may receive multiple copies of this questionnaire. Please answer only *one questionnaire* for your *oldest child* in the school.

Circle one in each category:

A. Grade of student   K - 1 - 2 - 3 - 4 - 5 - 6
B. Sex   F   M
C. Average Mark   A   B   C   D   E   F   S or I
D. Name of your child's school   _____

1. Which of the following statements best describes your judgment of the feelings of your son or daughter about going to school each day?

   Always looks forward to it with enthusiasm   _____
   Usually looks forward to it with enthusiasm   _____
   Frequently is indifferent about it   _____
   Often dreads the prospect of school   _____
   Always dislikes having to go to school   _____

2. To what extent do you think that the schools should emphasize preparation for college?

   More emphasis   _____
   About the same emphasis as now   _____
   Less emphasis   _____

3. To what extent do you think schools should emphasize preparation for a job?

   More emphasis   _____
   About the same emphasis as now   _____
   Less emphasis   _____

4. How would you characterize the quality of education offered in your schools?

   Excellent   _____
   Good   _____
   Average   _____
   Below Average   _____
   Poor   _____

5. How would you describe the standards (expectations) set by the teachers in your school?

   Much too difficult   _____
   Somewhat difficult   _____
   About right   _____
   Somewhat easy   _____
   Much too easy   _____

6. The following programs are currently in effect in some schools in this country. Please indicate those you believe are in use in this school and your opinion of their desirability:

	In Operation in This School				Your Opinion As To the Desirability		
	Yes	No	Don't Know		Favor-able	Unfavor-able	Don't Know
a. Choir	_____	_____	_____		_____	_____	_____
b. Instrumental music	_____	_____	_____		_____	_____	_____
c. Computer-assisted instruction	_____	_____	_____		_____	_____	_____
d. Computer skills courses	_____	_____	_____		_____	_____	_____
e. Independent study	_____	_____	_____		_____	_____	_____
f. Student involvement in school decision-making	_____	_____	_____		_____	_____	_____
g. No dress code requirements	_____	_____	_____		_____	_____	_____
h. Foreign language	_____	_____	_____		_____	_____	_____
i. Speech and hearing	_____	_____	_____		_____	_____	_____
j. Careers & Vocational Awareness	_____	_____	_____		_____	_____	_____
k. Learning Disability	_____	_____	_____		_____	_____	_____
l. Gifted Education	_____	_____	_____		_____	_____	_____

7. To what extent do you feel your child needs more personal attention from the school on such matters as study habits, personal hygiene, getting along with others, self-concept?

Someone is *always* available, according to my understanding, when he or she needs to discuss such matters. _____

Someone is *usually* available, according to my understanding, when he or she needs to discuss such matters. _____

I believe that my child would like to be able to talk to someone more often than he or she can now. _____

8. To what extent do you (and/or your spouse) discuss with your child such matters as study habits, personal hygiene, getting along with others, self-concept?

Very frequently _____

Frequently _____

Seldom _____

9. Do you feel your child needs more attention from the school in the development of —

	Yes	No
Self-understanding	_____	_____
Self-responsibility	_____	_____
Decision-making	_____	_____
Values	_____	_____

10. How frequently do you confer with one or more teachers, counselors, and/or administrators of your school in attempting to solve problems related to your child's education? Such problems might be related to the selection of extra classroom activities, the improvement of study habits, and social and/or academic development.

Four times a year or more	_____
Two or three times a year	_____
Once a year	_____
Not at all	_____

11. There is much discussion today about the behavior, attitudes, and discipline of students. How would you characterize the discipline in your school?

Too strict	_____
About right	_____
Not strict enough	_____

12. In your judgment, and taking into consideration the interests and needs of your child, what emphasis should elementary schools place upon the following post and/or extra classroom activities? Please use the appropriate number response in the spaces provided below.

1—More emphasis   2—About the same emphasis as now   3—Less emphasis

Art — special interest	_____
District Choir	_____
Picture Person	_____
Intramural (athletics)	_____
Stamp Club	_____
Student Government	_____
Service Organizations	_____
Educational Programs/Speakers	_____
Others: Specify	_____

13. Please give your general reaction to the following statements:

	Agree	Disagree	Don't Know
A. It is easy to make appointments to see teachers in this school.	_____	_____	_____
B. It is easy to make appointments to see the administrators of this school.	_____	_____	_____
C. There is effective communication between the school board and the community.	_____	_____	_____
D. There is effective communication between parents and the superintendent.	_____	_____	_____

234

PARENTS' QUESTIONNAIRE (cont.)

	Agree	Disagree	Don't Know
E. As a whole, teachers in this school are concerned about the individual student.	_____	_____	_____
F. The community is proud of this school.	_____	_____	_____
G. This school plays an important role in the life of the community.	_____	_____	_____
H. The school's location is suited to the needs of the community.	_____	_____	_____
I. Parking is adequate for school functions.	_____	_____	_____
J. The school uses its resources of both staff and money well.	_____	_____	_____
K. The school needs more financial resources if it is to continue to be effective.	_____	_____	_____

14. From which media do you obtain information about your schools? Please use the appropriate number response in the spaces provided below.

Radio	1 2 3 _____	1 Very frequently or frequently
Television	1 2 3 _____	
Local and/or general newspapers	1 2 3 _____	
Publications prepared by school personnel	1 2 3 _____	2 Sometimes
Staff and/or student appearances before community groups	1 2 3 _____	3 Never or almost never
School performances	1 2 3 _____	
School open houses	1 2 3 _____	
Staff affiliations with civic and community organizations	1 2 3 _____	
Personal contacts with school personnel	1 2 3 _____	
School social functions	1 2 3 _____	

15. To what extent have you (or your spouse) been involved in the school program? If you have not been involved frequently, to what extent would you be willing to become involved in the program conducted by the school? Please use the appropriate number response (see question 14) in the spaces provided below.

	Have Been Involved	Willing To Participate
Overall educational planning	1 2 3 _____	1 2 3 _____
Advisor for special instructional program	1 2 3 _____	1 2 3 _____
Planning and/or supervising supplementary educational experiences for students	1 2 3 _____	1 2 3 _____
Overall evaluation of this school's program	1 2 3 _____	1 2 3 _____
Planning and/or supervising aspects of the student and activity program	1 2 3 _____	1 2 3 _____
Educational and occupational information conferences	1 2 3 _____	1 2 3 _____
Others: Specify _____ _____	1 2 3 _____	1 2 3 _____

235

16. Would you welcome additional information about the school?   Yes_____   No_____
    If "Yes," please check the items below which would be of particular interest to you:

    Extra classroom activities available   _____
    Course content   _____
    Social work   _____
    Testing program   _____
    Library/audio-visual aids program   _____
    Recent changes and innovations in instructional and organization practices   _____
    Major problems (overcrowding, staff, etc.)   _____
    School costs and financial status   _____
    Others: Specify_____

17. How would you rate the following problems now being encountered in American education as they relate to this particular school? Please use the responses:

    1. A very critical area in this school.
    2. A somewhat critical area in this school.
    3. Not a critical area in this school.

    a. Student control and general discipline.   _____
    b. Financial problems; not enough money for the school.   _____
    c. Teacher unrest and dissatisfaction.   _____
    d. Indifference of parents in general to the school.   _____
    e. Student indifference to the school.   _____
    f. Inadequate or irrelevant courses of study in the school.   _____
    g. Drug or alcohol abuse among the students.   _____
    h. Clashes among various groups of students.   _____
    i. Lack of emphasis in the school on helping young people develop.   _____

18. How would you characterize the extent and degree of educational change and innovation in this school? (Check the statement that most nearly parallels your judgments.)

    a. There is too little educational change and innovation in this school.   _____
    b. There is just the right degree of educational change and innovation in this school.   _____
    c. There is too much educational change and innovation in this school.   _____

19. List the things you like most about the school. Include those things you feel are the school's strengths.

    _____
    _____
    _____

20. List the things you like least about the school. Include those things you feel are the school's weaknesses.

    _____
    _____
    _____

Thank you!

58 PUBLIC RELATIONS IDEA

In recent years, the news media have become fond of reporting community opinion on various issues. To do that, many newspapers conduct a poll on a regular basis to determine the opinions of citizens on a variety of topics. Most newspaper editors claim that their polls accurately reflect the prevailing thought of the community. Indeed, many of them claim that the polls accurately reflect community opinion within two or three percentage points.

Such polls offer an excellent opportunity for both a board of education and the administrative team to add to their knowledge regarding public opinion about the schools. In one community in recent months, the newspaper has run polls on such varied topics as whether citizens believed the community needed a new elementary school (only 35 percent thought so) and whether they wanted to see a foreign language taught in the elementary schools (more than 70 percent responded favorably). School boards can't base their plan of work or determine policy on the basis of polls. Fortunately, our schools are not governed in that way. But the poll does serve effectively as a trial balloon for many matters that the board may need to consider in the course of the year.

The opinions expressed regarding the attitudes about a school bond issue, for example, provide some evidence of the work the board must do if a school is really needed. If seven out of ten people want a foreign language taught, a board is obligated to investigate and study the issue.

If you use polls as indicators, keep one thing in mind. The results of polls are usually affected greatly by whether or not a price tag is attached to the question. When there is—as in the case of a new school—results are apt to be more negative than when there is not one.

Poll Parents About Emotional Issues Concerning Their Children

Parents have many desires for their children. Only one of these is the desire for a quality education. In fact, most parents take the idea of quality education for their children for granted. For the most part, parents believe—correctly or incorrectly—that students are receiving adequate instruction. As parents, however, they have many hopes and wishes concerning the "other" things their children will receive over the course of the K-12 years. They want friendship for their children—from other students as well as from teachers. They want their children to acquire good self-concepts, to learn discipline, and to build character. They also want their children to be included, liked, considered, respected, and kept safe. And they want *us* to make these desires become realities.

Is this an unfair request? Perhaps. But such desires can't be left out of our public relations plan—and it's far better for our success as educators that we accept these desires and have a plan to meet them as challenges. When it comes to public relations, these kinds of requests represent an opportunity for us. In fact, *any* time the public wants us to perform a service, we should be delighted. This is the best stance we can take to maintain the public's desire to have us do our job. After all, when the public asks more of us, it means that they still trust us and will continue to support us. Any business or professional in this position would be envied indeed. It is when our clientele doesn't think we are capable and looks elsewhere that we should be worried. Therefore, from time to time, we need to find out what *more* our public would like from us.

PUBLIC RELATIONS IDEA

At the beginning of the school year we often give parents a plethora of papers to fill out and return to the school. Let's give them one more—a sheet of paper which asks the following:

"IF WE COULD GIVE YOUR CHILD ONE THING IN ADDITION TO A QUALITY EDUCATION, WHAT WOULD THAT BE?"

(This sheet will be given to your child's classroom teacher[s].)

After you collect these papers, tabulate the responses schoolwide—not just for a single classroom. Then, categorize the replies under these headings:

1. Things which parents said they would like us to do for their children:
   -
   -
   -
2. Things that we are already doing:
   -
   -
   -
3. Things that we are not doing now, but are going to start doing:
   -
   -
   -
4. Things that we cannot do and why:
   -
   -
   -

When the lists have been compiled, publish your findings in your school or district newsletter. You will find that a number of parents cite requests and desires that you are already doing. They just aren't aware of them. There will also be things to which you say, "You know, we can do these things and here's how."

Finally, there will be those things that the school cannot do—for a wide variety of reasons: money, state law, or a chance that such action will deprive other children or be unsafe. There are legitimate reasons that we can't or shouldn't do something the public asks of us. Yet, these issues should be addressed with professional explanations. Likewise, we need to be aware that citizens don't expect us to do everything they would like, but they do want to know the reasons something can or cannot be done. It's when we ignore such suggestions and requests that we can lose support. And it needs to be said that when we answer a ridiculous request positively and professionally we gain the respect, sympathy, and support of many segments of our community. Our answer puts each segment as well as our entire community in a position to say, "It's amazing that the school does so much with all the demands that people put on it." On the other hand, when we don't face these issues empathetically and publicly, others can say, "They don't pay any attention to me either," or "They don't care what we want or think." In truth, it's the absurd request that makes us look good to the majority. That's why we should welcome such needs and requests from our public.

CHAPTER

VIII

EIGHT

WHEN
THE SCHOOLS
ARE CRITICIZED

"To give real service you must add something which cannot be bought or measured with money, and that is sincerity and integrity."
—Donald A. Adams

IN PUBLIC RELATIONS, PUBLIC CONFIDENCE REJOINS WITH TRUTH

In operations as large and complex as most public and private schools, things will go wrong. On occasion, our mission will be questioned in both class and extraclass activities. To expect otherwise is a mistake. Without anticipation of this fact, we may lose our credibility with the public and destroy the climate of confidence in dealing with issues when things do go wrong. This, of course, can sabotage any public relations effort.

Frankly, teachers, pupils, administrators, parents, and board members are human. Consequently, human mistakes and failures can and do occur. People sometimes make wrong decisions. They use poor judgment or behave erratically. Unfortunately, such behavior detracts from the positive attributes and successes of the school. When the negative occurs, it is not unusual for the school board, administrators, and teachers alike to want to keep the bad news from the public. Indeed, many board members and administrators may have been advised by their more experienced colleagues to keep the "dirty laundry" from public view. It's possible that there was a time when such advice was appropriate, but not in recent years. In fact, following such a course today can be one of the biggest mistakes a board, administrator, or teacher can make. Today, more than ever, there is truth in the old adage, "Two wrongs never make a right." This is almost always true insofar as public relations is concerned.

The Community's Right To Know

Whether we want to admit it or not, the community has as much right to know about the mistakes in a school system as it does the successes. Although it is often difficult for administrators, the board of education, or the school staff to acknowledge, acceptance of this basic fact will go far toward building a climate of mutual respect, confidence, and believability within a community. In truth, a stance of openness and honesty may go further in establishing a foundation of confidence than anything we do. If a community is kept informed of the schools' failures as well as their successes—as they occur—it soon learns that the board of education and the district administrators and teachers are honest and forthright with the public. When such is the case, the public is most likely to understand a particular failure and most apt to believe the successes. Indeed, when the school is open and truthful with the community, it will find that citizens will support the schools in the midst of most crises.

The news media are also more prone to be fair to the schools and educators where a climate of truthfulness exists. Even in those instances in which the news media may be biased against the schools out of some editorial pique, frankness and honesty on the part of the schools still have the best chance to pay handsome dividends. On the other hand, denial or cover-up will bring harsh and lasting consequences. If we think not, we are mistaken. In fact, the only way to regain public confidence after such incidents is to remove administrators and select new board members.

Examine Before You Move... "A Few" Is Not Everyone

We need to be aware of the need for disclosure for a very important reason. Schools may well be the most vulnerable institutions in our society. Whenever a national publication or telecast "exposes" certain problems, deficiencies of students, or faults in the schools, some people in almost every community become convinced that those faults afflict their own schools. They feel this way even if hard evidence proves otherwise. For instance, there are hundreds, perhaps thousands, of public and private school systems in which test scores *have not* fallen in recent years. In many schools, test scores have risen. Yet, a few people in each community where these successful systems are located will overlook the facts and conclude that their own schools are in the same boat with those schools whose test scores have declined. And they will act as if such is the case.

Nearly every school system has experienced individuals or small groups demanding that some action be taken on a certain issue. Their demands may be as commonplace as wanting children who live only a few blocks from school to be granted permission to ride the school bus for reasons of safety. Or they may be as inflammatory as demanding the removal of a book from the library. Not long ago, one school was faced with the demand to remove all lyrics from the music program which contained incorrect grammar—a demand which would have banned nearly all the folk songs and spirituals in existence.

We're not saying that demands from individuals don't have merit or don't deserve consideration. Quite the contrary, they do. In fact, a good public relations effort requires consideration of such demands. Educators need to remember, however, that the few people who make such demands do not represent everyone. There is no foolproof action we can take to keep perspective in this area, but a few suggestions are worth noting. And these actions often need to be taken with individuals or small groups rather than the whole of the district.

First, educators must remain current regarding trends, criticisms, and political comments about education. To be aware of these conditions is an absolute necessity if educators do not want to be taken by surprise, react out of ignorance, or believe that none in their community have concerns in some of these areas. It is wise to remember that it's not an event or a belief on the part of the public that can cause us to make public relations mistakes. Rather, it's us. Therefore, we need to develop an ability to address issues in calm, intelligent, professional, and creative ways designed to achieve solutions. And we have to have a working understanding that these stances are always weakened by the urgency inherent in surprise or lack of knowledge.

Second, we must remember that critics have been consistent companions of education throughout history. Equally important, their criticisms may or may not have relevance. At the very least, they do not represent the opinion of everyone. In fact, they often contradict the wishes of the majority. Too, it needs to be remembered that some of these critics have been attempting to make a "name" for themselves by being advocates of some cause or by being opponents of the school. A close look will reveal that they often reverse themselves at a later time.

The successful educator knows that no person should be ignored when he or she has comments to make about schools or education. At the same time, however, one person or even one small group with a unanimous point of view is not everyone. Nor does either represent everyone in the community. Consequently, the effective educator retains a sense of balance as he or she listens to such critics and their demands that the schools be changed or reformed to suit their beliefs and biases. This is what makes the schools in his or her district successful. The administrators in them cannot be baited. They are not reactionaries. They do not make public issues out of private criticism when such criticism does not warrant public discussion. But they do respond individually and privately—and they do try to win people over. And they never turn against anyone—privately or publicly.

PUBLIC RELATIONS IDEA

"I received a dozen calls!" Many superintendents have heard board members make that statement as a preface to some negative comment or complaint about the schools or school employees. It's as if they wished to substantiate the complaint they were to share.

Specifying the number of calls may be only a small exaggeration. However, the fact is that two or three complaints often become a dozen or more when communicated to the superintendent. This "stretching of the truth," although harmless in itself perhaps, may well distract from the maintenance of a balanced view about an issue in which there may well be legitimate differences of opinion.

It's important that board members listen carefully to those who contact them with complaints or criticism about the schools. It's equally important to keep those contacts in proper perspective. That's why one should keep a brief record of both the number and the substance of calls. Indeed, a small form might easily be developed and furnished to all board members—and administrators too. Then, when the comments are related to the superintendent or the board, the written record of the contacts can be produced. This practice will make it unnecessary to guess the number of calls and comments which are received.

There is enough criticism of the schools and school employees without the necessity of making an issue seem of greater importance than the realities. Yet, it's always important for the board and staff alike to know the extent of criticism. Keeping a record of contacts can help each board member to be factual and accurate in reporting on these contacts to both board members and the superintendent.

RUMOR: IGNORE OR CONFRONT IT

Abraham Lincoln is reported to have once remarked that if he were to pay attention to and try to counter every rumor, he might as well close up shop, for he would have time for no other business. His observation, made nearly 125 years ago, is equally valid today. Yet, in every community there are some rumors about education and schools that must be dealt with.

No one has yet been able to devise a specific way to stop people from being curious, nor should anyone want to. Neither have we found a way to stop people from hearing and repeating rumors, though we would like to. Yet, even a seemingly harmless story can hurt the morale and damage the image and efficiency of an entire organization. And it is certainly true that the career of more than one educator has been destroyed by rumor.

While school administrators and staff members can't direct their attention to every rumor about the school that circulates in a community, they do need to control their own actions and behaviors relative to a rumor. They must be absolutely certain that they do not contribute to the formation of rumors or elaborate on a rumor once it has begun. The best way to minimize rumors is to recognize the circumstances under which they are initiated and encouraged, and then attempt to avoid those circumstances. Unfortunately, it's amazing how many external rumors have an internal source. Pieces of information which eventually become rumors are magnified—some by what we say and do, and others by what we refuse to say or do once we hear a rumor or are asked about one directly.

A Major Culprit: Being Secretive

Nothing encourages rumors in a school system more than a secretive attitude on the part of the school board and administration. Many newspaper articles about a board of education holding an executive session have started rumors. Recently, one school board suddenly announced that they would hold an executive session and stated that the purpose of the session was to "deal with a personnel matter." The local newspaper editor wrote an editorial suggesting that board members were reviewing the performance of a superintendent. The editor questioned whether the board was unhappy with the superintendent. The editor then speculated that, if not the superintendent, the topic of discussion must be an elementary principal about whom there had been some public complaints. Following the appearance of the story, the superintendent contacted the editor and informed him that the executive session had been held to discuss a teacher's request for a leave of absence the following year. Unfortunately, the information came too late, for much damage had already been done.

It's important to note that the "secretive behavior" demonstrated by calling the executive session had many ramifications. First, it led to speculations that later became rumors in the community. Second, the effectiveness of the principal, the superintendent, and the board were reduced. Third, it was not a matter which could be cleared up quickly.

A close look will reveal that a rumor seems all the more interesting to people when someone in authority is trying to "keep it quiet." People like having something to talk about. Some enjoy it. Others "live" for rumors they can talk about, magnify, and perpetuate. If they do not have accurate information about the schools, some people will actually invent their own information to tell their friends and neighbors. Or at the very least, many people will eagerly listen to the inventions of others. (Remember the Law of Positive Reinforcement, p. 49) Just be aware that most of the information that is being protected in the name of confidentiality is often being held to meet the need for power. And as we said earlier, it's difficult to lead or create a good public relations program internally or externally without sharing power. That's because people want to have a measure of control over their own lives rather than have institutions control their lives for them.

PUBLIC RELATIONS IDEA

Newspaper accounts of board meetings often indicate that many school boards hold far too many executive sessions. As a result, hardly a year passes without our seeing legislatures address this issue. The intent of such legislation is to make the public business of governing bodies truly public. We may complain about how difficult the ever-increasing rules concerning executive sessions are, but the truth is that we bring them upon ourselves simply by discussing issues during executive sessions that should be discussed in public.

In reality, there are few occasions when an executive session is absolutely necessary. One occasion might be the development of a negotiation strategy. Another may be to discuss specifics about the performance of an individual employee. A third might involve a discussion about disciplinary measures concerning a specific student. Finally, there might be occasions when a board might need to discuss a pending lawsuit with its attorney. One is hard put to state additional instances in which an executive session is justified.

Yet, many boards routinely hold executive sessions prior to, following, or during every meeting. This is a practice that ought to be terminated. If not, the board can be assured that, sooner or later, the legislature will act to put a stop to such activity.

At a time when we talk a lot about the need for local control, we ought to pause and reflect as to why so many educational decisions are made elsewhere. Often it's because the behavior of local school boards has violated the democratic process. Holding unnecessary executive sessions is one of the most frequent violations. Perhaps an appropriate question for every board member is, "Is this executive session really necessary?"

With Rare Exceptions,
All Information
Should Be Made Public

Rumors flourish only in the absence of open, truthful, legitimate, accurate, and authoritative information delivered in a caring and considerate way. The best way to avoid and combat rumors is to put the facts and information about plans and the results of plans before the public at all times. Except for rare and exceptional instances, which include legal proceedings or protecting the required privacy of a person or persons, no information should be withheld from the public. And a wise school official always considers the likely outcomes of withholding information.

The successful administrator knows that employees, parents, and citizens are not going to stop talking about the things which affect them, their children, or their lives. This is a reality of life. He or she also knows that unless accurate and authoritative information is made available to people, rumors will often prevail and will be accepted as truth. That's why the successful board and the administration of the district conduct their decision-making and deliberative activities in an open and forthright manner in both positive and negative situations.

TAKING THE FIGHT OUT OF OPPONENTS...

It may sound facetious, but it's absolutely true: If you want people to avoid you, oppose you, or fight you, adopt certain specific behaviors. Be mean. Show your anger, disdain, and disapproval—privately and publicly. Use your power at every opportunity. Above all, avoid your opponents and openly exclude anyone who doesn't give you his or her kind words and complete loyalty, respect, and support. Finally, let people know—in no uncertain terms—that you'll be hostile if they get out of line or in your way. Then, you'll be easy to fight. That's because people can attack you both personally and professionally—with good reason and in good conscience. If you think not, you are mistaken.

If you really want to position yourself to lead people and conduct an effective public relations effort, you must adopt one stance: inclusion. You must approach both friend and foe respectfully, courteously, and empathetically. Believe it or not, people can't handle goodness when they are holding a grudge or clinging to a position they know is wrong or contains areas of gray. Therefore, being a genuinely good person and doing the right thing for the right reasons, in the right way has definite advantages in your public relations efforts. Opponents find it more difficult not to listen to you, accept your ideas or position, and follow you rather than their own demands.

Being genuinely nice is an accepted foundation for effective long-term leadership and public relations. It's also a basic rule for managing power and responsibility successfully. Look closely. People who abuse power are very easy to fight—because they almost always make four simply unacceptable mistakes when it comes to relationships with other people.

First, they believe and practice the adage, "You scratch my back and I'll scratch yours." Second, they honestly believe that if they're nice, people will walk all over them. Third, they label anyone who disagrees with them an enemy—and regard him or her as a personal danger. Fourth, they develop a formal or informal master plan for destroying that person as well as that person's ideas, opinions, and suggestions. Once they act upon any of these four beliefs, the stage is set for their predictable behavior—and their predictable failure in working for or with other people.

People who believe in these myths are convinced that they are right—and everyone else is wrong—and that their bad behavior is justified in any given situation. These stances also seem to give these people a sense of security when insecurity is the real creation. Adopting these stances, they think, positions them strongly with some segments of the community, wards off other attackers, and saves them intellectual wear and tear. It's true that many people don't feel any responsibility toward those who oppose them. Many also believe that the weak will jump on their bandwagon out of fear when they take such a stance. Some do—yet something else happens too. The opposition begins to prepare a case against them which may bring their house down.

Taking
The Tools of Fighting
Away From People

Remember, if you want to influence and lead people in a community as well as initiate a sound public relations effort, there are four practical rules you should follow. First, you must choose to be civil to all, including those who overtly oppose and avoid you as much as those who seem to dislike you—including special interest groups and the media. Second, your words and actions must be beneficial to all concerned—and detrimental to none. Third, you must be consistent in extending your help and professional friendship to all—in good times and hard times. Fourth, you must be willing to evaluate or re-evaluate what is being done in light of the criticism. You will never be believed or create credibility if you try to defend the school's positions without taking these four steps. Likewise, you'll never be able to defend the school's position when you, yourself, are neutral or opposed to these four guidelines. Rather, you must try to initiate change for those things that need changing. For sometimes the critics of education *are* right. Finally, keep in mind that these four practices can't be used to snare, delude, deviate, or manipulate. They must be sincere. They must be authentic.

Once you adopt these four characteristics, a fundamental value of overwhelming significance has been added to your professional style which makes you harder to fight. You've totally eliminated character assassination from other people's repertoire of opposition tactics. And character assassination is one of the ploys most widely used to discredit and defeat someone. Issues and ideas usually don't defeat people. Their characters do. Therefore, being "nice" allows you legitimately to disarm the biggest weapon of those who oppose your ideas and actions. It forces them to deal with the issues rather than focus an attack on your personality.

In truth, the vast majority of people don't know how to fight nice people. Many feel lost in a friendly conflict, for they only know how to feel justified and morally correct in fights. When the stereotype of a "bad" person is nonexistent, most people simply don't know what to do. They have lost the tools of their fight. Then, any attacking they do requires risk on their part. And risking is something people seldom do with their own lives if they don't have to. They will put another career or reputation in peril at the drop of a hat—but never their own.

When it comes to public relations, we know that it's often much easier to discredit a person than an idea. And it's easier if the person has both a personality and a stance which are easy to discredit. That's why we must realize that good people, nice people, considerate people, and caring people have the best chance of continually finishing first—even when they make mistakes. Equally important, we need to know that there are seldom any losses for us or anyone else when issues are settled in ethical, friendly, and inclusive ways. Remember, win-win is the goal of public relations. Therefore, keep in mind that "ready for attack" stances are degrading. They must be replaced by a belief that people are respected at all times. Issues may always be argued, of course. But people must never get destroyed. The debate can go on. But the issues being questioned or debated—not the people questioning or debating—must be the basis for our actions as well as our decision making. Then, everyone ends up being positioned to win. As professional educators, this should be our objective in working with people and perfecting our public relations positions, internally and externally.

62 PUBLIC RELATIONS IDEA

No matter how successful we may be, we will occasionally be confronted with a problem that assumes the magnitude of a crisis. And the problem may not be resolved on the basis of factual information. Worse, it may not even be resolved in a way that's best for the children. Instead, resolution may be on the basis of opinion and emotion. When this happens, we will usually find the outcome unsatisfactory.

Following a "crisis" we are often tempted to take immediate action to insure such an issue never arises again. However, immediate action following a crisis is likely to contain decisions that are an overreaction. Rather than curtail future problems, they often actually create new and unforeseen ones.

Here's one procedure which may help. Immediately following the resolution of a crisis, prepare a brief summary of the incident. The report should contain the issues which arose, the principal elements of the problem, and the way you managed resolution. Put this summary aside for a few weeks, perhaps even until summer. Then, after some reflection and allowing time for tempers to cool and emotions to settle, develop a policy or undertake some other remedial action—if needed—to prevent future problems. More often than not, letting time pass may well reveal that no new policy or action is actually essential.

It's not always desirable to wait, of course. However, when it's appropriate, we should postpone action. This will enable us to act in a less stressful environment. Letting a crisis cool before taking policy action often results in a better policy—and a better feeling about it, on the part of both the board and the community.

WHEN THE PUBLIC
ADDRESSES THE BOARD
OR AN ADMINISTRATOR

A public relations stance must contain a philosophy and a course of action to cover this very common occurrence. It is quite common for groups of citizens to approach or petition the board of education or administrators in a formal meeting to secure a redress of grievances. The grievances may be real or imaginary. The point of the approach or petition may be to change the curriculum or to pressure the board or administrators to take some action or to approve a particular program. Remember, the right to petition is one of our most cherished constitutional rights. More often than not, however, many boards of education and administrators do not handle the appearances by groups in such situations in a manner that is calculated to gain support of the schools.

Certainly, if we grant a favorable response to the petition, all may be well. But if the board or administration must deny the petition, the way in which it conducts the petition hearing is of paramount importance to relationships with the group and the community. Administrators often face such groups. However, let's look at an example that may be typical of the kinds of petitions a school board receives.

Suppose, for example, that the students in a small housing development do not qualify for bus transportation to and from school because they don't live far enough away. Perhaps state law or even board policy authorizes the district to provide transportation only for those pupils who live two and a half or more miles from school. Yet, the parents who live in the housing development, while acknowledging that their children do not qualify by reason of distance, regard the route that their children must travel when walking to school as exceedingly dangerous. Therefore, they petition the board to provide transportation for their children.

They have already approached the superintendent and have been informed of the board policy. However, the chief administrator has been unsuccessful in helping them to accept this reality. Now, they are before the board with their request.

The board listens to them. The president asks if individual board members have questions they wish to ask the petitioners...and this is when real trouble often begins.

Begin Petition Hearings
By Letting People
Have Plenty Of Time To Talk...

A close look will reveal that it is often board members' comments and questions that escalate citizens' requests into full-blown confrontations. That's why both in asking questions and in making observations, each board member should avoid sharing his or her personal philosophy and opinion with the petitioners. Perhaps a board member agrees with the petitioners. However, to indicate sympathy or support at this point is premature and may cause the petitioners to believe that their requests will be granted. On the other hand, the board member who is immediately opposed to the request and so states is equally guilty of creating a potentially explosive situation. If board members state strong opinions, either pro or con, about a petition when it is first presented, they make resolution more difficult—and can alter opinion about the schools in the entire community. This is especially true when board members respond with statements such as, "We can't afford it," "We don't make exceptions," or "I had to walk four miles to school when I was a child."

The best procedure is to let people talk, and give them plenty of time to do so. Ask questions to be certain each board member understands the petitioner's situation fully. In addition, ask to have the existing policy read aloud for the benefit of the board and others present, including the media. Then, request information as to whether there have been exceptions made in the past and the conditions under which exceptions have been made.

Once all pertinent questions have been advanced, a board should direct the superintendent to place the item on the agenda for a subsequent meeting. The board should ask the chief administrator to report at that time all of the facts as they may be known. This should include whether granting the request would be possible financially and whether any reordering of priorities would be necessary.

Finally, the superintendent should be asked to include a recommendation to the board for action. The petitioners should be invited to attend the subsequent meeting. All the facts listed in the report should be made available to the petitioners along with the superintendent's recommendation. The petitioners should then be offered an opportunity to present any additional information or question any data. Once this second meeting has been completed the board should reach a decision. That decision should be fair, consistent, firm, and supported with publicly stated reasons for its correctness.

We must realize, however, that procedure does not guarantee public acceptance. Nor does procedure automatically guarantee goodwill between the petitioners, or the community at large, and the board. However, it is a calm, reasoned, and careful approach which demonstrates that the board makes decisions on the basis of facts rather than emotions. This stance helps the board smooth feathers rather than ruffle them, the latter of which is bound to cause public relations obstacles.

Using such a procedure is wise and valid—for little and big issues alike—whenever the public petitions the board. After all, petitioners are exercising their constitutional rights. The method outlined here confirms these rights. And it's how board members themselves would want to be treated if they were petitioning a board of education.

63 PUBLIC RELATIONS IDEA

Many school board meetings have a substantial audience attending the proceedings. Those in the audience are citizens, representatives from special interest groups, teachers, and even students. Most school boards do not feel as threatened by these visitors as they once did. Yet, there is often an uncomfortable feeling present on the part of both the board and the audience that is not always conducive to relaxed and tension-free meetings. There are two techniques that board members can use that will help produce a more tension-free atmosphere.

First, the board can take the initiative in recognizing those in attendance for the first time. While it is possible that there may be so many new people present that individual recognition is not possible, that is not usually the case. When it is, the visitors are usually members of a group, and it will be possible to at least recognize the group.

Second, board members should take a few minutes to visit briefly with at least some of those in attendance. A few minutes spent in introducing yourself, a few words of conversation, or an expression of thanks for being in attendance at the meeting can help to make anyone feel good.

Good public relations in a school district is composed of many small actions on the part of the board and the educational staff. Most of these involve an application of the *human touch* to remove the coldness and impersonal feelings that exist about many schools and their governing boards. The above practices, when consistently used, will pay dividends because they will improve the climate in which school board meetings are conducted. And that is important for the decision-making process.

64 PUBLIC RELATIONS IDEA

Most school boards provide an appropriate time during each meeting for people to address the board. Many boards also allow individuals to speak at designated times to items on the agenda. Although this is a debatable practice, some school boards find that they are comfortable with it. Where the practice exists, there is sometimes the question of whether a citizen should be allowed to speak before or after the board's discussion of an issue. There is probably no single right answer to this question. But if the practice exists with your board, there are a few precautions that are wise to observe.

First, if a citizen is allowed to make comments following the board discussion but before a decision is reached on a matter, the president of the board should sum up the board members' discussion before a vote is taken. This will help prevent some articulate citizen from unduly influencing the outcome of the board vote—and surprising or perplexing some board members.

Second, the length of the individual's remarks should be limited. It is preferable that the patron be permitted no more than a few words.

Third, the remarks of citizens should be limited only to questions, in order that issues might be clarified for the person asking the question. Handling the matter in this manner is much more likely to shed light on the issue—and will avoid impassioned pleas from individuals for the board to vote one way or the other.

All in all, it is probably best to limit citizen input to the formal time designated for the citizens' forum. But where other practices exist, it is wise to control them so that the board does not forget who is responsible for making the decision. Remember, the board of education is responsible, not the audience.

65 PUBLIC RELATIONS IDEA

School board meetings, when held in public as they should be, offer one more opportunity for a board of education to communicate with the public. That is, they offer a practical opportunity for communication—if we give careful thought to the comments we make during school board meetings.

Unless we consider the impact of what we say and speak as clearly and concisely as possible, we are likely to be misunderstood or misquoted by the news media. Even when we use this cautious approach, it often happens that we make comments or statements we shouldn't.

For example, we may often make a comment when we really have nothing to contribute to the discussion. And frequently, our comment moves the board in a specific direction that does not permit members to deal strictly with the issue under discussion. Or, it may lead to an entirely new issue that the board is not prepared to consider.

There are specific times when we are prone to make needless comments. When we try to change the subject following a tense discussion is one of those times. When we try to hurry may be another. Too, we might be prone to talk when we think we have not contributed. Worse, we may talk when a board member or administrator gets approval for a comment—and we want approval too.

It is good to remember that one of the important contributions a school board member can make is to present an image to the public of being a knowledgeable, intelligent, and thoughtful member of the governing body. Thoughtless, careless, and off-the-cuff remarks seldom do much to create or enhance that kind of image. Thinking about what you say before you say it in a public board meeting is not only good advice, it is a requirement of good boardmanship.

66 PUBLIC RELATIONS IDEA

Administrators and board members receive many suggestions about how the schools ought to be operated, including advice about the curriculum, student discipline, and nearly every other conceivable aspect of education. Most of these ideas come from people with whom administrators and board members are in regular contact. Many of these ideas and suggestions are unusable, unrealistic, or impractical. Regardless of a suggestion's impracticality, it requires some response. While we are obligated to indicate the rejection of an idea, we don't want to "turn people off." After all, it is important that we continue to receive ideas.

People will not continue to offer ideas, however, if they feel that their suggestions are ridiculed or rejected without being considered. Therefore, remember the following:

● Express genuine interest in what people say to you and ask questions to make certain that you really understand their suggestions. In addition, make certain that they have communicated to you what they really intended.

● Don't turn down people's suggestions immediately. Show a degree of courtesy by taking a little time to think about them. Pondering their ideas may indicate value not apparent at first glance.

● Thank them for their interest in the schools and for wanting to help.

● Use some gentleness in rejecting an idea. While you need some measure of firmness in saying no, give your reasons for rejection and indicate that it is always possible that you are wrong.

It is important to remember that just as you like people to listen to you, employees and citizens of the community want you to listen to them. Acknowledge that reality by genuine concern and consideration.

HIDING
BEHIND FIGURES
ALWAYS HURTS PUBLIC RELATIONS

Without doubt, educators and boards of education are often placed in the position of having to make decisions they don't want to make. Few boards or administrators want to be forced to make the kinds of hard choices required when, for example, a textbook controversy arises or a tenured employee's performance is no longer adequate. There are a lot of other decisions we don't want to make because they may not be very important when compared with the larger scheme of events. Some school boards that want to give an excuse for a decision, rather than accept responsibility for it, have a habit of hiding behind figures. School administrators often develop the same bad habit. Here's how it works.

Suppose some community members desire a curriculum change with which the staff or board disagrees. Or there may be a demand for special education services to which the staff and the board object. Too often in such instances, a board and the chief administrator marshal statistical evidence to show that the school cannot afford such moves. Likewise, figures may be gathered to show that not enough students will participate in the program to justify such a decision.

Conversely, when board members or administrators want to accomplish something which is not particularly popular in the community, they often gather evidence supporting the action they want to take. For instance, the board and staff may want to install data processing equipment. So the financial considerations are computed and presented in such a way as to show the public how many dollars will be saved if the equipment is purchased.

We all know that the costs or savings inherent in any particular decision are powerful persuaders at a time when many families find it necessary to keep a constant hand on their pocketbooks. Unfortunately, the figures behind which a board and the administration often hide are sometimes little more than games to justify school action or lack of it. And when the final results are in, our figures may bear little relation to the real world. It's no wonder that the old saying, "The figures don't lie, but liars figure," is frequently heard through the public's and the media's complaints. That's why we need to be aware that the public may or may not accept our figures as readily as we think they do or think they should.

If Figures Are Used
As A Basis For Decisions,
Those Figures Will Be Used Against Us

Every decision that the schools make needs to be made on the basis of facts. Some statistics may well be involved in those facts. Indeed, certain decisions may be made because of the statistics. However, boards and administrators who state publicly that the reason for a decision is that "it costs too much" should know that they're trying to straddle the fence. We may think we are telling the public, "We would very much like to do what you propose, but we just can't afford to," when, in reality, we disagree with the proposal and are using statistics to avoid taking the heat. One-sided statistics soon come to haunt a board, as well as administrators and students. Those who oppose our decision may well use figures to show how stupidly we have acted. Then, we are placed in a position of having to defend our figures. This wouldn't happen if we did not hide behind figures in the first place.

When school officials use figures as an excuse for action or inaction, they are saying that financial considerations forced them to take a course they chose. How much better it would be to say, "We have examined the data. They are available for your viewing. We know that there are powerful arguments for more than one kind of decision. Nevertheless, in our judgment this is the best decision we can make."

When boards of education and educators do not use figures as an excuse for a decision—but instead take the stance that their decision is a matter of collective judgment based upon the evidence—they demonstrate sound leadership and invite public confidence. They are saying, in effect, that the decision is based upon their judgment—the board's and the staff's—as to how best to exercise the responsibilities of their office. This stance has the best chance to gain public acceptance as well as media support. And this is true regarding answering student requests as well. Make no mistake: Students will not respond in the ways we desire when we hide behind a stance of dollars. In fact, we may have developed a "cause" and not even be aware that *we* are the culprits—not our students.

CHAPTER

IX

NINE

PROMOTING SCHOOL EVENTS— SOME DEFINITE HOW-TO'S

"The secret of the world is the tie between person and event. Person makes event and event [makes] person."
—Emerson

There is a wide assortment of activities and events that occur at our schools each week and each year. And each year we experience a great deal of success in some areas and are faced with the problems of securing student, parent, and public attendance at other events. We have music programs, sporting events, theater productions, talent shows, debates, carnivals, award nights, fundraising dinners, end-of-the-year banquets, PTA and PTO meetings, open houses, and back-to-school nights, to name just a few. The following are some tips to use to take the trial and error out of promoting events—and, of course, to help your school meet with greater success and public participation in its multitude of activities.

Two Fundamental Mistakes
1. Not using a variety of methods to create interest. We become disillusioned and disheartened with our promotional efforts when we announce an upcoming event in our newsletter, and then parents tell us that they never got the information. The research concerning such communication tells us why this happens. At best, 42 percent of parents read any individual issue of your newsletter. And fewer than 42 percent read every announcement in the newsletter. This is the reason we must use a variety of methods to capture parent and public attention. We can never assume that one method and one method alone will do the trick and get the job done. Likewise, using the same method of promotion for every activity may prove less than effective.

The following Sensory Studies show precisely why.

Most people retain:
- About 10% of what they read *silently to themselves;*
- About 20% of what they *hear read aloud;*
- About 30% of what they *read silently* and *hear read aloud simultaneously;*
- Up to as much as 90% of what they *read silently* and *hear read aloud simultaneously*—providing the subject matter *relates to a personal interest* and when this process provides for and is augmented by *personal evaluation and discussion.*

THE RETENTION CURVE

In spoken exchange, people tend to forget...
- 40% of what they hear after only twenty minutes;
- 60% of what they hear after half a day; and
- 90% of what they hear after a lapse of seven days.

---

2. Not utilizing students in the early formation of activity promotion thus depriving them of ownership in the outcome. Students are, by far, our best press agents for school events. If students want something to be successful, they will hound their friends and family members to participate. This is especially true for students in the elementary grades, but applies to all other students as well.

Young people can have more energy, enthusiasm, tenacity, and ideas than we ever thought about having. And they can have a great desire to be important by making important things happen for their schools. That's why we need to trust representative students to participate in our early planning sessions. Whether it's getting parents to attend PTA meetings or increasing attendance at football games, given an important objective, students will usually come through in very significant ways. What you shouldn't expect is for students to buy into our concern after "the adults" have worked out all the important details. Likewise, you shouldn't expect parents to participate if you haven't communicated thoroughly with students. If parents ask their children about attending an upcoming event and the children don't know anything, or worse, don't support the idea that attendance is important or that attendance will be beneficial to parents, it is very unlikely that parents will attend—or have any feelings about the fact that they didn't.

PROMOTING TO PARENTS

We have already discussed the usefulness of the school newsletter in letting parents know what's going on in their schools. But we must also realize that a great deal of news gets "buried" in the newsletter. Likewise, some of your news reporting must be "scanty" by virtue of the amount of space available in the newsletter. That's why we must use other methods of promotion in addition to newsletters. Let's discuss a few.

FLYERS

Flyers are inexpensive, grab attention quickly, can be sent at the proper time, and give you plenty of room in which to put all the information needed to promote an event. Flyers can also permit you to include a reply device, if it is advantageous to do so. Often, when tickets or reservations are necessary, a reply device is mandatory to produce a decision to attend. (See Figure 9-1.)

Flyers Should Contain:

1. A large mast headline that names the event that you want publicized.
2. A short description of *where, when,* and *what time* the event is taking place.
3. Detailed information regarding *how* and *where* tickets can be purchased for the event or—in a more general sense—where and how people can take the desired action.
4. Price.
5. The importance and the benefits of participation. In many cases, many parents and members of the community may participate in an activity simply because it is for a good cause. Neglecting this information will reduce participation and sales significantly.
6. A convenient method for ordering or participating. Remember, ease and convenience are a large part of any sales effort. If tickets are hard to procure or if the parent must go to school to get them, you can count on the fact that something else is going to interfere with his or her participation. If, however, you make buying and attending easy—and you give parents a chance to "buy" via the telephone or via their child before the event—the chances are greater that your event will take precedence over anything else that comes up.

Production of Flyers

1. Photocopy or speed print.
2. Use colored paper! Remember, readership is 50 percent greater with color than with black and white.

Distribution of Flyers

1. Send flyers home with students.
2. Mail them out in an envelope to certain members of your public.
3. Fold them so they can be sent as self-mailers.
4. Insert flyers in grocery bags at local grocery stores.
5. Put on counters at other retail stores for local shoppers to pick up.
6. Place on windshields during other school events—on school property only.

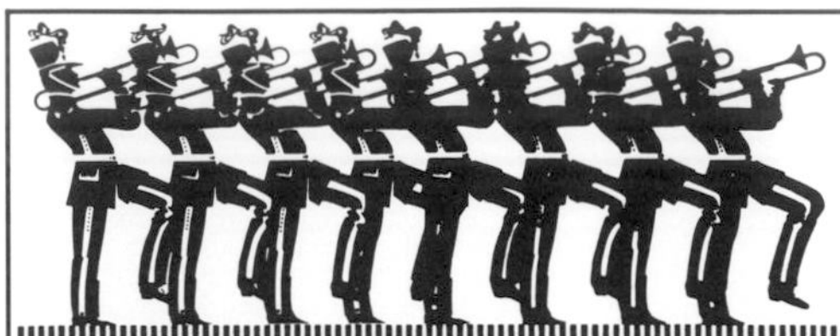

BAND BAR-B-Q FOR BOSTON

WHERE: *School Cafeteria*

WHEN: *Friday, October 2*
5:00-7:00 p.m.

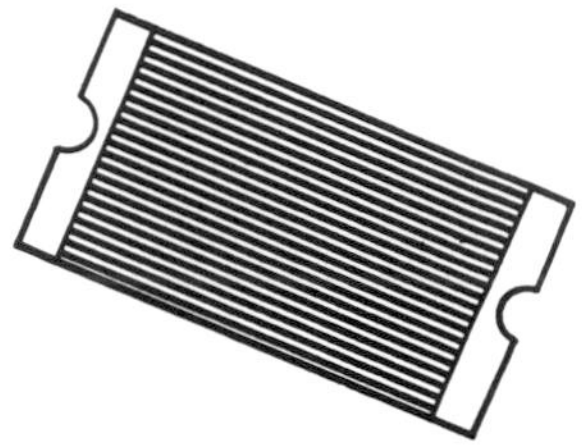

Tickets can be purchased by:
1. Calling the school office.
2. Sending money with the attached reservation slip to school with your child.

AVAILABLE: delicious ¼ chicken dinner - $3.50
which includes baked beans, potato salad, drink, and pie.

delicious ½ chicken dinner - $4.50
which includes baked beans, potato salad, drink, and pie.

The proceeds will be used to send the marching band to Boston.
(Details of the trip and why students will benefit from the experience)

Please reserve
_____ ¼ Dinners $3.50 _____
_____ ½ Dinners $4.50 _____

Make Checks Payable To:

_____

Figure 9-1

NOTES
HOME

Sending handwritten or typewritten notes home which are signed by a classroom teacher is almost guaranteed to get a great deal of attention from parents. Figure 9-2 illustrates how such notes can be used to announce an event or to remind parents of an event about which they have already received information.

Dear Mr. and Mrs. Smith:

Just a reminder about the fundraising Bar-B-Q on October 2. I sure would like to see you there. It means a lot to the students to be able to send the marching band to Boston this year with money from the Bar-B-Q. Tickets are still available.

$3.50 — A delicious ¼ chicken dinner including baked beans, potato salad, drink, and pie.

$4.50 — A delicious ½ chicken dinner including baked beans, potato salad, drink, and pie.

I hope you will make arrangements to come. I would love to have the chance to talk with you at the Bar-B-Q. You may send your money and the attached reservation slip to school with your child, or pay at the door. All we need is your reservation.

Sincerely,

Ann Barber

Mrs. Barber

- -

Please reserve:

\# _____ ¼ chicken dinners at $3.50 each   Subtotal _____

\# _____ ½ chicken dinners at $4.50 each   Subtotal _____

Total _____

Name _____ Phone_____
Make check payable to:

Figure 9-2

Note that the letter from the teacher includes all the informational elements of the flyer. This seems repetitive, but *it is necessary.* You can't rely on the hope that parents will have seen the first flyer or remember what it said if they have. In addition, the note is hand signed. Even if the letter is photocopied or mimeographed, the signature should be in ink and individually signed on each note to get the maximum benefits. And each letter should be hand addressed to the appropriate parent.

PHONE CALLS

There will always be a percentage of parents who will not respond to your newsletters, flyers, and personal letters. *This does not mean that they do not want to participate.* They may have merely delayed a decision on their response. That's when you can organize a group of parents or students to call the remaining parents. This is not as hard as it sounds. Whether using students or parents, telephoning is a very effective tool in gaining public participation.

For instance, a group of 20 parents from your PTA or PTO could reach 100 parents if each makes only five calls. Phone calls need to be handled very delicately, however. In no way should parents be pressured into participating *in anything*. Parents have too much to do already just raising their families and making a living—and pressure does not create good public relations. In addition, many parents are called frequently about participating in other events concerning or involving their children—from church to scouts to athletic teams. Therefore, the nature of your phone calls should *always* be to *inform*, not to strong-arm. The following is a sample phone solicitation. It should be typed and given to all who are making the calls.

EXAMPLE: "Hello. I'm Mr. Myers, calling on behalf of the school fundraising Bar-B-Q. I just wanted to make sure you knew about it and I wanted to let you know that we would very much like you to attend if possible. The money is going to help send the marching band to Boston. Are you planning on attending?" (End here if answer is yes, and say, "Great, I'll see you there!") If he or she is not sure, continue by saying, "It's Friday, October 2, from 5:00-7:00 p.m. Tickets are still available. I can take your order for tickets or you can call the school office by October 1." (Wait for reply). "Thanks and I hope to see you there." If the answer is no, say, "I understand. I hope you will consider attending next year, and thank you for your time."

Preselling Tickets To Parents For Sporting Events

Without question, schools can increase parent and community attendance at sporting events by selling tickets prior to the season. Again, a *flyer* is an important sales device. Many parents want season tickets—especially if their son or daughter is participating in the sport. Others would like to attend only one or two games or matches. That's why prebuying a ticket will help guarantee their attendance. Figure 9-3 is an example of how a flyer may be used to presell tickets to sporting events.

NELSON HIGH SCHOOL

Dear (Parents) (Supporter of Our School):

Nothing is more welcome to students than having (parents) (members of the community) show interest in their extracurricular activities. This note serves two important purposes.

First, we want to inform you of the sports season as it appears on the calendar.

Second, we want to give you the opportunity to buy tickets and reserve seats in advance if you should desire.

Sincerely,

Name

FOOTBALL

BASKETBALL

Date	Opposing Team	**Home**	Date	Opposing Team	Away
Date	Opposing Team	**Home**	Date	Opposing Team	Away
Date	Opposing Team	**Home**	Date	Opposing Team	**Home**
Date	Opposing Team	Away	Date	Opposing Team	Home
Date	Opposing Team	Away			

Tickets at gate: $2.00   Advanced sales: $1.50

(Reply device)

YES. I would like to purchase tickets in advance at the reduced rate. Please secure me:

_____ Season Football tickets at the reduced rate of (fill in)
quantity

_____ Season Basketball tickets at the reduced rate of (fill in)
quantity

_____ Tickets for selected games listed below
quantity

_____   _____

_____   _____

You may pick up your tickets at the school office on or after _____. If you will check the box, we will mail them to you.

☐ **Yes,** please send to me and add $1.00 postage and handling.

Make checks payable to _____

Figure 9-3

It's not difficult to see why and how this convenience measure will win increased parent and community participation. To meet the need for convenience more fully, you may wish to send the tickets to homes through the mail. Simply charge an insignificant $1.00 for postage and handling. You may even recruit the Pep Club to stuff the envelopes for mailings during a preseason evening meeting.

This procedure for selling tickets to parents and the community can easily work with a full season of plays, musicals, talent shows, and concerts as well.

Promotion Timetable

The chart below is a time line for properly promoting school events. Experience will tell you that using this combination of the various media to promote school events will produce maximum results.

PROMOTION TIMETABLE

1 month prior to the event	— Notice in your newsletter
3 weeks prior to event	— Flyer sent home with students, and placed in strategic locations in community
2 weeks prior to event	— Personal letter home from teachers
1 week prior to event	— Press release in local paper; public service announcements on radio
1 week prior to event	— Phone calls
1 week prior to event	— Have children remind their parents

Note: Save your flyers. The same flyers can be used year after year or every other year with only slight changes in dates and times. This practice of "re-use" helps to take some of the work out of designing and writing promotional pieces for the same event year after year.

PROMOTING TO STUDENTS

Promoting school events to students presents a different set of problems than promoting to parents. Among the events that we promote to students are schoolwide, class, and extraclass events such as dances, sporting events, talent shows, club sign-up sessions, and elections. Sometimes, the job is as easy as making an announcement—

and the event is so popular that every student *wants* to attend. However, this situation can change easily from year to year—from dance to dance. Students can change their minds in a matter of weeks as to what they think is an "in" thing to do and what they think is boring or silly. As we know well, students are swayed easily by what their peers think. Therefore, a major key in promoting events to students is to influence what *they* think about the events themselves.

**Involve
Students
From The Start**

If we want student participation in the extracurricular activities that we think are important, we must make each activity *their* activity from the start—and give them guidance. What's more, we have to realize that the involvement of a select group or token few students is not everyone—it is not representative of the entire student body. Often the more popular students—those involved in student council, sports, or certain clubs—are the ones who end up planning and directing all the activities. As a result, a whole group of students, which may be the vast majority, are left out of the planning, deciding, choosing, and promoting process. They are also the students who seldom attend school functions. And yet, these are the students who need to attend the most.

This is the reason it is wrong to have the student council plan all the big dances and other activities. The same students will be involved time and time again—and these students usually aren't successful in involving others outside their circle. Make no mistake regarding this reality. In fact, many of these students go to great lengths to promote the idea that it is "their" school, "their" dance, and "their" priorities that count. Though these students may give lip service to wanting all students to attend, not all students may feel welcome or be received well if they do choose to attend. That's why it's much better to have a student-body activities committee. This can be a very large group of students—because these students can be broken up into smaller committees to plan specific activities. This should not be an elected body. Rather, anyone who wants to be on a committee or who can be persuaded by the staff to serve should be allowed to do so. It's essential that teachers have a special hand in talking certain students into volunteering to serve on a committee. That is, it is important if total student participation is desired.

Teachers should get together at the beginning of the year and define the various groups of students that exist in the school. They should make sure each group is represented by at least three students on the activity committee. And sign-ups can be done in homerooms, in the cafeteria, or with *any teacher* during a specified week. This committee should be formed either early in the fall or during the spring of the second semester for the following year. The committees should have at least two meetings— either before second semester ends or immediately after first semester begins—to work on the planning of fall activities. The first meeting should be designed to explain the purpose of the committee, to formulate a list of upcoming events in the fall, and to designate which students will work on each activity.

The second meeting should involve getting down to brass tacks. At this meeting, students will break up into their individual committees to begin planning and working. Each committee should elect a chairperson to help facilitate the decision-making process. And teachers, counselors, or administrators should be on hand to help any nonactive or stalemated group as well as to give guidance to all groups. Each group should then decide when its next meeting will be held.

You will be amazed how this process helps to increase student participation from all the various groups of students in the school. For maximum results, the faculty should look at all the clubs and activities in the school and identify those students who are not participating. Then faculty members should try to match a student with an activity and convince that student to participate. The goal should be to place every student in both the curricular and extracurricular activities of the school.

THE ACTIVITIES HANDBOOK

Providing Each Student With More Than A List Of Activities

Many schools provide each student with an activities handbook at the beginning of the school year. Because this handbook is usually only a listing of information, it is rarely useful in gaining participation. That's because there is nothing in the handbook that compels a student to participate in a particular activity. A typical handbook entry would appear as follows:

> FRENCH CLUB—
> Open to students who are enrolled in French I, II, III, or IV. Meets once a month after school. We go to French restaurants, and one French play, and practice speaking French together. Sponsor, Mrs. Martin.

This entry is much better:

> FRENCH CLUB—
> Practice your conversational French in a fun atmosphere. This club enables members to get a real flavor of French culture as well as become more fluent in the use of the language. Enjoy our many activities: going to French restaurants, French plays, and French films together. We'd love to have anyone who will be enrolled in French I, II, III, or IV. Beginners welcome and appreciated. See Mrs. Martin, sponsor, in room 213 about signing up—anytime.

In order to put the handbook together, the existing clubs or teams should be asked to develop a list of benefits for belonging to the club or trying out for the team. Then, the sponsor should put the benefits together into a compelling and appealing statement

CLUB INFORMATION SHEET

GROUP NAME _____

Benefits of Joining or Participating

1.   6.

2.   7.

3.   8.

4.   9.

5.   10.

Statement which incorporates the above for the handbook:

How to Sign Up_____

_____

Sponsor _____

Special Considerations _____

Age, Taking special classes, Male, Female, etc.

Figure 9-4

about the activity. Every entry must be careful to explain how and where to sign up—and with whom students can make the arrangements for membership. *Remember, never send students to a room to sign up. Send them to a person.*

Included in the handbook should be a calendar of activities indicating dances, musicals, theater productions, and major sports events.

A form such as the one in Figure 9-4 should be supplied to every group and then turned in to the school secretary. This sheet may be photocopied.

PARENT
AND STUDENT
INFORMATION HANDBOOKS

Most schools issue a student or parent handbook year after year. Although educators like them because handbooks contain all the "how-to" and "information you need to know" in one place, most are not used by parents and students as much as they should be.

The most popular format from the parent's viewpoint for such handbooks is that which combines the essential information with a calendar that includes all the important school dates: beginning and ending dates, days off, vacations, picture days, graduation dates, fundraising events, grade card days, parent meetings, athletic events, and so forth. These calendars devote one 8 ½-inch-by-11-inch page to each month of the school year and the alternate pages to the "need to know" information. These calendars/handbooks are the most popular because they are so useful.

The following is a checklist of information that should be included in the handbooks:

A Checklist Of Information To Put In Your Handbook

Calendar Pages

☐ Students' First Day.
☐ Students' Last Day.
☐ Number of Pupil Attendance Days.
☐ Teacher Inservice Days.

☐ Parent/Teacher Conference Days.
☐ Legal School Holidays.
☐ Dates and times of athletic events.
☐ Dates and times of special
    events: musicals, plays, etc.

Additional Pages

☐ Letter from the Superintendent/Principal.
☐ Table of Contents.
☐ Names of the Board of Education Members.
☐ School address and telephone number of individual school/superintendent's office, plus office hours.

☐ Names and business telephone numbers of key personnel, i.e.
  ● Superintendent
  ● Secretary to Superintendent
  ● Business Coordinator
  ● General Office Secretary

- Curriculum Director
- Transportation Director
- Building Principals
- Building Secretaries
- Health Aides

☐ School hours, with specific information about when students should start arriving at school.

☐ Entrance requirements for students:
  a. Birth certificate.
  b. Age requirement.
  c. Transfer requirements.

☐ What to do when students transfer out of district.

☐ How long students are allowed to stay at school after school is out—and who is responsible for them in those nonclass hours.

☐ Rules for evening activities.

☐ Rules for visitors.

☐ Student fees.

☐ Rules for textbook disbursements.

☐ Policy on school supplies.

☐ How hall lockers will be assigned.

☐ Information concerning student insurance.

☐ Policy on proper dress.

☐ Articles not to be brought to school.

☐ Policy regarding personal property.

☐ Marking clothing.

☐ Policy on students and teachers receiving telephone calls.

☐ Information about student pictures.

☐ Policy on the distribution of flyers from local organizations.

☐ Use of building facility by outside groups.

☐ What to do when you witness vandalism of school property.

☐ How and to whom absences should be reported.

☐ What channels of communication people should use to solve a problem. For example: "Questions about instruction, discipline, or learning materials should be directed to your child's teacher(s); Questions about teachers or school policy should be directed to the principal; Questions about school board operations should be directed to the superintendent or board of education."

☐ Lunch program: price and details.

☐ Lunchroom conduct.

☐ What happens when students are dismissed early.

☐ The policy of the school in regard to vacations.

☐ Procedures that will be taken in severe weather conditions.

☐ When schools will have to call an emergency closing—include TV stations to watch and radio stations to listen to.

☐ Discipline policy.

☐ How tardies and truancy will be handled.

☐ Your policy about the privacy of students' records.

Academics

☐ When and how report cards will be issued.

☐ When parent-teacher conferences will be held.

☐ What the letter grades or symbols mean.

☐ How students make the honor roll.

☐ Provisions made by the school for students to stay after school for extra work.

☐ The homework policy of the school.

☐ Students' responsibilities for assigned work:
  a. During absences.
  b. With regard to late assignments.
  c. With regard to testing and evaluations.

☐ Services of the school in regard to academics.

☐ A listing of all the academic programs or courses with a short description of each.

☐ Use of the library services.

☐ Computer education.

☐ Listing and description of each extracurricular activity.

Health and Safety

☐ What health and first aid services are provided by the school.

☐ Rules and regulations in regard to the health of each child including what parents should do when their child becomes ill in school.

☐ What vision and hearing tests are given; dental program; physical exams for extracurricular sports.

☐ When a signed statement from a physician is required.

☐ Policy on health records, showers, and physical examinations.

☐ Handling communicable diseases.

☐ Handling a child after surgery.

☐ What you are doing to end an illness or injury in school.

POSTERS

Posters are one of the most effective ways for students to learn about an event as well as an effective way to create student interest and desire to participate. Posters are inexpensive to make and help the school hallways look bright and alive with activity. However, there are some things that students and teachers need to know about making posters which make this communication device successful in creating interest and inviting participation.

The greater the number of posters about one activity, the more effective posters become. Therefore, a number of posters concerning the same subject should be set up at strategic locations around the entire building. But the greater the number of posters displayed about several activities, the less effective they become for any one activity. Therefore, be careful about cluttered walls—and get old posters down immediately after the event.

Effective Placement

- School Entries
- Outside the gym
- Outside restrooms
- In the cafeterias—near food lines
- Above drinking fountains
- Outside library doors
- On large blank walls

Ineffective Placement

- On bulletin boards along with other posters and announcements
- On doors that stand open most of the time

Do's And Don'ts For Creating Posters

- ***Do make all the posters for the same event uniform.*** Quite often, different clubs and groups will be promoting activities at the same time. Therefore, if a particular group want recognition of *their* event, all their posters around the building should have the same look. If not, the increased impact caused by repetition will not result. Rather, it will appear that there are many events being publicized by the same group instead of just one. Just as radio and TV commercials gain recognition through a consistent look, so will posters gain recognition through uniformity. Remember, the Pepsi-Cola®

company does not change the look of each commercial aired. Rather, the same theme is used over and over again. In truth, you can easily identify the amateur promoters in your local community. They change their looks continually. The professionals do not.

The first time someone sees a poster he or she may notice only its color. But, the second time this person runs into a poster at a different location, he or she may notice the information on it. And every time this person passes this poster at other locations, it will be a reminder or reinforcement that there is an action that you want him or her to take.

• *Do use color.* One way of getting attention is by using colored poster-board. It's also one way of making all your posters for an event look uniform—even though there are several different students making them. Remember, readership is 50 percent greater with color than with black and white.

• *Do make the words on the poster various sizes.*

• *Don't try to do too much on a poster.* Cluttered posters won't be read. At best, a poster has about four seconds to gain attention and be read.

• *Don't clutter hallways with posters that forbid students to do things.* This creates a poor image for students—and for the public that views these posters.

• *Don't leave posters up after events.*

Use the following poster format for best results and for keeping things simple:

POSTER FORMAT

A. Event

B. Time and Place

C. Benefits

D. Where to buy tickets/price

E. Motivation slogan or brief appeal message

The format for posters will also make excellent ads for school newspapers and vice versa. (See Figure 9-5.)

Figure 9-5

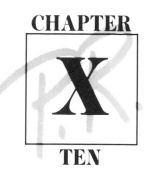

THE PHYSICAL PLANT

"The background reveals the true being and state of being of the man or thing..."
—*Juan Ramon Jimenez*

The values that are held by the administrative and teaching staff are communicated from the first moment a visitor steps through the school door. If the building is neat, clean, and orderly, one value is communicated. If it is dirty, cluttered, drab, and shabby—another is communicated. If the walls are covered by the artwork and achievements of students and staff, a visitor is likely to feel the pleasure and richness of additional values. If the walls are bare and sterile, a visitor is likely to experience different kinds of feelings, including depression and a sense of being institutionalized. In fact, consciously or subconsciously, a visitor might wonder how a building—so full of children—could appear so dead.

Maybe physical appearances shouldn't count for as much as they do—but they do. People are immediately affected by what they see, and their moods change because of it. When people enter our school buildings they ought to feel transformed from the moment they walk through the door. No matter what cares, worries, or concerns they brought with them, the school ought to be able to change or alter visitors' moods—at least for a little while. After all, this is one of the purposes of establishing a positive image via climate. The school building is the place where young people, professional educators, and support staff work. And this is the place where young minds are being shaped, ideas are being exchanged, and serious and important learning is taking place. Indeed, what important and exciting places our schools really are—and the physical environment ought to convey the important work being achieved within their walls.

The question is this: Do our buildings reflect the excitement and importance of what is really going on within our school walls?

Make no mistake: The school building not only reflects—in a very personal way—the feelings of the administrators and staff, but it also affects their productivity. In addition, the building reflects the administration's feelings toward parents and visitors to the school. So, let's start with a discussion of the administrator and his or her office.

THE PRINCIPAL'S OFFICE: THE IMAGE OF JUDGE, JURY, AND EXECUTIONER— OR CHIEF EXECUTIVE AND FACILITATOR?

The principal's office means many different things to many different people—teachers, parents, support staff, and children. Nevertheless, it's safe to say that no one has approached this office without hesitation, apprehension, or fear of reprimand at one time or another. Like it or not, that's the predetermined image school administrators often have, and the image is one that has been formed long before most administrators ever had their jobs.

Now, creating the *right* or positive image in an administrator's office is a tough job. That's because we may have to walk a tightrope between the different concerns of different people. First, the administrator is the chief executive officer of the school—an important position deserving an important image. Second, an expensive looking office may be criticized by staff, parents, and board alike. Third, some symbols may work against the impression we want to form. So here are some "do and don't suggestions" which address these realities, but give us and our offices the characteristics needed to ensure positive and constructive feelings toward us and the principalship.

Don'ts

1. Don't have an office that's cluttered with papers. Stacks of papers don't impress anyone—parents, teachers, or children. To other people, stacks of papers are like hanging a sign that says "I'm disorganized" or "I'm over my head in this job." What's more, clutter takes away from the impression that you want and need to make—that you are an important and competent manager of the whole of the school.

2. Don't keep all your memorabilia out where everyone can see it. In school work, it's almost impossible not to collect all kinds of tokens of affection from students, colleagues, and parents. Mugs, plaques, certificates, footballs, pictures, pencil holders, and posters are among these items of recognition. Although these gifts are nice to receive, they are apt to create a cluttered and unprofessional atmosphere in any office—including one that is nonexecutive in nature. Remember, your office should project the image that this is a vital and important place, where important decisions are made *in the present*. It should *not* be a place which serves as a memorial to you. Therefore, take care in selecting the objects you intend to reveal. Most of your mementos should probably be in your den at home, not in your office.

3. Don't have only large chairs in your office—if you are expecting to work with small children. On the other hand, don't have only small chairs if you want to meet with adults and want them to feel comfortable in your office. In truth, you need a place in your office to visit intimately with both children and adults.

4. Don't have a paddle hanging on your wall or behind the door—if you want to create the impression that you are more than a disciplinarian. If you have such an instrument, most of the students in your school know it is there and know exactly where it is located. Worse, it may be the most talked about item in your office—and may be synonymous with your image. In truth, many teachers will even tell children in class about your paddle as a means of instilling fear in the students. Some principals will even brag about their paddle. They shouldn't. You'll never find a banker bragging to the customers about a foreclosure or a businessman who wants a reputation for repossessing merchandise or a landlord who wants to be noted as an evictor. If you want to be regarded as a leader, mentor, advocate, counselor, and executive make sure your office reflects this decision.

Do's

1. Do hang your diplomas. Degrees earned are positive reinforcements and third-person supports to your qualifications and ability. And they help indicate that you are the learning leader in the school—not the chief paper pusher, head custodian, or chief disciplinarian. Just as in a physician's office, people are allowed to gain a feeling of credibility when you display your credentials prominently, but carefully and tastefully.

2. Do have pictures of children hanging on your walls and statues of children on tabletops, desktops, and bookshelves. We are in a child-centered business. If you go to the offices of General Motors, you won't find pictures of boats, dogs, or birds on their walls. They have pictures which denote their mission: automobiles. The art in your office ought to denote your values, priorities, and work. Therefore, to create the best possible image, hang some prints or photos on the walls where children are featured or pick out some outstanding photographs of students and staff, and display them prominently. Furthermore, don't forget to hang the work of students in your office.

3. Do put all your papers away every night when you go home. There's no way to leave papers on your desk and have people think that you are organized, efficient, action oriented, and on top of your work. Many administrators believe that a loaded desk denotes to all that they are very busy and have a lot of work to do. It does. However, it also makes people believe that you never get the work done—and maybe even that you can't get it all done. In truth, it reflects disorganization and makes others doubt that you can help them with their problems. If you want people—staff and public alike—to think of you as a leader, your office should reflect professional leadership.

4. Do dust your office and polish your desk. Dirt, cobwebs, and dust do not communicate many good or positive feelings toward the people who occupy such a place. And to many—especially other executives and organized teachers—such an office will be a total turn-off. Some administrators might say, "My office has a used and homey feeling." It may to you, but it doesn't to everyone else. The same is true for a merchant, doctor, or lawyer. You may have noticed that stores such as Wal-Mart even have attendants who do nothing all day *except* straighten and clean shelves as customers pass through. They don't even wait until the end of the day to perform such tasks because they want an image which reveals new, clean, fresh, and valuable merchandise. There's no doubt about it; if your office is dirty, you will not foster the necessary image to function as the chief executive officer in a school. Rather, you'll be regarded as a second-class person and second-class administrator who could never run a first-class school.

THE FACULTY LOUNGE—
A PLACE
FOR EVERYONE*

The subject of the faculty lounge comes up in discussions often whenever a group of administrators get together. And in many instances, administrators see so many negative aspects of staff lounge life that they have difficulty finding positive reasons to support the faculty rooms in their schools. Teachers and administrators alike realize that the faculty lounge is often the place where the majority of negative thinking and action occurs. We hear negative talk about the superintendent, principals, parents, kids, and the work of the school—in the lounge. That's why the lounge cannot be left out of any public relations effort. Many times an administrator's first reaction to the negative talk and happenings in the lounge is to wish he or she could close the place or at least make a rule that staff members could not dump their discontent there every day. At times, many administrators might have wondered, "Why should a principal encourage staff members to whine and feel sorry for themselves by providing them with a place to do it?" However, knowing that closing the faculty room would be an unwise or impossible action, many administrators choose to pretend that the room and its problems do not exist. Some administrators refuse to go in the lounge. Some know they aren't welcome. Indeed, some teachers won't go to the lounge either. They find the lounge depressing, unprofessional, and even disgusting.

---

*Excerpts taken from *V.I.P., Views, Insights, & Perspectives,* a publication for administrators written by Dr. Jack L. Larson, and published by The Master Teacher, Inc.

The Faculty Lounge
Meets Specific Needs
Of Teachers

As we ponder the faculty lounge we need to remember that teaching is a lonely profession. Even though teachers are surrounded by people all day long, they carry out their work in the "adult loneliness" of a kids' world. Their work in the classroom gives them little opportunity—compared to other professionals—to share thoughts and hopes with other adults. When staff members are together at school, it is often to share supervision of children, such as during assemblies or playground activities, or in team teaching. Even during staff meetings, teachers spend the time listening and they have little direct involvement with one another. And evening activities with parents or students do not change this condition significantly. Often, the extent of teachers' socialization with one another at such events is a nod of recognition, small talk, and a mere hello and goodbye. Social events just for teachers aren't held frequently enough to fill the need for regular contact and conversation with colleagues. The only refuge many teachers have from the loneliness caused by lack of adult contact—which is inherent in school life—is the faculty lounge.

The lounge also provides daily relief from pressure and stress. Many teachers need the psychological security of knowing they have a private and comfortable space, away from students, where they can "let down" and unwind. The faculty lounge is one of the few places teachers can go during the day to relax semi-privately, rest, and enjoy a few uninterrupted moments alone or with other adults. As building and equipment costs soar and space becomes tight, teachers' need for an "oasis" becomes even stronger.

The faculty lounge is so important to teachers that it is often an item negotiated between the board of education and the teachers in their education association or union. As we all know, most teachers believe that the board of education and the school administration have an obligation to provide them with a special place that is "theirs," where they can rest, work, visit, and post notices on bulletin boards. Whether we think so or not, the lounge meets these vital needs. Yet, to become the place of its intentions, special teaching is a must. Without some ground rules, the lounge will not serve all the people in a school for the purpose of its creation. Rather, it will serve only some.

Actively Supporting
The Faculty Lounge
Is To The Administrator's Advantage

Whether administrators agree with this point or not, they should recognize that actively supporting the faculty lounge is to their advantage. It demonstrates to teachers that the administrator is aware of their wants, needs, and the stresses on them—and that he or she cares about their welfare. Showing concern for the pleasure, comfort, convenience, and happiness of faculty members says loudly and clearly that administrators believe that teachers count. The administrator who supports the existence of the faculty lounge, and who works to make it as attractive as possible, is actively supporting teachers by establishing a climate conducive to productivity and satisfaction.

The faculty lounge also provides an opportunity for the administrator to develop friendships, visit constructively, and demonstrate professional leadership. Therefore, rather than ignoring the faculty lounge and letting negative leadership emerge there, the administrator should make his or her presence felt in positive and constructive ways. By getting involved and exhibiting the leadership which makes the lounge a place where *everyone* wants to be, the administrator encourages the development of positive attitudes and behavior throughout the faculty.

The faculty lounge also benefits administrators by contributing to the cohesiveness of the entire staff. The wise administrator cherishes the team concept in the school because he or she knows that it's essential to good climate. Coming together regularly as a group on an informal basis is conducive to teachers' getting to know one another both personally and professionally. And this is absolutely necessary for a feeling of faculty comradery. Every school has plenty of built-in cliques as well as splits among staff members. Though the faculty room does not eliminate the potential for divisiveness, without the lounge the staff is likely to gather in small, private cliques all over the school—always alone and always in their exclusive places. The damage done by these cliques may far exceed that of any negativism generated in the faculty lounge.

Planning
The Physical Environment
Of The Faculty Lounge...

Any faculty lounge, but especially one that has been a breeding ground for staff unrest or despondency, cannot be transformed into a positive place very quickly. Furthermore, the principal's attitude alone toward the staff members and the faculty lounge, though very important, will not alter the feelings emanating from that room. Equal attention must be focused on the physical setup and environment of the room itself.

Too often, the faculty lounge remains just that—the faculty's room. The administrator provides the space and then adopts a "hands-off" policy, leaving the faculty alone to furnish and decorate the room in whatever way they can manage. In some schools, teachers bring in old couches, chairs, cast-off toasters, or hot-plates—anything from their homes that is no longer needed. The result is the creation of a faculty lounge which resembles a mismanaged Goodwill store. A drab, cramped, disheveled, dirty room filled with secondhand furniture and tin cans for ash trays does not increase staff morale. It sure doesn't make teachers feel very good. It doesn't make them feel that they are important and responsible people doing important work. Nor does it make them feel that they are partners with administrators. Rather, it makes them feel like second-class people who work and live more poorly than all others.

For these reasons, every administrator should make some promises to the staff concerning the faculty room. You might promise, for instance, that the lounge will have:

1. Good equipment.
2. A clean appearance.
3. An annual budget.
4. Sufficient space.
5. Daily maintenance.

Then, develop a plan for fulfilling these promises. Invite representative staff members to form a lounge-planning committee with you. Whether you're fortunate enough to be in on the development of a brand new faculty lounge or are simply wanting to upgrade an existing one, you should keep certain questions in mind and help the committee do the same. Here are a few of the questions you should consider:

● *How will the faculty room be used?* Will it be primarily a lounge where staff members can rest and relax before and after school and during the planning period? How will it be made a pleasant place for all rather than for a select few? Will it be used as a staff lunchroom? Will it be a place for the entire staff or teachers only? (See p. 198 on inclusion of support staff.) Will it be a workroom for teachers? How will smokers and nonsmokers be accommodated? Remember, the smokers will *find* a place to go. Will the lounge be all of the above? The answers to these questions form the basis of your needs assessment and subsequent planning.

Without doubt, staff members may very well have differing answers to these questions. For instance, some teachers don't like the workroom-lounge combination because they feel that paper cutters, duplicating machines, typewriters, and other equipment take up valuable space and create noise which detracts from the relaxing atmosphere of the lounge. Others are enthusiastic about the workroom-lounge, because they can take care of necessary tasks while enjoying refreshments and visiting with fellow staff members in the lounge. Therefore, when deciding how the faculty lounge will be used, it is very important to take a poll or let the staff vote.

● *How large should the faculty room be and where should it be located?* The faculty lounge should be big enough to accommodate comfortably the largest number of staff members who are likely to be in it at one time. It should be a pleasant room, preferably with windows, and located so that it is easily accessible to all. If it's located off the beaten track in some corner of the building, it may seldom be used by some teachers. Therefore, carefully select the location. Above all, don't relegate the faculty room to a leftover space after all the room assignments have been made. This is an important area insofar as teachers' morale, productivity, and satisfaction are concerned.

- *What furnishings, equipment, and maintenance does it need?* The answer to this question depends, of course, on the answers to the preceding questions. But in general, tables for small groups and couches or easy chairs should be provided. A refrigerator, a sink with hot and cold water, cabinets for storage, a coffee pot, magazine and display racks, and a bulletin board are many of the items also needed. Make sure there is adequate lighting and ventilation. All furniture should be attractive, comfortable, and in good repair. Art work on the walls, as well as green plants, is a nice touch. Consider utilizing the talents of staff members, such as the home economics teacher or art teacher, to create a decor that is pleasant, inviting, and conducive to relaxation.

Make sure the custodian places the faculty lounge on his or her workload of obligations. The faculty room should get more than a quick sweep with the custodian's mop or broom. The administrator might request that the room be ready and the coffee pot turned on by the time the first teacher arrives in the morning. The administrator might also request that the custodian check the room over and clean it a couple of times a day as well as once before he or she leaves at night. Sometimes, the custodian's attitude reflects the feeling that because the faculty room is messed up by adults, "they" should keep it clean. Yet, this is seldom the attitude that businesses take toward their employee lounges. Therefore, make clear that the lounge is a priority. Especially, make sure that it is not a space that the custodian cleans only when he or she has time. This task is accepted more easily if the lounge is for all—cooks, custodians, aides, and the rest of the school team.

- *What responsibilities will staff members have?* The items for which the staff will assume responsibility should be defined from the outset. Staff members should share the cost of coffee and other drinks. A soda and candy machine might be obtained and monitored by a faculty committee. Other committee responsibilities might include use of the room, decorations, bulletin board policy, and other issues relating to the total operation of the room. The lounge committee should fully represent the wishes of the faculty.

Architect Lawrence Perkins of Chicago was once asked, "Why have beautiful schools for kids?" He replied, "For whom else then?" A similar remark may well be made about the school personnel and the faculty lounge. Whatever involvement you may have administratively in planning, equipping, budgeting, and arranging for maintenance of the faculty room, it is paramount to provide evidence that you *believe* in the importance of the faculty room and the people who use it. This cannot happen with a "hands-off" approach. It can only result when you hold to the functions of administration: to be a facilitator of the work of the school. And remember, the lounge *is* a part of the school.

THE CAFETERIA

The cafeteria is one of those places where bad public relations news can begin and then be carried home to parents. The cafeteria is everybody's room. It belongs to students, to faculty, to support staff, to visitors, and to administrators. For many people, it's the "time-out" room—especially for students. Here students are able to talk openly and freely. They are also able to get up and move around. Lunch time is the longest period for most students that isn't organized for them and totally controlled by adults. This change of pace is both healthy and beneficial. Students need the time to eat, to relax, to let off steam, to talk with their friends, to be alone, to walk around freely—rather than sit in an assigned seat—and to "breathe." For students in the upper grades, this "break" becomes even more important because recess has long been a benefit of the past. And yet, as administrators, we know that if there is one room where trouble, mischief, and loud noise are likely to occur, it's in the cafeteria. After all, free time often brings unconstructive behavior.

The quality of the food and the variety of choices are big issues with students as well as with the adults who eat in the cafeteria. If the food is regarded as good and appropriately cold or hot, then students are more likely to have a happy and satisfying time in the cafeteria. However, students are prone to bad behavior, including food fights, when the food is poorly prepared—or when students are bored with the choices. And it is hard to please people with food. After all, we even get "tired" of the food at home. There are few mothers and fathers who haven't heard the same complaints about the food at home that our cooks hear about the food at school.

That's why many schools have a plan and a program for the cafeteria just as they do for other aspects of school life—one in which students, teachers, administrators, and cafeteria workers all have a voice—and a responsibility.

67 PUBLIC RELATIONS IDEA

Choose a committee. Ask representatives from each of the following groups to be on the committee: two teachers, six students, two cafeteria workers, and an administrator. Brainstorm your ideas for the cafeteria. Your goal is to come up with:
1. A position statement for your cafeteria.
2. A promise to your target-group students.
3. A list of positive ideas intended to make the promise and position realities.

Remember, there is no such thing as a bad idea—only some ideas that are better than others.

EXAMPLE:

Cafeteria

Position: We want to make the cafeteria period the most pleasant period possible for teachers, students, principals, and cafeteria workers alike.

Promise: We promise good food at good prices and a varied menu—all in a calm and relaxing atmosphere.

Positive Ideas:
1. Serve family style
2. Play music
3. Have flowers on the tables
4. Have a committee that makes the rules and evaluates the food
5. Have a suggestion box
6. Have a "no cutting in line" policy
7. Allow students to sit where they want
8. Cook Appreciation Day

Do this exercise in conjunction with the people motivators, Chapter III, p. 31.

Obviously, some of the above ideas are better than others. But some of them are very good. Remember, administrators and teachers can't be the purveyors of all truth or total perfection. That's why we must learn to involve all those who are going to be affected by our plans and processes. This is best achieved by asking them to help us create those plans and processes.

HALLWAYS

Hallways are the passageways to the various places of learning in a school. They lead to classrooms, offices, restrooms, cafeterias, gyms, and libraries. All people in the school, including visitors, travel these passageways. They are the only places used and seen by everyone every single day. Whether we want to admit it or not, what happens and what is seen in hallways affect learning—for the hallways are often where the moods of students and teachers are formed before and after leaving class or leaving for the day.

While classrooms take on the identity of the individual teachers who teach within them, hallways are a collective expression. They are the expression which administrators, staff, teachers, and students establish together. Therefore, as much as any other place in the schools, hallways reveal the values and priorities of adults and their attitudes toward students and vice versa.

Hallways are also areas of individual freedom and privacy. Thus, hallways are a source of concern for teachers, administrators, and students. It's this concern that causes many administrators and teachers to concentrate on the rules and regulations for hallways—rather than on creating a congenial and interesting space for students to pass and relate to other people. Yet with the use of a little creativity, we can set the tone for real student body recognition and achievement in our halls. Our walls can become the billboards for student and teacher awards, honor rolls, and curriculum and extraclass opportunities. The walls can contain lists of the most improved students, most creative students, and most caring students. The halls can display athletic awards, music and theatrical awards, and individual birthdays. When we attempt to create a congenial atmosphere in the hallways, there will be no doubt to students, staff, and visitors that there are many positive, exciting, and rewarding events going on within our schools.

68 PUBLIC RELATIONS IDEA

Choose an advisory committee. Ask representatives from different groups to serve on a twelve person committee: three teachers, six students, two aides, and one administrator. Allow the committee to brainstorm ideas for hallways.

EXAMPLE:

Hallways

Position: We want our hallways to be colorful and exciting representations of the activities and opportunities of our school. In addition, we want our hallways to motivate students and teachers alike toward greater achievement.

Promise: We promise that we will have groups of students and teachers working on ideas for the hallways at all times—and we won't allow the hallways to become drab, tattered, or negative.

Positive Ideas:
1. Have certain clubs or classes responsible for certain hallways
2. Have art classes display their work
3. Have a banner where students can write positive graffiti
4. Have a "congratulations" bulletin board
5. Make specific plans for each club throughout the school
6. Purchase art for hallways
7. Name halls after famous people or local people
8. Make hallways convenient for visitors
9. Create welcome signs

Do this exercise in conjunction with the people motivators, Chapter III, p. 31.

It should be noted that this same process can be applied to any aspect of school life whether we want to improve other physical locations or the image of certain programs, clubs, or classes.

CHAPTER

XI

ELEVEN

DRESS— AN IMPORTANT PUBLIC RELATIONS INGREDIENT

"The body is the shell of the soul, and dress the husk of that shell; but the husk often tells what the kernel is."
—Anonymous

HOW DO YOU LOOK?...

IT DOES MAKE A DIFFERENCE

Talking to another person about the way he or she dresses and looks is not an easy task or an attack-free subject. Neither is urging people to bathe daily, wash their hair, brush their teeth, or use deodorant on a regular basis. Because these important hygienic topics are so intimately personal, seldom are they discussed in groups—much less individually and directly. As the saying goes, "Your best friend won't tell you." It's true, your best friend won't. And if he or she does, at best, we're apt to either justify our habits or tell him or her, "It's none of your business," and resent the friend.

It's even difficult for many teachers to talk to children about these personal subjects. There are countless times when teachers are compelled to ask a counselor, nurse, physical education teacher, or administrator to "talk to one of my students" about a cleanliness or hygiene problem. The same is true when a teacher or administrator has these problems. Nobody wants to or will discuss the situation with him or her. The subject is just "too sticky."

Likewise, students would like to talk to teachers and administrators about being allowed to dress certain ways. And this issue is equally sticky. As adults, we don't want to see students dressing just any way. Neither do parents. Some parents will even ask us to talk to their child or set rules at school that will make the issue easier to control at home.

Most of us sense—if we don't actually know or have tested data—that people's appearance can and does affect their personal pride. It affects how they think, how they act, and how much they learn. Therefore, we usually put some parameters or limits on what students should and can wear to school. However, as educators, we ourselves don't want any—and won't permit any—limits, recommendations, or parameters to be set for us.

An Overlooked Advantage

A professional teacher or administrator needs all the help he or she can get to relate better to human beings. Proper dress and good grooming are easy professional attainments. They may be gained so easily that many people completely overlook the value and importance of appropriate dress and good grooming to their professional image. Whether we realize it or not, how we look has a great deal to do with people's acceptance of us—both personally and professionally. This includes the acceptance of us by students, parents, colleagues, and the public alike. Many educators may argue that clothes and appearance should not be that important—that the "inner person" is the important thing. Even though this may be true, the experienced person knows that often, how one dresses determines whether he or she gives other people a chance to know that "inner person." Clothes may not make the person, but they help others accept the person.

Business and industry have long accepted the importance of dress. Most restaurants have uniforms. So do many automobile garages and paint shops. Doctors wear smocks, nurses have uniforms, and executives wear suits and ties. The list goes on and on. Yet, the reason dress is mandatory in these occupations is that it is known, without question, that appearance is a powerful influence. It represents a standard. And unless the standard is met with compliance, customers won't accept the work as being very skillful and a worker's advancement in the organization will probably not be achieved. We can argue all we want, but dress *is* important. And important people dress in important ways. As educators, if we want people to think we are important and do important work, we need to comply with a professional dress code. If not, we will lose the battle of image and public relations.

We have seen teachers who were in a real position to help a child and his or her parents, but the parents were "turned off" the minute they saw the teacher. Yes, this teacher may still have his or her individual identity protected, but the child he or she intended to help was the loser—and so were the teacher and the school. Often, we must sacrifice a little of our individual identity and all of our selfishness to be a professional teacher in the eyes of others. This is a reality of professional life for all professionals, including educators.

The truth is, similar standards of accepted dress apply to most of the professions. A lawyer *could* wear a pair of Bermuda shorts in a hot courtroom—but he or she won't. If the lawyer could not relate to a jury, his or her client would be the loser—and so would the lawyer.

Your Personal Reflection

Teachers or administrators who don't think students measure them by their dress are foolish indeed. Appearance is very, very, very important to children. The minute a teacher walks through the door, students "size him or her up." You either pass or fail the test. Whether you wear heels and hose, a suit and tie, or a tight dress, all result in either a professional or unprofessional image conveyed to students. Whether you brush your teeth, comb your hair, shine your shoes, or use perfume or cologne reflects to all with whom you associate how smart, how considerate, and how aware you are—of yourself and others.

It also reflects how important you think your profession is and how important you think students are. Students are taught at home, in scouts, via the media, in the elementary grades, in health and physical education courses, and in home economics classes, the importance of good grooming. They are taught appropriate dress for appropriate occasions. They learn how to dress for a picnic, religious worship services, a party, and for work. Of course, these students should expect to see their lessons practiced by their teachers. If these lessons are not reflected in the appearances of professional teachers, what opinions can we expect the students to form?

The truth is that many students get dressed in the morning in homes where both the mother and father are dressing for work. The child may see the father dress in a suit and tie, or in jeans. Likewise, the child may see the mother dress in a suit, a dress, or slacks. Children may form the opinion, over time, that both mother and father are going to jobs that are important simply because both dress in suits. These same children then go to school and make judgments about teachers based on how the teachers dress in comparison to the children's parents. If the teachers are not dressed in an executive style, the children may conclude that teachers are not very important people in our society. If you think not, watch television tonight and observe how dress is taught to us continuously. It doesn't take a bright child to see that tennis shoes, jeans, slacks, and sport shirts are not the dress of executives. One thing is certain: Education is the most important of all professions. Very few people will find success in the world today without passing successfully through our classrooms. Yet, educators will never be found among the most *respected* of all professionals until our dress complies to certain standards. That's how vital dress is to the individual and the whole of the school.

PERSONAL CHOICE
VS.
PROFESSIONAL CHOICE

Most of us do our very best to make choices about clothing that will make us look not only successful, but attractive as well. As we do, many of us make the wrong choices. What we choose for attractiveness and flair often works against our desired image of professionalism and trustworthiness.

John T. Molloy, author of *Dress for Success** and *The Woman's Dress for Success Book*,* has done valuable research that helps the professional take some of the guesswork out of dressing for maximum success with superiors, colleagues, and customers. His research started with a series of experiments done in Connecticut schools. Through these experiments he concluded that the type of clothing worn by teachers substantially affects the work and work attitudes of students.

He tested two groups of male teachers: The first wore a casual look—penny loafers, a tie, and a shirt, slightly open at the collar. The second group of teachers wore traditional black lace-up shoes, a conservative suit, and a conservative tie. The outcome: The students worked harder and longer for the teachers with the conservative look.

Through additional experiments, Molloy discovered that the look people respect, trust, and associate the most with success is the executive look. Please note that this doesn't mean that all people necessarily like this look or that it's appropriate for every worker on the job, but it is the look people trust and respect. Likewise, as Molloy has continued in his research, he has discovered that we *change* our attitudes regarding proper and professional dress. Therefore, we need to keep abreast of these changes to keep in tune with the perceptions and judgments of our various publics.

The Executive Style—
The Best Dress
For Both Teachers And Administrators

Several years ago we at The Master Teacher were asked to go to work with a group of over 100 administrators for three days. The schools in the district were suffering from teacher strikes that had gone on for three years in a row and they were going into their fourth year. Open disdain, disrespect, suspicion, and even hatred for these administrators had developed among teachers. We had very little time to work with these administrators. After much consulting with our professional staff, we decided to ask them to do two things to change their image. First, we had them say to teachers during and after the strike, "I missed you and the kids missed you." Second, we asked the administrators to change their dress. In essence, we asked them to start

---

*John T. Molloy, *Dress for Success* (New York: Warner Books, Inc., 1975) and *The Woman's Dress for Success Book* (Chicago: Follet Publishing Co., 1977).

dressing in agreement with the research which indicated how a person in an administrative position should dress to command maximum respect. We asked them to start dressing like executives. And our advice was very specific for both men and women administrators. We took these two steps first, and saved the leadership and management training for later.

The result was that within 60 days, administrators reported—to a person—that teachers' attitudes toward them had begun to reverse or had actually completely reversed. They couldn't believe the results. Now, administrators were seen as knowledgeable, caring, considerate, and respected advocates for learning and teaching.

Why do we put so much weight on the ability of dress to have changed teacher attitudes and perceptions? The reason is both simple and complex. The administrators in the district were willing to try to change their hostile attitudes toward some or all teachers to attitudes of advocacy. But people want more than advocates—they want *successful* advocates. And in this case, teachers had to be able to look at their administrator every day and say, "You know, this person looks pretty competent and is trying to carry out his or her responsibilities in a professional way. Maybe I ought to listen to what he or she has to say." This is why the administrators' new executive style had such an impact. Relationships had to get better as a result—and people actually started working together with a new esprit de corps.

Another example from our personal experience should have special interest to our female readers. Half of the executive positions at The Master Teacher are held by women. About seven years ago, before we established a dress code, women managers were having a great deal of difficulty being taken seriously by suppliers as well as by some teachers, principals, superintendents, and board members. Make no mistake, we have always had high standards for dress. The women in our organization dressed well. They were all well groomed. But they were not always dressed for maximum respect. As a result, salesmen would make passes at them, call them "hon," or refer to them as the "little gal in the front office." Many suppliers wouldn't even take "no" for an answer. Instead, they would go over the female manager's head, ask the superior to make the decision and, many times, wouldn't even come through with their deliveries on time.

Now, at The Master Teacher, with only a change in dress, not many women experience any of these indignities any more. Women are treated quite differently. They are seen as authoritative decision makers, and are treated respectfully. Their "no's" mean no—and they command the respect to have promises and deadlines met on time. More important, educators and suppliers seek them out and they enjoy an equality that many women do not yet enjoy in the professional world. And all we changed was dress.

Remember, Leon Lessinger said the first two ingredients to a healthy and successful self-concept are a person's ability to say: First, "I feel successful," and, second, "Other people feel I'm successful." As educators we are already successful. Most of us can count our successes every day. But we deserve to *feel* more successful. And as a profession, we need others to believe that we are successful too. After all, success without recognition usually renders the success less meaningful.

A close look will reveal something we may not have considered before. We have this nation's children under our influence for twelve or more of the most formative years in their lives. We are their teachers. Only part of what we teach them will come through our instruction. The rest will be taught by the unspoken influence of our modeling. The way these students of ours present themselves in the world of work will in large measure be determined by how we present ourselves in our work. It is a huge responsibility that we must not take lightly—for them or for ourselves.

The Traditional Business Suit
Commands Maximum Respect
In Almost All Business Circles

For men, executive dress consists of the traditional two- or three-piece business suit. In every piece of research, it outscored the sport jacket for respect and credibility. This suit is gray, navy, khaki, or beige rather than red, green, or light blue. It is pinstriped, subtle plaid, or solid. The executive look always includes a long-sleeve shirt in white, light blue, or possibly another pastel color—solid or pinstriped. Knit, polyester, and ribbonweave shirts, as well as plaid, polka dot, floral, and paisley patterns are not acceptable executive dress.

The tie is probably the most important feature of professional dress for men. If a man's profession prohibits him from wearing a suit, a tie will always add credibility. Ties should be silk or a polyester that looks like silk. They may be solid colors or patterned with small polka dots or even-spaced stripes or motifs such as those on the rep or club tie. Bow ties and ties with large symbols are not considered part of the executive style.

For women, the skirted, unvested suit is the foundation for the executive look. Women who want to command respect will refrain from wearing slacks or pantsuits in the work setting, if possible. A woman's suit should be a solid color, tweed, or subtle plaid. Wool or woolen blends and cotton or cotton blends are preferable to polyester. Navy, black, gray, tan, and khaki command more respect than red, green, light blue, or pink.

Dresses are also considered part of the executive look, but they should be of a solid color or small patterned fabric—never flowered. Sundresses, dresses with puffy sleeves, flowered dresses, and dresses with large geometric patterns are not seen as executive style. A blazer is a great addition to a woman's wardrobe and can be worn with skirts or dresses. Blouses are preferable to sweaters, and plain blouses with bows or ties are peferable to blouses with lots of ruffles. The best shoe for the executive style is the basic pump. Strappy high heels and boots are associated with evening wear or sportswear. (See Figure 11-1.)

Female teachers often reject the notion of dressing like an executive for school. They say that dealing with young children requires them to bend down, sit on the floor, work with paints and paste—all of which are hard to do when one is "dressed up." Female teachers of the older students say that students wouldn't be able to relate to them if they dressed in an executive style. In regard to these objections we suggest that teachers rethink how they would like to be perceived by students and the public. If they want respect and to be regarded as professionals they will conclude that they should dress one way. If they want to be "with it" they will conclude that they should dress another way.

MEN	
What Is Executive Dress?	**Not Executive Dress?**

1. Traditional-cut, vested suit
   a. Fabric: wool or wool blend; cotton or cotton blend
   b. Color: gray, navy, khaki, light brown
   c. Design: pinstripe, subtle plaid, solid
2. Long-sleeve shirt
   a. Fabric: Oxford cloth
   b. Color: light blue, white, sometimes pink
   c. Design: small pinstripe, solid
3. Tie (always)
   a. Fabric: silk or polyester that looks like silk
   b. Design: solid, even-spaced repeating pattern (small polka dot) rep, or club
4. Shoes
   a. Style: cordovan, wing tip, or plain lace; some slip-ons if not too much metal on them
   b. Color: black, brown
5. Socks: dark, over the calf
6. Top coat: beige
	1. Sport jacket: European, fitted cut
	   a. Fabric: polyester
	   b. Color: red, green, light blue, dark brown
	   c. Design: loud plaids
	2. Short-sleeve shirt
	   a. Fabric: knit or polyester
	   b. Design: plaid, polka dot, floral, paisley, pictures, ribbon print
	3. Tie
	   a. Color: solid black or solid purple
	   b. Design: large symbols, pictures
	   c. No tie
	   d. Bow tie
	4. Shoes: patent leather or crepe-soled
	5. Socks: ankle length socks in bright colors
	6. Top coat: black

WOMEN	
What Is Executive Dress?	**Not Executive Dress?**

1. Skirted, unvested suits
   a. Fabric: tweed, wool or wool blend, cotton or cotton blend
   b. Color: navy, black, gray, tan, khaki
   c. Design: solid, subtle plaid
2. Dresses
   a. Color: preferably dark
   b. Design: small pattern (not flowered)
3. Blazers: navy or camel
4. Blouses (preferable to sweaters)
   a. Design: with bows or man tailored
5. Shoes: basic pump, medium heel
6. Hose: plain, skin-color
	1. Slacks, pantsuits, sportswear, pinstriped suits
	2. Dresses: sundresses, dresses with puffy sleeves, flowered dresses, or dresses with large geometric patterns
	3. Sweaters
	4. Blouses with ruffles
	5. Shoes: strappy high heels
	6. Hose: black, white, colored, patterned

Figure 11-1 Executive Dress

Even if we make the decision to dress professionally, male and female teachers both cite money as one of the main barriers between them and a professional wardrobe. And although it does take money to buy good clothes, we must consider the fact that it takes money to do many of the things that we value—continue our education, drive nice cars, and entertain ourselves and our families. How we spend our money is a decision we make and we make it daily. If we want to build a professional wardrobe we must make a decision to budget to do so, just as we do for other major expenses.

As professionals, we need the vision to know that we can be all dressed up and still have no substance. That's not the point. The point is this: Images are very powerful. People *are* affected by how we look. People make immediate and lasting judgments based upon how we dress. Right or wrong, good or bad, this is the reality.

It doesn't take great perspective to understand that when we dress as professionally as we can for the tasks we must perform, we can be far more effective in influencing people. And considering that our effectiveness on the job is often dictated by how influential we are with students, colleagues, parents, and superiors, this valuable key to success cannot be taken lightly. That's why we cannot afford to overlook our appearance. Remember, clothing may not make a person, but it surely can be a contributing factor in the unmaking of him or her.

MORE POSITIVE PUBLIC RELATIONS IDEAS

"Just as our eyes need light in order to see, our minds need ideas in order to conceive."
—Nicolas Malebranche

Times of year when we need special events:
1. Before school bcgins
2. After students begin new classes, a new semester, a new trimester, or summer school
3. Before and after grade cards
4. When academic schedules are chosen/determined
5. When new curriculum is offered
6. During holidays/break periods
7. During preregistration
8. Contract time
9. End-of-school week

IDEAS FOR ADMINISTRATORS TO USE WITH STAFF MEMBERS

PUBLIC RELATIONS IDEA #69
Let staff members know about district concerns—on a regular basis. Staff shouldn't learn about anything "second hand."

PUBLIC RELATIONS IDEA #70

Send birthday cards and other appropriate cards to colleagues. (Don't leave the job up to the staff hospitality committee.)

PUBLIC RELATIONS IDEA #71

Set up a bulletin board and post laudatory materials and articles—for both teacher and student information.

PUBLIC RELATIONS IDEA #72

Staff morale is never universally high or universally low. Rather, it's cyclical in nature. Consequently, morale may be high one month and low the next. One of the times when morale is often lowest occurs in the winter, especially in late February or early March. At this time employees could use a bit of a boost to renew the enthusiasm to do the best possible job. Unfortunately, school board members and administrators may take the attitude that they employ and pay people—and that should be effort enough on their part. While that may well be true, it doesn't do much for improving instruction in the schools. Rather than taking this view, a board as well as administrators should do something to boost morale. Next winter, why not try one of the following:

Arrange to have some small token of appreciation placed on all teachers' desks before they arrive at school on Monday morning. The token might be an apple from the principal with a thank you note attached. A thank you note from the board of education is also a good idea. Or an administrator might try to involve parent organizations in implementing an activity. Another possibility is to release employees early some Friday. Even if the early release is permitting them to leave immediately when school is dismissed, it says to the teacher, "We care."

If finances or legal agreements prohibit any of these actions, then a simple note of appreciation delivered to each teacher and signed by the students or a board member can be used. These small touches, if not overdone, can be a big morale booster. At a time when there's much talk about teacher stress and burnout, a simple act can say, "We care"—and can boost morale.

PUBLIC RELATIONS IDEA #73

Have administrators teach a class occasionally...and have teachers switch classes with colleagues once or twice each year.

PUBLIC RELATIONS IDEA #74

Meet with each staff member informally at least once in a grading period, whether you think it's needed or not.

PUBLIC RELATIONS IDEA #75

Once a year, you might have teachers from your school switch classes with teachers from a nearby school. Or your teachers might substitute in a "comparable" district (prearranged). Then, take a realistic look at how you treat substitute staff members at your school.

PUBLIC RELATIONS IDEA #76
Ask teachers and support staff to attend one board meeting a year. And administrators should attend as many board meetings as possible.

PUBLIC RELATIONS IDEA #77
Form an "Innovative Ideas Advisory Council" of teachers and administrators...just to brainstorm, identify problems, and develop a total awareness of your school.

PUBLIC RELATIONS IDEA #78
Use the weekly bulletin to build an awareness of trends in and plans for departments and clubs within your school.

PUBLIC RELATIONS IDEA #79
Organize an all-school brainstorming hour to get numerous workable communications ideas—ideas uniquely appropriate to your school.

PUBLIC RELATIONS IDEA #80
Get a Polaroid camera and use it to take pictures of all substitute staff members serving your school. Post the pictures each day—tell who the substitutes are and for whom they are substituting, and encourage a warm welcome.

PUBLIC RELATIONS IDEA #81
Assign new teachers a "buddy" and give them one of last year's yearbooks. Put up a bulletin board in the staff room with the new teachers' pictures, names, and subject areas as well as hobbies and family information.

PUBLIC RELATIONS IDEA #82
Provide planned opportunities for staff members to share information picked up at workshops and conferences.

PUBLIC RELATIONS IDEA #83
Have a "family day" at your school—during an evening or on a weekend—when staff members can bring their families to see where they work, meet colleagues they work with, and see what they do.

PUBLIC RELATIONS IDEA #84
Try using the telephone for follow-up calls to substitutes. Ask them how their day at school went, and what suggestions they have to improve the effectiveness of substitutes in your school.

PUBLIC RELATIONS IDEA #85
Call absent teachers during the day and wish them well.

PUBLIC RELATIONS IDEA #86
Reserve part of your staff bulletin board for "good news."

PUBLIC RELATIONS IDEA #87

In the spring of the year, it's not uncommon to read that a college or university has recognized one or more outstanding teachers by award, cash grants, and public acclaim. These outstanding teachers may have been selected by the students, administrative officials, or a jury of their peers. Regardless of the method used, one or more faculty members are recognized and rewarded each year for their performance. They are representative of all teaching excellence.

Unfortunately, these practices aren't common to every public or parochial school. They could be. Even in the small system, two or three thousand dollars could be set aside each year to reward teachers who are recognized for excellence. In one recent situation, a local businessman and a professional individual agreed to establish a trust fund, the income from which was sufficient to award a significant cash reward to several teachers each year. Any teacher may be nominated for the award. A committee composed of teachers, administrators, and citizens decides upon the recipient.

Do all teachers like this procedure? Certainly not. Some have very strong objections and claim that the selection is too political. Perhaps it is. Regardless, the individuals selected for recognition each year have some definite attributes that appeal to students and parents—and the students under their direction do achieve. Such awards are also evidence that a board is willing to designate certain teachers as desirable models.

Recognizing teacher excellence with rewards is not the only way to reward and encourage superior teaching. However, it is well worth considering.

PUBLIC RELATIONS IDEA #88

Let the person who's been responsible for a program or activity get the credit he or she deserves. Let him or her make the report to the faculty or the board of education.

PUBLIC RELATIONS IDEA #89

Give "Teacher of the Week" or "Teacher of the Month" awards. A good internal public relations program includes efforts that reward a great many people. Good programs don't attempt to single out one person at the expense of many. "Teacher of the Year" awards fall into this category. There is one winner and many losers. In such a climate, losers don't try very hard. How much better it would be to consider a "Teacher/Colleague of the Week/Month" award which enables you to reward 9 to 36 teachers. This practice also creates an image in the minds of the public that their schools have a great number of important and creative teachers instead of just a few.

PUBLIC RELATIONS IDEA #90

A useful practice as you visit classrooms is to be on the lookout for specific techniques, practices, materials, or classroom environments that other teachers would be interested in knowing about. When you see something that should be shared, ask the teacher you are observing if he or she would take some time at the next department or faculty meeting to explain or demonstrate the technique or practice. You will be pleasantly surprised how eager teachers are to show what they are doing in the classroom. It should be noted that teachers appreciate this kind of sharing, because they are seeking success and working to be better at what they do.

PUBLIC RELATIONS IDEA #91

Do not make calls to your colleagues through your secretary. Above all, do not keep your colleagues waiting on the line while you transact other "more important" business.

PUBLIC RELATIONS IDEA #92

Caution your staff members, and be on the alert yourself, for criticism of your colleagues' schools and school practices. Be especially concerned about teachers who are shared between two or more schools and who carry "messages"—often damaging—from school to school. Work out strategies with your administrative colleagues and, if you feel comfortable, with the travelling teachers to reduce these comments. One strategy may be for the administrators involved to hold occasional meetings of a nonthreatening, information-gathering nature, to hear the interests and concerns of the teachers who serve them jointly.

PUBLIC RELATIONS IDEA #93

Remember, there are other schools in your community—or nearby. Invite groups of students from neighboring public, private, and parochial schools to participate in activities with your school. These activities need not be competitive. Rather, they can provide opportunities for students to come together, discuss, and collaborate upon issues facing the young people of the community.

PUBLIC RELATIONS IDEA #94

Ask a different teacher or department head to host each scheduled faculty meeting. Meetings should be held in the individual's classroom or department. During the first ten minutes, have the host staff member tell others about special instructional techniques, curriculum, and other areas of his or her program. This type of scheduling gives the staff an overview of all the school's programs.

PUBLIC RELATIONS IDEA #95

Publicly recognize school employees at every level for exemplary service to the schools and to the community.

PUBLIC RELATIONS IDEA #96

Include bus drivers as one of your priority audiences. Invite them to staff meetings. Let them know how important they are to your school.

PUBLIC RELATIONS IDEA #97

Show the board of education the outfits they've been buying. Have a mini fashion show before the board meetings. Show board members physical education outfits, varsity uniforms, band uniforms, etc.

IDEAS
FOR ADMINISTRATORS
TO USE WITH STUDENTS

PUBLIC RELATIONS IDEA #98

Hold monthly informal "rap" sessions involving staff and students or principal and students. These can be held after school.

PUBLIC RELATIONS IDEA #99

Publish your answers to questions about pertinent issues in student newspapers. You may want to do so in a regular column.

PUBLIC RELATIONS IDEA #100

Have a monthly student birthday calendar posted in the hallway—with students' birthdays on it. Be sure to add new students when they arrive.

PUBLIC RELATIONS IDEA #101

Hold news conferences for reporters from the student paper.

PUBLIC RELATIONS IDEA #102

Form special student advisory committees to study problems and make recommendations.

PUBLIC RELATIONS IDEA #103

Send thank you notes to students who go beyond the call of duty...or who do good work consistently.

PUBLIC RELATIONS IDEA #104

Call students who have been absent more than two days, wish them well, and offer help.

PUBLIC RELATIONS IDEA #105

Encourage the staff to make phone calls to ill or absent students.

PUBLIC RELATIONS IDEA #106

Call all "A" students to the office immediately following the distribution of grade cards and offer congratulations and encouragement.

PUBLIC RELATIONS IDEA #107

Call all students to the office who have improved a grade, and offer congratulations.

PUBLIC RELATIONS IDEA #108

Call all students to the office who have a low grade. Counsel them and offer to help.

PUBLIC RELATIONS IDEA #109

Have an "Alumni Day" for former students who are in your community. This is a good time for junior high students to return to their elementary school and tell the elementary students what it's really like "up there." (This idea works well with senior high students, too.)

PUBLIC RELATIONS IDEA #110

It's part of our culture to find a reason to celebrate in almost everything. We have victory celebrations following sports contests. We have parades to mark the start of county fairs and to observe St. Patrick's Day and Thanksgiving. But one celebration that we don't see often enough is a celebration of learning. Yes, we do have graduation exercises for students when they complete their high school course of study, but that hardly seems adequate to recognize the tremendous amount of learning that occurs from the time a child enters kindergarten until he or she graduates from school as a young adult.

We ought to find ways to celebrate progress in learning more often. Here is one that stresses academic achievement. Identify graduates of your schools who have become successful in various fields of endeavor. Select a date during the year and invite them to return to spend a day with students from selected grade levels. That will give students an opportunity to interact with these successful graduates. Ask one or more of them to address the entire student body. Top off the special day with a "Celebration Of Learning" banquet and invite key officials from the community to celebrate the occasion with you. Above all, focus your celebration on the academic achievement and progress of current students as well as former students.

Such a celebration can build pride, generate support for education, and create motivation for students in one event. Finding ways to celebrate learning is a responsibility we all have—if we want our schools to receive the attention and support that they deserve.

PUBLIC RELATIONS IDEA #111

Teach about the foundation, mission, and operation of the school through units in regular social studies courses to help students understand about the school system and its administration, budget, curriculum development, and general operation. A principal may want to teach this unit.

PUBLIC RELATIONS IDEA #112

Hold an all-school T-shirt day on which everyone—including the principal—wears a T-shirt with a positive theme.

PUBLIC RELATIONS IDEA #113

Hold a "Dream Week" during which students are encouraged to talk about their dreams for their lives and to reach toward those dreams.

PUBLIC RELATIONS IDEA #114

Place suggestion boxes around the school and let it be known that suggestions are read. (You may have to "prime the pump" with a few of your own suggestions.) When people know you're listening, they'll contribute.

PUBLIC RELATIONS IDEA #115

Assist students in a study of how the school board functions.

PUBLIC RELATIONS IDEA #116

Have a telephone for students' use which is financed by student body funds.

PUBLIC RELATIONS IDEA #117

Reverse roles with students occasionally.

PUBLIC RELATIONS IDEA #118

Have "tooth" envelopes. Use the envelopes for sending home the teeth that *finally* come out at school—with a note from the teacher or principal. Those are tender moments that parents don't want to miss.

PUBLIC RELATIONS IDEA #119

Take a small group of students to your home for dinner. (Ask the parents first.)

PUBLIC RELATIONS IDEA #120

Call students who are entering a new school or a new grade before school starts. (This idea is especially effective with first-graders).

PUBLIC RELATIONS IDEA #121

Have "rug meetings" with younger students. Get down to their physical level and talk about school issues that they want to talk about.

PUBLIC RELATIONS IDEA #122

Have an honor banquet for those students who raise their grade point averages significantly.

PUBLIC RELATIONS IDEA #123

Form a group patrol squad made up of students to patrol the school before and after school or on weekends.

PUBLIC RELATIONS IDEA #124

Start a Student Outreach Program for student/peer tutoring. Many schools have similar programs in which students from high school help students from lower grades—gaining much newspaper publicity in the process.

PUBLIC RELATIONS IDEA #125

Use talented students to write news releases about student awards, student productions, and other activities for local papers and radio stations.

PUBLIC RELATIONS IDEA #126

Have students in special foods classes prepare meals and then serve them to adults including senior citizens, business leaders, and other community members.

PUBLIC RELATIONS IDEA #127

Have students sign up to be "I care" counselors. The purpose is to say, "I care about myself, my classmates, my teachers, and my school." "I care" counselors can perform countless acts of caring—from helping children find classes the first day to opening lockers to having classmate and teacher appreciation days.

PUBLIC RELATIONS IDEA #128

Have incoming sixth-graders from feeder elementary schools visit the junior high for a day with their parents. Show students how the school operates while the principal and other staff members discuss the junior high program with parents.

PUBLIC RELATIONS IDEA #129

A "student-school attitude" survey can help you know the status of your relationships with students. Release results to the public through the media.

PUBLIC RELATIONS IDEA #130

Structure homerooms to involve students in school. Use written discussion guides with which teachers lead discussion of school problems. Then, have teachers relay students' suggestions to the principal.

PUBLIC RELATIONS IDEA #131

Occasionally incorporate a "Time-Out Hour" in the school day during which student council representatives can lead discussion on specific topics or identify general student concerns and questions. Results can be compiled by the student council and distributed for further discussion both among students and by teachers at faculty meetings.

PUBLIC RELATIONS IDEA #132

Establish a "teacher advisor system," similar to the homeroom system, in which all professional staff members in the school sit down with 18-20 students to discuss a wide variety of concerns and events. Some such groups have even met for breakfast before school. This provides students a specific staff member with whom they can identify.

PUBLIC RELATIONS IDEA #133

Try a student advisory board of education with members elected from elementary, junior, and senior high schools. This group can actually meet with the board once each semester, but would not vote. These students would be involved with policy development and long-range planning for the school system.

PUBLIC RELATIONS IDEA #134
Invite board members to visit schools and talk with students and teachers.

PUBLIC RELATIONS IDEA #135
Have children in different grades write special interest stories to appear in the newsletters.

IDEAS
FOR ADMINISTRATORS
TO USE WITH PARENTS

PUBLIC RELATIONS IDEA #136
Plan visits to the principal's office that are fun and informative. Let the secretary explain what she does, what the procedures are, and the services the office provides. If parents want to sit at the principal's desk, let them. (Watch how many parents laugh, carry on, and how many will act stern or will put their feet up on the desk.)

PUBLIC RELATIONS IDEA #137
Set up a "buddy system" for new parents in the community.

PUBLIC RELATIONS IDEA #138
When school opens this fall, we may find that from 10 to 40 percent of the families with children in school are new to the community. What these newcomers perceive and expect schools to be may be entirely different from those in your community.

As a result, we may find newcomers proposing changes and offering criticisms which cause the schools problems. It's easy to label such parents as troublemakers. Worse, we may hope that they will soon move on to another place. Many of these problems stem from the fact that new families have little or no understanding of the curriculum, specific programs, or what the schools are attempting to achieve in their new community. Because their new schools seem different from their former ones, they begin to raise questions and offer criticism. That's why it can help if each attendance center arranges for an orientation of all new parents.

The principal of each school should invite new residents to meet the teachers, administrators, and at least one board member. A brief program that provides some explanation of the curriculum and goals of the board should be presented. It should be informative and professionally done. Ideally, new parents should learn something about how the entire school system operates—and be informed of special programs and opportunities available for their children. Indeed, having two or three such orientation meetings during the year may prove profitable. The meetings won't solve every problem or answer every question, but they're a good start. At the very least, they will establish a basis for good communication and relationships between new parents and the schools.

PUBLIC RELATIONS IDEA #139
Put together a slide show about your school or district for homes, service clubs, and realtors. Remember, realtors don't just sell homes, they also "sell" schools.

PUBLIC RELATIONS IDEA #140
Conduct general tours of your school periodically. Have an open house the Sunday before summer vacation starts. The media and the clergy in your town can help you announce the event.

PUBLIC RELATIONS IDEA #141
Have a regular (Dads') (Moms') breakfast and invite parents to stay as long as they wish to observe the school in action.

PUBLIC RELATIONS IDEA #142
Sponsor "Parents' Work Night" during which parents get together and build something the school needs. Senior citizens can help, too.

PUBLIC RELATIONS IDEA #143
Host mother-daughter, father-son school activities.

PUBLIC RELATIONS IDEA #144
Videotape lunch period (or any other period of interest) and play it back for parents at a later time.

PUBLIC RELATIONS IDEA #145
Use "Happy-Gram" forms on which teachers can write "good news" notes. This will encourage teachers to share with parents positive news about their children.

PUBLIC RELATIONS IDEA #146
Have a slide presentation on each new school program. Set up times to show the programs to parents and make them available to service clubs.

PUBLIC RELATIONS IDEA #147
Have an inservice program for school secretaries which stresses the importance of their public relations role. This session can be very productive. School secretaries are the voice of the school and are often the best known or most frequently contacted school employees in the attendance area.

PUBLIC RELATIONS IDEA #148
Keep track of telephone queries posed to school personnel. These are among the most important questions that need answering in meetings, newsletters, etc.

PUBLIC RELATIONS IDEA #149
Send invitations to parents to eat lunch with their children once a year in the school cafeteria.

PUBLIC RELATIONS IDEA #150

Revive the old parent-staff talent show.

PUBLIC RELATIONS IDEA #151

Ask teachers to phone parents and invite them to back-to-school nights.

PUBLIC RELATIONS IDEA #152

If you have professional public relations people among the parents in your schools, set up a public relations advisory committee. They'll come up with suggestions and aids you never dreamed possible. And they'll be pleased with your recognition of their talent.

PUBLIC RELATIONS IDEA #153

When student work is on display somewhere in your building, send a note to each student's parents inviting them to drop by to see it.

PUBLIC RELATIONS IDEA #154

Tell parents when you're available for calls...and encourage them to call with any questions.

PUBLIC RELATIONS IDEA #155

Give parents suggestions regarding how to spend time with their children during the summer. Give them a list of community resources, places to visit, etc.

PUBLIC RELATIONS IDEA #156

Help a parent tutor his or her children.

PUBLIC RELATIONS IDEA #157

Install a coffee cup rack for parents in the staff lounge. It's a good way to keep the welcome mat out for those who are always helping.

PUBLIC RELATIONS IDEA #158

Schedule a parent-teacher conference in a student's home. (It'll help teachers see what it's like for some students to come to school.)

PUBLIC RELATIONS IDEA #159

Let the students in various classrooms cook an evening meal for their parents. While they're eating, let the students tell what they're learning.

PUBLIC RELATIONS IDEA #160

Host a "New-Parents Night," inviting all the new parents in your school personally.

PUBLIC RELATIONS IDEA #161

Open the school gym for parents to play basketball or volleyball. Tournaments between parents whose children are in different grades are possible. For example, first-graders' parents could play third-graders' parents, and so forth.

PUBLIC RELATIONS IDEA #162

If working with an advisory group, be sure to summarize at each meeting how the advice they have previously given you was used. If the idea they suggested can't be implemented, tell them so.

PUBLIC RELATIONS IDEA #163

Run a videotape of school activities for parents to watch while they're waiting for their conference with the teacher.

PUBLIC RELATIONS IDEA #164

Inform parents in elementary school about junior and senior high programs in an attempt to reduce fear as well as build greater parent interest in secondary schools. Capitalize on early parent interests and "bring them along" as their children advance into high school.

PUBLIC RELATIONS IDEA #165

Use student work in your newsletter to parents—poems, artwork, sayings—making sure you check the work for spelling and punctuation.

PUBLIC RELATIONS IDEA #166

Hold monthly school visitation days. Instead of only one parent night a year, have one day a month set aside for parents' visitation. Parents can be invited alphabetically to avoid overcrowding.

PUBLIC RELATIONS IDEA #167

Hold a "What My Family Is Proud About" night in the gym. Each participating family sets up its own little booth displaying something family members do together.

PUBLIC RELATIONS IDEA #168

Send a blank report card home to parents in which parents have a chance to grade the school.

IDEAS
FOR ADMINISTRATORS
TO USE WITH THE COMMUNITY

PUBLIC RELATIONS IDEA #169

Invite special luncheon guests from different segments of the community to the school to update them on programs and to solicit suggestions.

PUBLIC RELATIONS IDEA #170

Elementary schools may invite a different policeman or fireman to eat lunch with students weekly or monthly.

PUBLIC RELATIONS IDEA #171

Type up a monthly school building or school-system-wide news "tip sheet" for mailing to all media. This gives plenty of advance notice about potential news for feature stories, and results in very good coverage. And send a copy to all school principals to encourage their own contributions to the tip sheet.

PUBLIC RELATIONS IDEA #172

Have mini-tours for special groups, including business people, senior citizens, nonparents, and teachers from feeder schools.

PUBLIC RELATIONS IDEA #173

Be sure to let key communicators know when you have followed up on concerns they have shared with you.

PUBLIC RELATIONS IDEA #174

Have a "press review" at the beginning of the school year. Invite the media people who cover your school or district in for coffee and a quick look at what this year will be like in your school—new people, new programs, new directions, new policies, etc.

PUBLIC RELATIONS IDEA #175

Hold a brief seminar with realtors. Provide them with a fact sheet on your schools. All you need to do is invite them in—and they'll help you get appropriate information to new residents about your school(s).

PUBLIC RELATIONS IDEA #176

Put up a marquee at elementary schools to advertise upcoming classroom as well as school events.

PUBLIC RELATIONS IDEA #177

Schedule student art displays for restaurants, banks, libraries, the shopping centers, and other well-trafficked locations in your community.

PUBLIC RELATIONS IDEA #178

Have student tour leaders or student hosts for visitors to your school. There's nothing more infectious than student pride; and playing positive, authoritative roles such as host and hostess gets students talking positively about the school.

PUBLIC RELATIONS IDEA #179

Have a map of your school campus available for visitors, and include "You are here" marks.

PUBLIC RELATIONS IDEA #180

Help your school publish a neighborhood map—one that shows more than the location of the school. This is great for new residents, and it is even better as a classroom teaching tool. You may even want to designate "safe homes" in the neighborhoods where children can go when in trouble. You might also mark safe crossings, signal crosswalks, and dangerous intersections.

PUBLIC RELATIONS IDEA #181

In many of our communities, schools have ceased to celebrate or even recognize many occasions that are important to our state and nation. A celebration of such occasions cannot help but draw favorable attention to the schools, not only from those who do not have children in school but from those who do as well. One possibility that's often overlooked is to recognize, in the schools, events which are significant to the community—or should be—such as Arbor Day. Students can be encouraged to take the initiative in planting trees or shrubbery on the school grounds. Likewise, there are many "patriotic" holidays that may not be noticed by the schools any more such as Veterans Day, Columbus Day, the special day set aside to honor the settlement of the state, or the date when the state entered the Union.

PUBLIC RELATIONS IDEA #182

Take your school choir/band to a convalescent home, to the park, to the mall, or downtown for "brown bag" lunch programs for the public.

PUBLIC RELATIONS IDEA #183

State and federal rules and regulations pertaining to the identification, testing, and placement of students in special education programs have become complex and lengthy. While educators and board members generally understand how they work, parents and other citizens usually don't. Rather, the rules may appear so complicated to people not familiar with them that they seem frightening.

Thus, it's important—even necessary—for every school or district to do two things. First, devise a means of informing parents about the various programs as well as their requirements. Second, explain the procedures used for delivering special education services to children.

You'll find it helpful to prepare packets of materials that identify and explain the programs. In the packet, detail rights and provide information about services and programs available to special education students after they finish their work in the secondary schools. Several organizations or advisory groups that exist to aid parents will be happy to assist you in preparing the packets.

If the public thinks special education programs already take more attention and resources than they deserve, it's helpful to know that taking the initiative in informing parents is good public relations. It will serve to build a better climate of trust and appreciation. You will be pleased at the positive comments that you will receive as a result of these efforts.

It's unlikely that state and federal rules will be simplified in the future. Thus, explaining programs and procedures to parents takes some effort and time, but it's effort and time well spent—and no parent deserves less.

PUBLIC RELATIONS IDEA #184
Designate a telephone number on which you can record messages pertaining to school events. The messages can be used to answer the general, normal questions that parents are interested in and ask all the time: When are football games? Where can tickets be purchased? When are report cards coming out? The messages might also include information about adult meetings, deadlines, activities, or school plays. You can offer up to two minutes of messages and make the number available 24 hours a day, seven days a week. This service may solve the problem of citizens who become frustrated because they can't find certain answers or information about the schools.

PUBLIC RELATIONS IDEA #185
Host a weekly luncheon meeting of a service club such as the Rotary, Kiwanis, or Lions Club once each year.

PUBLIC RELATIONS IDEA #186
Develop a group of volunteers from the community who can discuss local history, talk about occupational possibilities, or demonstrate specific skills to students. Volunteers can increase learning opportunities for students and will be out in the community talking about their positive experiences at school.

PUBLIC RELATIONS IDEA #187
Have students write notes of thanks to the media for coverage of a school event.

PUBLIC RELATIONS IDEA #188
Develop a group of administrators, teachers, and students who can talk to the civic group about the school or specific programs in your community.

PUBLIC RELATIONS IDEA #189
Have a "Senior Citizen Recognition Day" when senior citizens are invited to the school for a tour of the classes and facilities, and to have lunch.

PUBLIC RELATIONS IDEA #190
Create bumper stickers to promote attendance in school. They can read, "Regular School Attendance Is Necessary" or "I Go to School Every Day."

PUBLIC RELATIONS IDEA #191
Create buttons with a positive slogan for each child in the school to wear. Change the slogan periodically.

PUBLIC RELATIONS IDEA #192
Have a balloon lift, promoting the school and the slogan with media coverage of the lift. Attach names of students to the balloons. As the balloons are found and contacts are made back to the school, report in your newsletter the names of students whose balloons were found—and at what location.

PUBLIC RELATIONS IDEA #193

Have a "Special Person Day" during National Education Week. Invite community members who have done something special for your school or community. The visitors will have a chance to visit the school and the faculty, and have lunch with students.

PUBLIC RELATIONS IDEA #194

Have a weekly cable TV program that is produced and directed by (high school) students. Use the school's camera and technical equipment.

PUBLIC RELATIONS IDEA #195

For parochial schools, have a weekly newsletter printed in the parish bulletin.

PUBLIC RELATIONS IDEA #196

Conduct weekly radio programs on different school topics.

PUBLIC RELATIONS IDEA #197

Invite representative groups of parents to have early morning breakfasts at your school. Solicit their concerns and suggestions for improving the school(s).

PUBLIC RELATIONS IDEA #198

Invite the people in accounting and purchasing to visit classrooms so they can see the results of their work.

PUBLIC RELATIONS IDEA #199

Send copies of your school newspaper and honor rolls to other schools.

PUBLIC RELATIONS IDEA #200

Have an informal meeting with the board of education during which students can demonstrate the school curriculum through speeches, essays, or math and science fairs. Invite the parents and community to attend.

IDEAS
FOR BOARD MEMBERS
TO USE WITH STAFF, STUDENTS, AND THE COMMUNITY

PUBLIC RELATIONS IDEA #201

Getting people involved in the schools not only enables us to secure their understanding and support, but we gain from their insight, knowledge, and skills as well. That's why we need to use advisory committees. These committees may range from a building principal's advisory committee, to an advisory committee for a specific vocational subject, to committees appointed by the board of education to study and make recommendations on particular aspects of curriculum, class size, or school facilities.

Regardless of the purpose, we can't appoint people to advisory committees and expect them to function effectively and democratically with little or no help from us. Advisory committees need specific instructions—not only as to their purpose, the extent of their authority, and the use that will be made of their recommendations, but also in the way they are expected to operate.

The members also need some instruction on ways to make their meetings productive, ways to collect data, the extent of staff assistance that will be provided, and how the outcomes of their study and deliberation are intended to be used.

Many complaints are heard about advisory committees. Most of them stem from failure to orient volunteers and committee members properly and to specify their mission. When we do these things, however, and provide the committee with some instruction on effective ways to hold meetings, we will find little to complain about. Moreover, the members of the committees will receive greater satisfaction from their service. And that is a plus for the school in terms of good feelings and support by the committee members.

PUBLIC RELATIONS IDEA #202

Board members should be viewed as having wisdom and insight in governing the schools. But it's important to show personal sides as well—if people in the community are going to see us as helping and caring too. That's why it is worthwhile to encourage news stories focusing on the personal sides of school board members' lives from time to time.

These profiles should spotlight the human side of a school board member. They ought to describe the board member as a person, as a learner, as a parent, and as a leader. The stories ought to include information about hobbies, special interests, and recreational activities of the board member and his or her family. And they should also identify people who have been important as role models in the board member's life. It's also worthwhile to mention the books and events that have most influenced the board member.

It is important that the public see board members not only as personable human beings, but also as learners and role models for students and educators. And make no mistake, such stories offer a great benefit: They can help make school board members more visible in the community. Citizens can see board members as important governing officials—just as they do city, county, and parish officials.

We are often told not to hide our light under a bushel. And every board member ought to take this advice. But unless a board takes the initiative and arranges for these news profiles, it's unlikely that the personal and human sides of school board members will be communicated to the public.

PUBLIC RELATIONS IDEA #203

A number of practices can be designed to provide parents and other community members with an opportunity to experience the life of a teacher or student during the

310

school day. For example, parents may sit in on one of their child's high school classes. Or parents can follow an abbreviated version of their child's schedule during a back-to-school night. In addition, American Education Week is a good time for a citizen to take the place of a regular teacher in a classroom for a portion or even all of a school day. Likewise, it is a good idea for students to spend a day shadowing a business person, professional person, or public official in order to get some idea of what work outside the school is like.

A board might use a similar practice to give administrative personnel a morale boost during the school year. For example, a board member could take the place of an administrator who is assigned supervision responsibilities for a school activity. A board member can assume the role of a principal or assistant principal at an athletic contest, music program, or play. There, he or she can perform the responsibilities of crowd control and supervision, which are a part of an administrator's ongoing duties. When board members choose such actions, they can "get a feel" for the work of the administrator, as well as appreciate some of the responsibilities the administrator has—many of which fall outside the school day. And this practice lets the administrator know that a board cares and understands. It is not appropriate for board members and school employees to exchange places often—but it can be of value as both a learning experience and a morale booster if a board follows this practice once a year.

PUBLIC RELATIONS IDEA #204

Regardless of what we may think about the practice, schools can make considerable use of citizen committees. These may vary from formally structured committees for vocational education to special purpose committees appointed to complete a specific task. An interesting problem arises, however, when vacancies occur on committees that are continued year after year.

We are frequently faced with the need to replace a committee member who has resigned or whose term of service has expired. It should be an easy task to replace a committee member, but, unfortunately, that is not always the case. Sometimes, one of the most troublesome tasks is agreeing upon an individual to be appointed to some committee. Sometimes it is so difficult that the appointment is postponed or steals valuable time from several board meetings. Worse, it sometimes results in hard feelings and even embarrassment for a citizen whose name is proposed but who fails to secure a majority vote of the board for appointment.

One technique that can be used is to maintain a bank of names for standing committee appointments. The bank is created by submitting names in advance—which are agreed upon—as eligible for automatic appointment when committee vacancies occur. The bank of names need not be large. Depending upon the size of the system and the number of committees, it might be as many as twenty or as few as four or five names of people who are interested in the schools, who have some skill in working in groups, and who have agreed to be considered for committee work. While the committee bank is not the only solution to resolve a chronic problem, it's one possibility that's worth exploring that can save us time and problems.

PUBLIC RELATIONS IDEA #205

The daily responsibilities of administrative work and board service often tend to obscure a broader view of the school board's and administrators' work. When that happens, we can become bogged down in trivia that is seldom important and nearly always confusing to the community, students, and employees. More important, a lack of overview can prevent achieving the quality school system we desire.

We need to be aware that this situation is likely to occur with any of us. That is why it is wise to develop a procedure for periodically redefining the dimensions and magnitude of our work. One way to do this is to seek advice outside the district.

At least once a year, we should sit down with one or more advisors from outside the district and ask for a review and critique of the board's activities during the past year. The board should also explore with the advisors the way in which a board ought to work with the chief administrator and the community. It is not expected that the advice of consultants should be accepted without question. But it can help the board to view its activities in a more objective manner, and it is an important aid in self-examination of past work.

These consultants can be secured at nominal cost through the state School Board Association, a state university, or independent consultants such as The Master Teacher. While the cost is usually small, a board will find that the investment pays long-term dividends. Special consultants can help the board to maintain effective working relationships with the chief administrator and other employees. More important, they will aid the board and administrators in keeping work focused upon the real responsibilities. That can be a vital step toward educational excellence.

PUBLIC RELATIONS IDEA #206

In many communities, parent-teacher associations aren't as active as they once were. In fact, many local parent groups no longer affiliate with the state and national organizations—and refer to themselves as parent-teacher organizations.

Many of these organizations limit their activities to a few programs and a fundraising event during the year. The funds raised are spent on equipment, supplies, materials, library books, or to underwrite the cost of an educational trip for students. Indeed, most of the funds are spent for things that are a legitimate responsibility of the board. In truth, if needed by the schools, they should have been provided by the board.

While boards usually insist that the funds of these organizations be spent in conformance with board policy, they give little other direction—even when the funds may be used for unimportant purposes. Yet, the board ought to be used to give some direction as to how these funds might be best used to improve the education of students. Your board may want to consider one of these possibilities.

Some of the funds might be used to provide opportunities for nonparents to participate in school activities. Most adults report that they haven't visited the schools in years. When one realizes that about 70 percent of the households today have no children in school, it becomes obviously important that these people have some contact.

Another sound expenditure is to purchase art objects for the schools. A few pieces of sculpture, paintings, or prints can do much to brighten up schools and add a dimension to the education of each child. Yet, these purchases are not ones that a school board is likely to make unless it has outside assistance. Using funds in these ways can provide education and enjoyment now as well as in the future.

PUBLIC RELATIONS IDEA #207

The creation of attractive grounds offers a real challenge. The foot traffic on the playground is so heavy that it's difficult for grass to survive. Nevertheless, attractive playgrounds are important—and can be created and maintained.

A first step is to secure the services of a landscape architect who can create plans for planting and for placement of playground equipment. The plan should be a complete, long-range document of what the board wants to accomplish as a final product. And it should include a step-by-step plan that will enable a school system to make some progress each year in attaining the results envisioned.

Funds for the maintenance of school grounds are nearly always limited. And once a board decides to do something, some people may criticize the board for spending money on a "noneducational" item. However, excellence in a school system is exhibited on many fronts, and "inviting" school grounds can help to establish the feeling of a quality school system.

A board may be reluctant to begin such a plan. If it does, however, it will find that the community will respond positively. Not only will the board receive expressions of appreciation, it may discover that there are individuals and groups who want to contribute money, materials, or time to the project. Further, attractive grounds just might create a positive model for the entire neighborhood. And business, industry, executives, real estate agents, and the chamber of commerce sell the schools continually. That's why this help will be supported.

PUBLIC RELATIONS IDEA #208

In many communities, employees and lay citizens alike refer to the central administration offices with humorous and even derisive names. Some of the more common references are "House of Many Errors," "The Ivory Tower," and "Downtown." There are other terms that are less amusing that are used to express disdain for the board of education and central office. Whether humorous or not, all these descriptive phrases have a negative connotation that detracts from the educational image of the school system.

There's no way to prohibit the use of such terms if people want to use them. And even if we could prohibit them, we shouldn't. The truth is, however, we're often equally guilty of using similar terms when referring to the administrative offices.

If we find that such a situation exists in our community, we need to give some thought to improving the image. One way to address the problem is to be certain that an appropriate name is designated for our central office. We could, for example, name the office after an important personage or historical figure—just as we often name school buildings. Even a descriptive term such as The Center for Elementary and Secondary Education might be considered. Regardless, the central office of a school system ought to have a name that denotes, in some manner, that caring, knowledgeable, considerate leadership is housed there.

Will such a step ensure that derisive terms will no longer be used when referring to our central office? Not necessarily. But if we want to create and maintain a positive image with the public, we can at least find a way to refer to the central office with a positive term or statement. This is part of our responsibility.

PUBLIC RELATIONS IDEA #209

At least once every month, set aside a few minutes on the agenda for *anyone* to speak to the board. You might even want to call this procedure *The Citizens' Forum*. The first 20 minutes is the best time. Let anyone in attendance address the board. Deny this privilege to none, whether it is an individual or a group. This includes interest groups, parents, teachers, or students. School boards who have used *The Citizens' Forum* find that it provides a realistic way for citizens to air their concerns as well as their complaints. Use but two guidelines. First, limit presentations to 10 minutes each and 20 minutes out of each meeting. Second, make an effort to answer all questions if you can—and let others in the audience reply. Address unanswered questions at the next meeting.

Using this technique can sometimes cause some uncomfortable moments, especially when comments are made that a board may not want to hear. Yet, it may be far less uncomfortable to hear the comments now than allow citizens' concern to grow into a full-blown problem. More important, it is one more way in which citizens can communicate with their board of education, and it eliminates the complaint that "one can never talk to the board of education." And if the board is willing to have an open forum at *every* meeting, nobody can ever legitimately complain that he couldn't make it to one monthly meeting that did have *The Citizens' Forum*.

PUBLIC RELATIONS IDEA #210

Whether large or small, schools have a number of extracurricular award assemblies and banquets each year. The purpose of these occasions is to recognize students' achievement and celebrate their participation in the activities of the school. Unless board members have a child participating in an activity, they usually don't attend these school functions—except on rare occasions. They should be invited for several reasons. First, these occasions are, or can be, good public relations activities. Likewise, board members ought to satisfy themselves that these events are organized in a manner that indicates organizational efficiency, care, and concern for students. It's easy for award banquets and assemblies to be handled in a very careless and informal way. Sometimes, the attention is focused on everyone but students.

Attendance also provides an opportunity to meet and visit with citizens who are often strong supporters of both the academic and extracurricular programs of the schools. This fact is reason enough for every board member to attend as many of these functions as possible. After all, we need to pay as much attention to the supporters of the schools as we do the detractors.

The most important characteristic of extracurricular activities is that they provide a way to motivate students in school work as well as building a climate of enthusiasm among both kids and their parents. Board members who regularly expose themselves to this kind of enthusiasm will find that it's easier to keep their own attitudes positive in the day-to-day decision making that is required of them. It's easy to forget about young people as we make educational decisions. However, attendance at a banquet or award assembly will make it easier to remember that the schools are for the children.

PUBLIC RELATIONS IDEA #211

In many places, the schools are used to solicit funds for everything from United Way to special education, and to distribute everything from advertisements for crafts classes to tickets to free movies. Worse, these actions have become a common occurrence. Indeed, significant demands are placed upon the schools when they are used to solicit funds for various charities or used as distribution systems in place of the postal service. Those demands often take a considerable amount of educational time. This ought to be a concern of every administrator and school board for several reasons.

First, using the schools as distribution systems seems to give tacit endorsement of the literature that comes home with the student. No matter how the schools may be criticized, people still consider them honest and well meaning. Why do anything that might undermine this public trust?

Second, the distribution or collection of material and money is bound to take some school employee's time—be it principal, secretary, or teacher.

Finally, the number of agencies, businesses, foundations, activities, and individuals who want to use the schools to solicit funds or distribute advertising has increased dramatically. And many of them utilize so-called educational materials to gain the schools' assistance. Most of these materials are quite poor despite the exaggerated claims made for them. Consequently, a board ought to consider a policy that either limits or eliminates the school's participation in these activities. Adopting such a policy does not mean that the schools are uncaring about charitable activities. It simply means that school comes first. While you may receive some criticism from these organizations for taking such actions, you'll receive a silent note of thanks from most parents.

PUBLIC RELATIONS IDEA #212

A successful board of education celebrates its victories—not only because of the personal satisfaction that it brings, but also to draw both employee and public attention to the event. For example, the passage of a school bond issue might be acknowledged and celebrated in a public meeting. Students' achievement test results being above the norm is cause for some employee and public celebration. When a particular instructional program has successful outcomes, it's time for public recognition of both teachers and students—and a brief celebration at the next board meeting. Successful conclusion of negotiations with employees is, likewise, a reason for celebration—jointly by the board and teachers. Time ought to be set aside for these important, successful occasions.

There are many successes in education. We must stop and enumerate them from time to time. In the process, we will find more achievement than we think. Celebrating these successes in public not only adds to our own optimism about education and pride in our work, but also serves to draw public attention to school accomplishments and the benefits schools offer students and the community. These overt acts of enjoyment can create positive public attitudes about education in general and our schools in particular. And they can have the same impact on teachers and administrators as well.

PUBLIC RELATIONS IDEA #213

If your board is experiencing difficulty in getting parents and other community representatives to attend board meetings, you may want to consider establishing a continuous student/staff recognition program. Time can be set aside during one board meeting each month to recognize and honor outstanding performance on the part of students, teachers, and members of the support staff by presenting them with certificates of commendation from the board. By recognizing several students, teachers, and members of the support staff each month, attendance will be increased because parents will willingly bring their children, and members of the professional staff who are singled out for special recognition will bring their spouses as well as other family members to the meeting. This gives the school board an excellent opportunity to showcase the greatest resource in the school: The children as well as the staff who work with the children on a daily basis. If handled correctly, this part of the monthly agenda can become a very significant event in the life of the community. Those extra people now attending meetings of the school board, and especially those who have either been recognized or witnessed a member of their family singled out for special recognition will leave the school board meetings with positive feelings and attitudes toward the board and the school. In addition, they will have had an opportunity to observe the board conduct its regular business meeting, discuss issues of concern, and take action designed to fulfill the board's responsibility of providing a quality education for the children of the community. School boards that have implemented this kind of special recognition program for students and staff members have found they now have a new cadre of advocates in the community.

PUBLIC RELATIONS IDEA #214

It often happens that board members spend a lot of time on school-related matters that the staff of a school are paid to do. Yet, at the same time, they spend little time on matters that they as board members could best do. As an example, board members are expected to represent people. Therefore, they need to have a good feel for what citizens think about education and their schools, what things please them, and what things irritate them as well. Unfortunately, however, many school board members do not have that sort of feel. Instead, the "feel" that they have is influenced and determined by their friends, acquaintances, and the calls of criticism and complaint that they may receive.

A board member can improve on that feel by making a half dozen telephone calls each week. This is how. The board member places telephone calls at random to households in the community. When the party is reached, the board member should identify himself or herself, state the purpose of the call, and then spend a few minutes discussing education and the schools, gathering suggestions and ideas for change or improvement, and emphasizing the importance of education to the party being called.

A half dozen calls made each week result in over a hundred citizens being contacted each year. Multiplied by each board member's efforts, these contacts will effectively broaden the base of citizen participation in the schools.

Not every call made using this procedure will turn out to be a pleasant or informative one, but that can be valuable too. It helps to remind us that it's a real world in which we live. Using the telephone to contact households throughout the year can provide positive benefits to you as a board member. More important, however, it can provide positive benefits for the schools.

PUBLIC RELATIONS IDEA #215

School boards, even in the smallest communities, often have a number of visitors in attendance at their meetings. These observers may range from teachers and parents to representatives from community groups, special interest organizations, or even those who are considering the possibility of becoming board candidates at some future date. Overall, those in attendance usually represent various beliefs, have various interests, and conduct themselves in varying ways. Many boards of education have found that it is quite worthwhile to have a list of rules or regulations for those in attendance. The list is usually printed on one sheet or in a small brochure and made available to those guests attending the meeting.

The list of rules should contain at least some of the following information:

A. A brief message of welcome.
B. The legal duties and responsibilities of the board.
C. The conditions under which visitors may address the board.
D. The way in which the board's agenda is constructed and disposed of.
E. Other information that may be desirable for the visitors to know.

The construction of such materials can help to insure that board meetings are conducted in a business-like and civilized way. Whether you have many or few visitors, now is a good time to develop your list of rules. With the increased emphasis upon citizen involvement in local government activities, it's likely that the number of visitors attending board meetings will increase in the coming years. Outlining the rules for visitors now may prove to be farsighted and a good way to improve public relations.

PUBLIC RELATIONS IDEA #216

It is vitally important for every school board to establish a good working relationship with state legislators who represent the area in which their schools are located. Unfortunately, many boards overlook this fact. It's an oversight which should be corrected—immediately.

Legislators are often acquainted with individual members of a board, but not with the total board and its views regarding pending educational legislation. This is one of the reasons we are often shocked and frustrated by the legislation which governs the operations of our schools. This year is a good time for the entire board and administrative team to resolve that situation. Association representation is not good enough. Your legislative contact must be personal and direct when a need for communication with legislators arises.

You can begin by inviting your legislators to a breakfast, luncheon, or dinner session with your board, superintendent, principals, and even a select group of teachers. State the reason for the gathering: to meet the board personally and discuss educational problems of mutual concern. The initial meeting can be brief, but there should be an agenda during which you can ascertain the manner in which your legislators wish to be contacted about educational legislation. It should be mutually understood how the board and administration will handle its responsibility for doing so. Likewise, follow-up meetings should be planned to assure continuous contact.

The most appropriate meeting time is before the legislative sessions begin. Call your legislators today. These meetings may prove to be among the most beneficial you have during the year.

PUBLIC RELATIONS IDEA #217

Here is a suggestion that many boards of education have found helpful in working with their legislators. First, recognize when your state legislature is in session, and take advantage of it. As each legislative bill concerning education is introduced, your district's administrative staff should summarize the bill briefly, determine its impact upon the local school district, and send the information to each of your legislators along with a recommendation of support or opposition. It's also a good idea to make your recommendations known to the press at the same time.

You will find that your state legislators will soon begin to depend upon both the summaries and your recommendations. You will be surprised how quickly your district will have more influence than you thought possible. This, of course, is not the only means of working with and influencing legislators that you can or should use, but it is a resourceful and effective start.

PUBLIC RELATIONS IDEA #218

It's always a bit startling to realize how quickly the school year passes. The months pass before we get around to doing some things we resolved to do. Maintaining periodic contact with legislators is often one of those resolutions.

The construction of a calendar which indicates how, when, and under what conditions we will be in contact with our legislators during the coming year can prevent this from happening again. While a board of education will want to construct the calendar to fit its own situation, here are some suggestions which may be useful.

The calendar should include a time for a general meeting with legislators well in advance of the legislative session. Specific arrangements should be made for legislators to discuss the upcoming educational issues. Board members should be especially concerned about legislation which is likely to have an impact upon their schools. The meeting should also be designed to inform legislators of action items in which the board of education is interested.

The calendar should include a time for a general meeting with legislators well in advance of the legislative session. Specific arrangements should be made for legislators to discuss the upcoming educational issues. Board members should be especially concerned about legislation which is likely to have an impact upon their schools. The meeting should also be designed to inform legislators of action items in which the board of education is interested.

The calendar should indicate predetermined dates and times during the year when the legislators will be contacted. Equally important, it should also specify the board member or administrator who will have the responsibility for making each individual contact.

Finally, the calendar should include a date for a meeting with the legislators at the end of the session. The purpose of this meeting should be to provide a report of legislative action as well as an evaluation of the work of legislators on behalf of the schools. The adoption of a formal schedule for contacting legislators is important—if board members expect to avoid letting the legislative session pass without regular and consistent contact with their legislators.

PUBLIC RELATIONS IDEA #219

If our schools are to gain the community's attention and support, a board of education, administrators, and staff must be highly visible. We must be involved in community activities and governance beyond the one or two school board meetings each month and school programs. Nearly every board finds that it must compete for public attention with city, county, or parish governments as well as with hospital and mental health boards, the chamber of commerce, and a host of other organizations and activities.

We can enhance prestige and influence by seeking some involvement with these groups. The board of education can, for example, meet periodically with other governing bodies to discuss items of mutual interest. Individual school board members and administrators can hold membership in the chamber of commerce as well as serve as liaisons with other governing bodies and attend their meetings on occasion. A board and administrators can do these things, but they won't unless there is a plan for involvement.

As we get organized at the start of each fiscal year, plans should be made for meeting with other governing bodies. Specific assignments for individual members of the board to act as liaisons with important groups should be decided. The board president should contact the organizations involved and explain the purpose of the liaisons. He or she should explain the board's desire to keep abreast of various activities in order to foster maximum cooperation.

Naturally, some board members will maintain that they don't have time for such activities. Some may insist that their knowledge about the other governance activities is sufficient. In some very special instances, this may be true. But for the vast majority of us, it is not the case. And unless plans are made and followed, a board and administrators cannot assume their proper leadership role in the community.

PUBLIC RELATIONS IDEA #220

Without reservation, morale can be best enhanced when teachers and administrators are aware that something has been accomplished during the year. That's why it can be a worthwhile exercise to have teachers and administrators alike jot down one thing that they have accomplished during the school year and of which they are especially proud. As an illustration, you might request a short paragraph about something teachers have done to improve the mastery of the basic skills—then publish or review these accomplishments publicly.

You will be surprised at the many ways teachers and administrators are working to improve the quality of education in your community. If all of the contributions are compiled and returned to the staff in the form of newsletters, those accomplishments will probably make a very impressive picture. Teachers and administrators will have an improved outlook about their own work and that of their colleagues. They will be much more informed as they discuss education with their friends and neighbors—and the ground work will be established for continuous improvement.

PUBLIC RELATIONS IDEA #221

How much does the board of education really know about what goes on in the classroom? Aside from rumors, what do you know about programs? Here is a proposal which will start the board on the road to being truly informed about the real reason for the schools' educational programs.

Select and place on the agenda one key area of the curriculum each month, and request that those teachers and supervisors who are more responsible for it provide a report to the board. The following format is suggested to insure that the best information is available and that some interchange can take place.

Prepare a written summary of two to three pages which describes the curriculum area and its major objectives or activities. The following should be included:

1. A description of the program.
2. Progress-illustrations of the kinds of activities and successes which are evident.
3. Consideration of problems—these may range from facilities to materials or other areas that the board must be involved in or must approve.

An open discussion should follow after a 10- or 15-minute highlight has been presented. However, it's important that the written report be in the board's hands along with the agenda in advance of the meeting. This allows the board time to consider what questions or comments it might have for the meeting.

Experience shows that it's what the board and the community don't know that poses the real problems in education. Program reports can maintain communications with the board of education and the community as well.

PUBLIC RELATIONS IDEA #222

School board members are busy people. Most of them don't have a lot of time during daylight hours to devote to board service. Yet, a board member can secure a better overall feel for his or her work and for how the schools operate by setting aside two or three days during the year to participate in some school activities.

If board members were to devote only one day a year to learning more about the schools for which they are responsible, the following suggestions would help them spend this day wisely. Ride two bus routes, one in the morning, and one in the afternoon. Eat lunch with students at one of the schools. Observe three or four academic classes and visit with a building administrator. Look in on students in music and physical education, and also observe the work with special children, including the learning disabled, those with speech problems, and the emotionally disturbed. Attending a parent organization meeting in the evening can round out the day's experience.

On the surface, such visits may seem simplistic and not particularly worthwhile. Yet, even one day spent visiting schools can provide a board member with a better understanding of the total operation of the schools. Observing teachers and other employees in action provides information about the quality of their work. Getting a feel for student attitudes can prove very insightful as well. In making school visits, however, a school board member should not confuse the board's policy-making responsibility with the administrative responsibility of the school.

Spending a day or two in the schools during the course of the year is part of the personal education program all board members should undertake—if they want their work to be the best it possibly can be.

PUBLIC RELATIONS IDEA #223

If you've thought about the possibility but haven't tried it yet, seriously discuss taking an administrator-board of education retreat. Two of the best times to take a couple of days for such a meeting are after school adjourns for the summer or after the hectic days of beginning school in the fall. Set aside a time and place where the board and administrators can be together "away from it all" without interruption. For best results, organize activities for the two days to provide both work and play together.

For the first session, you might try a theme like, "Planning to Achieve District Goals." Discuss ways to achieve goals working together as a team, not only for the entire district but in individual attendance centers as well. Most important, design the meeting to be both practical and specific. You might wish to kick the session off with an outside consultant or speaker, but that is not necessary.

If the retreat is kept short and is well balanced with work and play, you will experience many positive results. First, board members and administrators will get to know one another on a more personal level. Second, board members will increase your foundation of education knowledge and better understand how schools work in reality. Third, both will develop a new sense of equality and *esprit de corps* which did not previously exist. Finally, you will find that both the administrative personnel and the board are working together on common goals and problems during the course of the year. Over a period of two or three years, you will find that the retreat idea can pay big dividends in improved morale and in performance in your district from both the administrative and board of education points of view.

PUBLIC RELATIONS IDEA #224

An effective and exciting school system depends much on the board to build a climate of enthusiasm. A community is unlikely to have good schools unless there's enthusiastic and optimistic leadership. Yet, school boards are often guilty of not recognizing the importance of this fact.

Consider this situation. The typical administrator, no matter how capable, is faced with a constant barrage of criticism about education, the performance of employees, and curriculum. Although he or she may not be criticized personally, the constant exposure to criticism has a wearing effect. It undermines both physical performance and the ability to think and plan effectively. Although most boards are aware of this, they seldom stop to think they might do something about it. Yet, they can and they should. They can offer administrators encouragement. They can give praise and commendation at critical times when administrative performance has been sound.

PUBLIC RELATIONS IDEA #225

Many school boards fail to assume the obligation they have to orient new members to their elected or appointed offices. Instead, they leave the entire matter to the superintendent. While superintendents conduct this activity quite well within the legal restraints that they have, orienting new board members is a duty in which every board of education ought to be closely involved.

Men and women who are new to the board have much to learn. For instance, what are the board's policies? What issues do board members face? What issues does the existing board see on the horizon? These are only a few of the questions for which new board members seek answers. A superintendent of schools should not be placed in a position where he or she is left alone to answer them. This is a board responsibility. It is important that poor decisions or controversy not result from the lack of knowledge of new board members. Communication between new and old members of the board is the first step in such a foundation.

Every school board should plan an orientation schedule for new board members. Perhaps no more than five or six hours need to be set aside for this activity. But the time should be well planned. At a minimum, it should provide an overview of the board's present work and review policies from which the board operates. Also included should be the issues with which the board expects to be faced in the immediate future. New board member orientation should be conducted in an open and public meeting. And remember, this practice not only provides orientation for new board members, it can also serve as an orientation for the community, news media, and the employees of the district as well.

INDEX OF PUBLIC RELATIONS IDEAS

KEY WORD	IDEA: PAGE
COMMUNITY:	
Communication (with)—	2:47, 3:48, 7:95, 8:98, 9:123, 10:124, 12:124, 15:125, 18:125, 20:126, 22:126, 28:152, 30-31:153, 33:179, 34:181, 56:228, 58:237, 60:244, 66:254, 139-140:303, 146:303, 148:303, 162:305, 169:305, 173:306, 175-177:306, 179-180:306, 181-183:307, 184:308, 188:308, 190:308, 192:308, 194-196:309, 199:309, 207:313, 209:314, 214-215:317
Involvement—	64:252, 152:304, 170:305, 172:306, 185-186:308, 189:308, 197:309, 204:311
Recognition—	193:309
MEDIA:	
Communication (with)—	7:95, 26:145, 171:306, 174:306
Recognition—	27:146, 187:308
PARENTS:	
Communication (with)—	11:124, 13:124, 14:125, 16-17:125, 19:126, 23:129, 24:135, 25:139, 52:226, 55:227, 56:228, 59:238, 118:300, 138:302, 144-145:303, 151:304, 153-156:304, 158-160:304, 163-166:305
Involvement—	11:124, 136:302, 141-143:303, 149:303, 150:304, 161:304, 167-168:305
Morale—	137:302
Recognition—	157:304

INDEX OF PUBLIC RELATIONS IDEAS (Cont.)

KEY WORD	IDEA: PAGE
SCHOOL BOARD:	
Committees—	201:309, 204:311
Communication (with)—	97:297, 221:320
Image—	61:246, 65:253, 208:313
Involvement—	40:188, 134:302, 203:310, 206:312, 210:314, 211:315, 214:317, 219:319, 222:321
Legislators—	216-217:318, 218:319
Morale—	62:249, 212:316, 223:321
Orientation—	225:322
Recognition—	202:310
Relationships—	62:249, 63:252, 205:312
STAFF:	
Climate—	6:76, 57:228, 73:294, 77:295, 90:296
Communication (with)—	5:55, 29:153, 33:179, 34-36:181, 37-38:182, 41:189, 69:293, 70:294, 74:294, 76:295, 78-79:295, 91-92:297, 98:298, 198:309, 220:320
Family—	83:295
Grade Cards—	48:224, 49:225
Image—	42:203
Inservice—	39:187, 82:295, 147:303
Meetings—	94:297
Morale—	4:53, 41:189, 72:294, 81:295, 85-86:295, 112:299, 220:320

INDEX OF PUBLIC RELATIONS IDEAS (Cont.)

KEY WORD	IDEA: PAGE
Orientation—	32:154
Planning—	1:43
Productivity—	4:53
Recognition—	71:294, 87-89:296, 95-96:297, 213:316, 224:322
Student Requests—	45-46:222
Substitutes—	75:294, 80:295, 84:295

STUDENTS:

Communication (with)—	1:43, 38:182, 47:223, 50-52:226, 98-99:298, 108:298, 111:299, 114-115:300, 120-121:300, 128:301, 130:301, 132:301
Image—	44:217
Involvement—	43:216, 53:227, 67:281, 68:283, 93:297, 101-102:298, 109:299, 113:299, 116-117:300, 119:300, 123-125:300, 126-127:301, 129:301, 131:301, 133:301, 135:302, 159:304, 165:305, 178:306, 181-182:307, 188:308, 194:309, 200:309
Morale—	4:53, 47:223, 54:227, 67:281, 68:283, 104-105:298, 110:299, 112-113:299, 129:301, 191:308
Recognition—	100:298, 103:298, 106-107:298, 122:300, 213:316
Visitors—	53:227

327